PLEASE RETURN T
BY THE DUE DATE
TULSA CITY-COUNT

FINES ARE 5¢ PER DAY; A
MAXIMUM OF $1.00 PER ITEM.

ANGLO-SAXON LITERATURE.

ANGLO-SAXON LITERATURE.

By JOHN EARLE

AMS PRESS
NEW YORK

Reprinted from the edition of 1884, New York
First AMS EDITION published 1969
Manufactured in the United States of America

Library of Congress Catalog Card Number: 70-101909

AMS PRESS, INC.
New York, N.Y. 10003

PREFACE.

THE bulk of this little book has been a year or more in type; and, in the mean time, some important publications have appeared which it was too late for me to profit by. Among such I count the "Corpus Poeticum Boreale" by Dr. Gudbrand Vigfusson and Mr. York Powell; the "Epinal Gloss" and Alfred's "Orosius" by Mr. Sweet, for the Early English Text Society; an American edition of the "Beowulf" by Professors Harrison and Sharp; Ælfric's translation of "Alcuin upon Genesis," by Mr. MacLean. To these I must add an article in the "Anglia" on the first and last of the Riddles in the Exeter Book, by Dr. Moritz Trautmann. Another recent book is the translation of Mr. Bernhard Ten Brink's work on "Early English Literature," which comprises a description of the

Anglo-Saxon period. This book is not new to me, except for the English dress that Mr. Kennedy has given to it. The German original has been often in my hand, and although I am not aware of any particular debt, such as it would have been a duty and a pleasure to acknowledge on the spot, yet I have a sentiment that Mr. Ten Brink's sympathising and judicious treatment of our earliest literature has been not only agreeable to read, but also profitable for my work.

15, NORHAM ROAD, OXFORD,
March 15*th*, 1884.

CONTENTS.

CHAPTER	PAGE
I.—A Preliminary View	1
II.—The Materials	28
III.—The Heathen Period	59
IV.—The Schools of Kent	79
V.—The Anglian Period	98
VI.—The Primary Poetry	119
VII.—The West Saxon Laws	150
VIII.—The Chronicles	169
IX.—Alfred's Translations	186
X.—Ælfric	207
XI.—The Secondary Poetry	225
XII.—The Norman Conquest, and after that	243
Index	259

ANGLO-SAXON LITERATURE.

CHAPTER I.

A PRELIMINARY VIEW.

ANGLO-SAXON literature is the oldest of the vernacular literatures of modern Europe; and it is a consequence of this that its relations with Latin literature have been the closest. All the vernacular literatures have been influenced by the Latin, but of Anglo-Saxon literature alone can it be said that it has been subjected to no other influence. This literature was nursed by, and gradually rose out of, Latin culture; and this is true not only of those portions which were translated or otherwise borrowed from the Latin, but also in some degree even of the native elements of poetry and laws. These were not, indeed, derived from Latin sources, but it was through Latin culture that those habits and facilities were acquired which made their literary production possible.

In the Anglo-Saxon period there was no other influential literature in the West except the Latin. Greek literature had long ago retired to the East. The traces of Greek upon Anglo-Saxon literature are rare and superficial. Practically the one external influence with which we shall have to reckon is that of Latin literature, and as the points of contact with this literature are numerous, it will be convenient to say something of the Latin literature in a preliminary sketch.

The Latin literature with which we are best acquainted was the result of study and imitation of Greek literature. But the old vernacular Latin was a homely and simple speech, much more like any modern language in its ways and movements than would be supposed by those who only know classical Latin. The old Latin poetry was rhythmical, and fond of alliteration. Such was the native song of the Italian Camenæ, unlike the æsthetic poetry of the classical age, with its metres borrowed from the Greek Muses. The old Latin poetry was like the Saxon, in so far as it was rhythmical and not metrical; but unlike it in this, that the Latin alliteration was only a vague pleasure of recurrent sound, and it had not become a structural agency like the alliteration of Saxon poetry. The book through which juvenile students usually get some taste of old Latin is Terence, in whose plays, though they are from Greek originals, something is heard of that rippling movement which has lived through the ages and still survives in Italian conversation. Reaching backwards from Terence we come to Plautus and Ennius, and then to Nævius (B.C. 274–202), who composed an epic on the first Punic war. He lamented even in his time the Grecising of his mother-tongue. He wrote an epitaph upon himself.

to say that if immortals could weep for mortals, the Camenæ might well weep for Nævius, the last representative of the Latin language.

The splendour of classical Latin was short-lived. The time of its highest elevation is called the Golden Age, of which the early period is marked by the names of Cicero and Cæsar; the latter (the Augustan period) by the names of Virgil and Horace. There is a fine forward movement in Cicero, who studied the best Greek models; but gradually there came in a taste for curious felicity suggested by the secondary Greek literature. This adorned the poetry of Virgil; but when it began to spread to the prose, though the æsthetic effect might be beautiful in a masterpiece, it was apt to be embarrassing in weaker hands. Æsthetic prose appears in its most intense and most perfect form in Tacitus, the great historian of the Silver Age. As new tastes and fashions grew, the oldest and purest models were neglected, and, however strange it may sound, Cicero and Cæsar were antiquated long before the end of the first century.

The extreme limit of the classical period of Latin literature is the middle of the second century. The life was gone out of it before that time, but it had still a zealous representative in Fronto, the worthy and honoured preceptor of Marcus Aurelius. After this last of the Good Emperors had passed away, the reign of barbarism began to manifest itself in art and literature. The accession of Commodus was a tremendous lapse.

The point here to be observed is that the classical

Latin literature was not a natural growth, but rather the product of an artificial culture. It presents the most signal example of the great results that may spring from the enthusiastic cultivation of a foreign and superior literature. And it is of the greatest value to us as an example, because it will enable us better to understand the growth and development of Anglo-Saxon literature. For just as Latin classical literature was stimulated by the Greek, so also was Anglo-Saxon literature assisted by the influence of the Latin. And as the classical student seeks to distinguish that which is native from that which is foreign in Latin authors, so also is the same distinction of essential importance in the study of Anglo-Saxon literature.

The influence of Greek upon Latin literature was so far like that of Latin upon Anglo-Saxon, that it was single and unmixed. But then the influence of Greek upon Latin was altogether an external and invading influence, like the influence of Latin on modern English; whereas in the case of Anglo-Saxon the literary faculty was first acquired through Latin culture; the Saxons were exercised in Latin literature before they discovered the value of their own; they obtained the habits and instruments of literature through the education that Latin gave them.

Up to the end of the classical period the Latin had not yet attained, in literature, the position of a universal language. It was rather the scholastic language of the Roman aristocracy. There was but one field in which it occupied the whole area of the Roman world, and that was the field of law. To this we should add the Latin poetry, which was also absolute in its own domain. In every other subject Latin was a second and a subject literary language, the supreme language of literature being Greek. Greek was the chief literary language even of the Roman Empire. Of the two languages, Greek was by far the more convenient for general use. Human thought is naturally serial, and the language that is to be an acceptable medium of general literature must, above all things, possess the art of moving forward. In this art the Greek was far in advance of the Latin, and the curious culture which produced the Latin classics had, indeed, been productive of much artistic beauty, but had withal entangled the movement. It is not in Latin but in Greek books that the knowledge of the ancient world has been preserved. The greatest works in botany, medicine, geography, astronomy were written not in Latin but in Greek, even in the most flourishing times of the Roman power. It is sufficient to mention such names as Dioscorides, Galen, Strabo, Ptolemy. The greatest works in history, biography, travel, antiquities, ethics, philosophy were also written in Greek. Such names as Polybius, Plutarch, Josephus, Pausanias, Dionysius, Epictetus, Lucian will give the reader means of proof. Fronto could not prevail with a Roman emperor, his old pupil, to prefer Latin to Greek. Marcus Aurelius wrote his "Meditations" in Greek. The language of the infant Church, even in Italy and the West, was not Latin, but Greek. The names of the first bishops of Rome are Greek names, the Christian Scriptures are in Greek, and so is the oldest extant Liturgy—the Clementine—which seems to represent the practice of the West no less than of the East. Not only the Canonical Scriptures of the New Testament are in Greek, but also those which were partially or for a time received, as the Epistle of Clement, the Hermas, the Epistle of Barnabas. And a further set of writings beyond these and inferior to these, but ultimately of great popularity, were in Greek : I mean the legendary and romantic apocryphal writings, such as the Acts of Peter and Paul, the Acts of Pilate, and many others.[1] This latter set was already growing in the second century, and reached their mature form in the time of Gregory the Great.

It is not clear how early Latin began to be used as the official language of the Church, but everything points to an important change soon after the middle of the second century. Before that time, Justin, living at Rome, and writing (A.D. 138), for the Roman people to read, a defence of Christianity, which was addressed to the emperor Antoninus Pius, wrote it in Greek ; but before long another apologetic writer, Minucius Felix, wrote in Latin. This coincides with other indications to mark a great transition in the latter half of the second century. Up to this time two languages were in literary currency, a foreign scholastic language and an æsthetic vernacular. It was chiefly the wealthy class that sus-

---

[1] A translation of these writings is given in Clark's "Ante-Nicene Library," vol. xvi. Among the "Acts of Pilate" are contained the so-called "Gospel of Nicodemus," which is the fountain of that favourite mediæval subject, "The Harrowing of Hell."

tained these literary languages in Rome. When in A.D. 166 the Oriental plague was brought to Italy with the army returning from Parthia, cultivated society was wrecked, and the literary movement was greatly interrupted in both languages. This was a blow to the artificial culture of Greek in Italy, just as the plague of 1349 and following years was a blow to the artificial culture of French in England. After A.D. 166 a check was given to progress, which lasted, in the secular domain, until the sixteenth century.

Let us spend a moment upon the sequel of the old literature, before we come to the new, which is our proper subject here.

Under the altered times that now ensued, the continuity of classicism is seen in two forms of literature —namely, philological criticism and poetry. The acknowledged model of Latin poetry was Virgil, and his greatest imitator was Claudian, who had made himself a Latin scholar by study, much as the moderns do. Claudian is commonly called the last of the heathen poets. He has also been called the transitional link between ancient and modern, between heathen and Christian poetry.[1] One characteristic may be mentioned, namely, his personification of moral or personal qualities, a sort of allegory destined to flourish for many centuries, of which the first mature example appears in the "Soul's Fight" of Prudentius, the Christian poet, who was a contemporary of Claudian. The school study of the classics produced grammars, and two authors became chiefly celebrated in this branch,

[1] North Pinder, "Less Known Latin Poets," p. 486.

namely, Donatus and Priscian. Their books were standards through the Dark and Middle Ages.[1]

There was one department of prose literature in which Latin was undisturbed and unsophisticated. This was the department of law and administration. The legal diction escaped, in a great measure, from the influence of classicism; it kept on its even way through the whole period, and as it was an ordinary school subject under the empire, the language of the law books exercised great influence in the formation of the prose style that continued through the Middle Ages.

We now come to the new Latin literature with which we are intimately concerned.

By the side of this diminished stream of the elder literature there rose, after the middle of the second century, a new series of writings, new in subject, and new also in manner, diction, and spirit. The phraseology is less literary, and more taken from the colloquial speech and the usage of everyday life. It seems also to be, in some measure, the return-language of a colony: some of the earliest and most important contributions come from Africa, where Latin was now the mother-tongue of a large population, and that country appears to have escaped the ravages of the plague.

The first of these books is one that still bears

---

[1] Donatus was Jerome's teacher. His name grew into a proverb, insomuch that an elementary treatise of any sort might in the fourteenth century be called a "donat." Priscian was a contemporary of Boëthius. His grammar was epitomised by Rabanus Maurus in the ninth century.

considerable traces of classicism. It is entitled "Octavius," and is an apology for Christianity by Minucius Felix. But immediately after him we come upon a chief representative of this new literature, which aimed less at form than at the conveying of the author's meaning in the readiest and most familiar words. This is strikingly the case with the direct and unstudied Latinity of the first of the Latin fathers, the African Tertullian, in whom the contrast with classicism is most pronounced. In him the old conventional dignity gives place to the free display of personal characteristics, and no writer (it has been said) affords a better illustration of the saying of Buffon—"the style is the man."

Another African writer was Lactantius, to whom has been attributed that poem of the Phœnix, which most likely served as pattern to the Anglo-Saxon poet.[1] It consists of 170 lines, hexameters and pentameters; terse, poetical, classical. This old Oriental fable, as told by Ovid, was short and simple: "There is a bird that restores and reproduces itself; the Assyrians call it Phœnix. It feeds on no common food, but on the choicest of gums and spices; and after a life of secular length, it builds in a high tree with cassia, spikenard, cinnamon, and myrrh, and on this nest it expires in sweetest odours. A young Phœnix rises and grows, and when strong enough it takes up the nest with its deposit and bears it to the City of the Sun, and lays it down there in front of

[1] Other Latin poets who touched this subject are—Ovid, "Metam.," xv., 402; Martial, "Epigrams," v., 7; Claudian's First Idyll, a poem of 110 hexameters, is entirely devoted to it.

the sacred portals." Such is the story in Ovid ; and there we know we have a heathen fable. But in the poem of Lactantius, it is so curiously, and, as it were, significantly elaborated, that we hardly know whether we are reading a Christian allegory or no. Allegory has always been a favourite form with Christian writers, and more than one cause may be assigned for it. Already there was, in the taste of the age when the Christian literature arose, a tendency to symbolism, which is seen outside the pale of Christianity. Moreover, the long time in which the profession of Christianity was dangerous, favoured the growth of symbolism as a covert means of mutual intelligence. Then Christian thought had in its own nature something which invited allegory, partly by its own hidden sympathies with Nature, and partly by its very immensity, for which all direct speech was felt to be inadequate. But what doubtless supplied this taste with continual nutriment was that all-pervading and unspeakable sweetness of Christ's teaching by parables. The Phœnix was used upon Roman coins to express the aspiration for renewed vitality in the empire ; it was used by early Christian writers[1] as an emblem of the Resurrection ; and in the Anglo-Saxon poem the allegory is avowed.

To Lactantius also has been ascribed another book in which we are interested. This is a collection of a hundred Latin riddles under the obscure name of Symposius, which name has by some editors been set

---

[1] Clemens Romanus; Tertullian, " De Resurrectione Carnis," c. 13. See Adolf Ebert, " Christlich-Lateinische Literatur," vol. i., p. 95.

aside in favour of Lactantius for no better reason than because of some supposed Africanisms. Aldhelm speaks of these riddles under the name of Symposius.

A new literature thus rose up by the side of that which was decaying, or had already decayed. This new literature was the fruit of Christianity; it was more a literature of the masses than any that had been hitherto known; it was marked by a strong tinge of the vernacular, and it was separated in form as well as in matter from the old classical standards. The spirit of this new literature was characterised by a larger and more comprehensive humanity. It was animated by those principles of fellow-feeling, compassion, and hopefulness, which were to prepare the way for the structure of human society upon new foundations. This, rather than the classical, is the Latin literature which we have to follow; this is the preparation for modern literature, and its course will be found to land us in the Saxon period.

After the triumph of Christianity, this new literature was much enlarged, and it appropriated to itself something of the grace and elegance of the earlier classics; and whether we speak of its contents, or of its artistic character, we may say it culminated at the end of the fourth and the beginning of the fifth century in the writings of Augustine. In his time we find that the contrast between profane and sacred literature is already long established: the old literature is called by the pagans liberal, but by the Christians secular.

The removal of the seat of empire to Constantinople had ultimately the effect of substituting Greek for Latin as the language of administration in the East. On the other hand, the growth of the papal power in the West favoured the establishment of Latin as the sole language of the West, to the neglect of Greek. Thus East and West were then divided in language, and Latin became universal in the West. In Anglo-Saxon, the people of the Eastern Empire are characterised simply as the Greeks (Crecas).

The heart of the new Latin literature was in the Scripture translations. Many exercised themselves in translating, especially the New Testament. Augustine says the translations were beyond number. But the central and best known of these many versions is thought to have been made in Africa. In A.D. 382, Damasus, the bishop of Rome, induced Jerome to undertake that work of revision which produced the Latin Bible, which is the only one now generally known, and which is called the Vulgata, that is to say, the received version. Older italic versions, so far as they are extant, are now to us among the most interesting of Christian antiquities. In the early centuries, and throughout the whole Middle Age, the Scriptures took rank above all literature, and their influence is everywhere felt.

The sack of Rome (A.D. 410) drew forth from the pagans a fresh outcry against Christianity. They sought to trace the misery of the times to the vengeance of the neglected gods. This accusation evoked from St. Augustine the greatest of all the apologetic treatises, namely, his "City of God" (De Civitate Dei). This great work exhibits the writer's mature and final opinions, and it may be said to represent the maturity and culmination of that Latin literature which began after A.D. 166, and continued to progress until it was half quenched in barbarian darkness. The "City of God" has been called the first attempt at a philosophy of history; and, again, it has been called the Cyclopædia of the fifth century. It lays out before us a platform of instruction on things divine and human, which reigned as a standard for centuries, even until the theology and philosophy of the school-men had been summed up by Thomas Aquinas.

To this great work a companion book was written by Orosius, who had been Augustine's disciple. This was a compendium of Universal History, and it was designed to exhibit the troubles that had afflicted mankind in the ages of heathenism. It became the established manual of history, and continued to be so throughout our period; and Orosius was for ages the only authority for the general course of history. This explains how it came to be one of the small list of Latin books translated by Alfred.

We have no sooner reached the culmination of that Christian literature which began after the depression of A.D. 166, than we find ourselves in the presence of another great fall. The sack of Rome in 410 shook the minds of men as if it were the end of all things. The fifth century was a time of ruin, but also it was a time of new beginnings. Three great events are to be noted in this fifth century: 1. The Western Empire came to an end; 2. The Franks passed over the Rhine into Gaul, and became Christian; 3. The Saxons passed over the sea to Britain, and remained heathen until the close of the sixth century. These three events group together by a natural connection; it was the expiring empire that made room for the Frankish and Saxon conquests, and these two conquests have been, and are, fertile in comparisons and contrasts, and reciprocal action, not only through our period, but till now and onward.

About A.D. 500, Avitus, bishop of Vienne, wrote a Latin poem on the mighty acts of Sacred History—(De Spiritalis Historiæ Gestis); and this book has been regarded as the original source of some passages in Cædmon and Milton.[1] The poem is in five books, of which the first three—1. On the Creation; 2. The Disobedience; 3. The Sentence of God—form a whole in themselves; while the remaining two books, which are nominally on the Flood and the Red Sea, are really on Baptism and the Spiritual Restoration of Man. So that the whole work comprises a Paradise Lost and a Paradise Regained.

We now come to a book which, though not by a Christian author, is so manifestly influenced by Christianity, and has been so fully recognised by the Christian public, that it must be included in our list —viz., "The Comfort of Philosophy," by Boëthius. Gibbon even called it a golden volume, and one which, if we consider the barbarism of the times and the situation of the author, must be reckoned of almost incomparable merit. It was composed in the prison to which Theodoric had consigned the wisest of the

---

[1] Siever's "Der Heliand," p. 18, and references; Guizot, "Histoire de la Civilisation en France," 18^e Leçon.

old Roman patriciate; and it is commonly regarded as closing the canon of Roman literature. It was translated into all the vernaculars, Alfred's translation into English being the first, and Notker's into High German being the second.[1] Other works of Boëthius lived through the Dark and Middle Ages, especially his translations of Aristotle, which were standards for the student in philosophy.

From this time we see a world fallen back into a wild and savage infancy, and we shall witness the gradual operation of a spiritual power reclaiming, educating, transforming it. The subject of Anglo-Saxon literature derives, perhaps, its greatest interest from the fact that it represents one great stage of this process.

As we approach the Saxon period we must take particular notice of a new agency that now comes on the scene. The institution of monachism was one of considerable standing before the date at which we are now arrived, but it had never yet found any function of systematic usefulness. Benedict of Nursia is called the father of monks, not because he first instituted them, but because he organised and regulated the monastic life and converted it to a powerful agency for religion and civilisation. Benedict was born in 480, and he died at Monte Cassino in 543. The Benedictine institution is the great historical fact which demands our attention in the early part of the sixth century.

An eminent Benedictine was the Roman Pontiff Gregory, surnamed the Great. He was born in 540,

[1] For the Latin text, and the bibliography, there is an admirable little edition by Peiper, Lipsiæ, 1871.

and died in 604. He designed the conversion of the Saxons. He was a great author, though he was ignorant of Greek. We will here notice three of his works—the "Commentary on Job," the "Pastoral Care," and the "Dialogues."

The first of these is remarkable as a specimen of that mystical interpretation of Scripture which characterised the exegesis of the Middle Ages, and of which manifold examples occur in the Homilies of Ælfric, who names Gregory as one of his sources.

The "Pastoral Care" is worthy of its name as a book of direction and advice from the chief pastor to his subordinates. It is full of grave practical wisdom, animated by the Christian spirit and the love of souls. For prudence it is worthy of the pontiff who solved Augustine's questions, as we read in Beda's history. In this book we discover the true and legitimate source of the power of the clergy, and we verify the words of Joseph Butler, who said that if conscience had power as it has authority, it would govern the world. The power of the clergy is sometimes explained as a stratagem; he who reads this book will see a deeper root to that power; he will see that if trickery made that power to fall, it was something else that caused it to rise.

A greater contrast than that between the "Pastoral Care" and the "Dialogues" it is hardly possible to conceive. We cannot wonder that the identity of authorship has been questioned, and that the "Dialogues" have been attributed to another Gregory. The difficulty is, however, lessened if we consider the widely different conditions of the readers addressed.

At a time when an old civilisation and a crude barbarism were intermingled and living side by side, the one was written for the highest, the other for the lowest in the intellectual scale. The "Pastoral Care" was addressed to the Roman clergy, with whom, if anywhere, something of the old culture still lingered. The "Dialogues" were intended for the barbarians. The book is addressed to Theodolinda, the Lombard queen. It is a book full of wonderful, not to say puerile, stories, in which a religious lesson or moral is always conveyed, but not always one that carries conviction to the mind of the modern Christian. It reflects the policy of converting the barbarians by condescending to their tastes, and belongs to the same system as that increase of pomp and ceremony which was due to the same motive. This book far outran the former in popularity. It was among the earliest of Latin books to be translated into vernacular languages. Gregory's writings were very influential on popular religious literature throughout the Dark Ages, and nowhere more so than in England, where he was honoured as a national apostle. There exists an Anglo-Saxon translation of the "Dialogues," but it has not yet been edited.

The time of Gregory the Great was the time in which, to use Dean Milman's words, "the human mind was finally Christianised." This triumph, as usually happens, was overdriven. We see a too jealous exclusion of secular literature, and a too credulous and favourable disposition towards Christian legends. This was the time when the secondary apocryphal literature reached its maturity, and was grouped in collections. An active labourer in this pious work was Gregory of Tours. He contributed the "Miracles of St. Andrew," and possibly other pieces. This period, from the middle of the sixth into the early part of the seventh century, is the period of the greatest literary activity of the monasteries of Gaul, and the apocryphal collections seem to have been made in some of these.[1] If the Christianised Latin literature reached its highest excellence in the time of Augustine, it discovered its extremest tendency in the time of the two Gregories.

There is yet one form of literature that claims our attention. The Greek romances of love and marvellous adventure were probably discountenanced in Christian families, and we may regard the secondary Apocrypha as a kind of pious substitute for such entertaining works of fiction. But there was one of these old heathen novels that held its ground, that can be traced in more than one early monastic library, and that was translated into every vernacular —Anglo-Saxon first. This was the Romance of Apollonius of Tyre, from which comes the story of that Shakespearean play, "Pericles, Prince of Tyre."

The books which we have noticed between the second and the seventh centuries may be allowed to represent that Christianised Latin literature which is the historical bridge between the ancient classical and the modern vernacular literatures. The latter had as yet no existence. In Mœsia, on the shores of the Danube, a Gothic dialect had been immortalised

[1] R. A. Lipsius, "Die Apokryphen Apostelgeschichten und Apostellegenden," Braunschweig, 1883, p. 170.

by Scripture translations from the Greek as early as the fourth century; but nothing of the kind had as yet appeared under the Latin influence in the West. The Merovingian Franks left no vernacular literature; on the contrary, they rapidly lost their native speech, and adopted that of the conquered nation.

The Franks and the Saxons had been neighbours in their native homes, speaking almost the same mother-tongue; but their migrations led them into new regions in which they again proved neighbours under altered conditions. Each was to take a leading part in the formation of modern Europe, but they were to be divided in that office, their lots being severally cast with the two great constituent factors of modern civilisation. The one was to lead the Romanesque, the other the Gothic division. The Franks became assimilated to the Romanised Gauls, and formed, with them, one Latin-speaking Church; they raised the standard of orthodoxy against the Arianism of the other barbarian powers, and the Frankish king was decorated with the title of Most Christian; the history of that Church was written in Latin by Gregory of Tours. This work, upon which he was engaged from A.D. 576 to 592, bears strong marks of literary degeneracy. Gregory complained of the low state of education in the cities of Gaul. He became a historian only from a sense of necessity, and for fear lest the memory of important events should perish. He has been called the Herodotus of the Franks, and the Herodotus of barbarism. The history of the Church in Gaul after the absorption of the Franks is not one of quickened progress but of crime and torpidity. Gregory the Great justified his mission to the Saxons on the express ground that the Church of Gaul, whose natural duty it was, had neglected it. The history of the Merovingian Franks stands in disadvantageous contrast with the early vigour of the Saxon Churches. The first great elevation of European culture was to spring, not from among the Franks, but in the remoter colonies of the Saxons.

The English conversion began A.D. 597; and two religious foundations were quickly established:—
1. The Minster of St. Saviour, afterwards called Christ Church, and now Canterbury Cathedral; 2. The Abbey of SS. Peter and Paul, outside the walls of Canterbury on the east, which was afterwards called St. Augustine's. Of the foundation of schools nothing is heard at this time; but a generation later, A.D. 631, we find the Kentish schools taken as a model for schools to be founded in East Anglia by Felix.[1] It is an interesting question whether these were the missionary schools, or whether they were schools which kept up the traditions of Roman education in a degenerate form like the schools in Gaul. On the ground that our oldest document is a Code of the first converted king, it has been too easily inferred that before this time the Saxons were wholly destitute of literary appliances. Were the fact more certain than it is, the conclusion would be weak. There are in the Chronicles certain archaic annals which have been thought to be a possible product of the heathen period.

[1] Bede's " Ecclesiastical History," iii., 18.

A PRELIMINARY VIEW. 21

The second home of culture was in Northumbria. A wonderful combination of influences met on this favoured soil. In the extreme province of the empire, there had been a concentration of military force, to keep the Picts in check; the centre of Roman government on the island had been at York, and here, if anywhere, something of the civilisation of Rome would naturally remain.

Another important influence was the Irish, or, as it was then called, the Scotian. It is true that the first evangelist in order of time was Paulinus, who came from Kent, and represented the Roman mission. But the savour of the Gospel was first received through the teaching of the Irish missionaries, of whom the foremost name is Aidan. Never did any people embrace Christianity with such entire heart as the Irish; and much of their lofty devotion was communicated to the Angles whom they converted.

Upon this, when they were prepared to profit by it, supervened the mission of Theodore and Hadrian, who implanted the seed of learning, with great ability, at an opportune moment, and with the most abundant results. Under the warmth of a first love, all these advantages were moulded together, and resulted in making Northumbria for three or four generations the centre of European culture. The seat of this culture was York, the old Roman capital, and its culmination was under Archbishop Egbert (734–766), and his successor Albert. The great writings of this period are in Latin, and the chief names are Aldhelm, Eddi, Winfrid (Bonifacius), Danihel, Beda, Alcuin. Of vernacular prose the chief remnant is a series of

Northern Annals, between A.D. 737 and 806, which have been embodied in some of the Southern Chronicles. But what specially characterised this period was a rich development of sacred poetry, some remnants of which are perhaps extant in our "Cædmon." But our fullest knowledge of this old poetic strain comes back to us from Old Saxony, where it was propagated by the Anglian missionaries, and it survives under a thin disguise in the poem called the "Heliand."

In Aldhelm we see that this new learning was not solely ecclesiastical, but that there was something in it which aimed at recovery of classical learning. He was distinguished for his elaborate study of Latin metres, and his commendation of the pursuit. He wrote poems in Latin hexameters, and among these a Collection of Enigmas, which bore fruit in the later Anglo-Saxon literature.

The latter part of the Anglian period produced Alcuin, the distinguished scholar who was engaged by Charles the Great to organise his new schools. So we see the lamp of culture pass from Anglia into Frankland, shortly before the time when Anglia was overrun by the Danes and almost all the monuments which were destructible perished.

We may dismiss the Anglian period with the remark, that its achievements are all the more distinguished from the fact that they belong to a time when the whole Continent was in the thickest darkness, that is to say, the seventh and eighth centuries.

Under Charlemagne a new start was made for the restitution of literature. He drew learned men to his court, Alcuin from England, Paulus Diaconus from Italy. Thus he made a new centre for European learning, and France continued to sustain that character down to the latter end of the Middle Ages. His chief agent in this great work of enlightenment was Alcuin, who was educated at York under Egbert, who had been a disciple of Beda. And so we see the torch of learning handed on from Northumbria to the Frankish dominions in time to save the tradition of culture from perishing in the desolation that was near. Among the names that adorn the annals of revived learning under Charles himself, we must mention Smaragdus, because Ælfric acknowledges him as one of his sources. The book referred to would hardly be the " Diadem of Monks," a selection of pieces from the Fathers with Scripture texts, worked up as it were into a Whole Duty of Man, although Ælfric would be likely to know this book ; but for the composition of his Homilies it is more likely that Ælfric would have drawn from another book by Smaragdus, namely, his commentary on the Epistles and Gospels for Sundays.

Men who have left their names in history now followed in the work of sustaining the revival of learning. We must mention Rabanus Maurus, whose Scripture commentaries were used by the poet of the "Heliand"; and Walahfrid Strabo, who wrote on plants and had a taste for Greek etymologies.

The revival of secular learning brought in its train a strong development of speculative theology. The ninth century is marked by controversy on the Eucharist, and on Predestination. The former of these controversies had an effect upon Anglo-Saxon literature, which requires us to record one or two main facts in this place. Paschasius Radbert, a monk of Corbey, who was for a short while Abbot of that famous monastery, wrote a treatise (the first of its kind) on the Eucharist, maintaining the change in the elements. The opposite side was taken by Ratramnus (otherwise called Bertram), a monk of the same house. His views were adopted by Ælfric in the tenth century, and were embodied in a Homily, which was welcomed by the English reformers of the sixteenth century as an antidote to the doctrine of transubstantiation. Haymo, bishop of Halberstadt, who had studied at Fulda, maintained the doctrine of the material change in its most extreme form. He was also a commentator upon the Scriptures, and Ælfric used his commentaries, but only "sometimes."

The Danish scourge beggared the land, as in all other respects, so in learning and in all the liberal arts. We who had formerly sent instructors to other nations, were now suitors for help in our destitution. The same national deliverer who rid us of the destroyer, was also the restorer of education. If he cannot be said to have effectually restored learning, at least he laboured with so much earnestness at the task that he may be said to have bespoken an ultimate though delayed success. Alfred is not more famous for his great battles than for his great literary efforts.

The literary restoration of his time is supported by the Carlovingian schools, and in this we may see a repayment in the ninth century of that help which

A PRELIMINARY VIEW. 25

Charles had received from England through Alcuin in the eighth.

Different in its origin is the remarkable spring of religious and intellectual life in the tenth century. Ever since the synod of Aix-la-Chapelle in 813, the religious spirit in Gaul had manifested itself in the stricter discipline of the Benedictine monasteries, and this movement reached us in the middle of the tenth century. The Benedictines had a famous school on the Loire at a place then called Floriacum, now Fleury or St. Benoît-sur-Loire, and some leading men in England were in active relations with this house.[1] In the eclipse which the nominal seat of Christianity was under in the tenth century, the light of the Church shone in France and England. The reforms of Æðelwold and Dunstan and Odo are the transmission of this movement to our island.

This great movement has only time to take shape enough to declare itself when it is again interrupted by troublous times, invasions, and wars, and changes of dynasty, and before any length of peace is again allowed, by the decisive and final blow of the Norman Conquest, which brought with it more than a change of dynasty. It changed the whole body of the governing and influential classes, not from one stratum to another within the Saxon nation, but by the introduction of a ruling class from another nation, speaking another language, and one of a different family.

The new language thus brought in was no barbarous

[1] It was destroyed by the Calvinists in 1562.

dialect, but the most cultivated of the Continental vernaculars. It was the other great factor of European literature. It had begun to be cultivated later than the Saxon, but then it had ages of culture at its back. The strength of this language was in its poetry —just the element which had stagnated in England. The French taught not only the English but all Europe in poetry. All modern European poetry is after the French model.

After the Conquest Saxon literature had a stronghold in the great religious houses, and here it continued to be cultivated until far into the twelfth century. This was due not only to the patriotic sentiment, but also to the interests of their several foundations. The chief Anglo-Saxon works that we have from the times after the Conquest are concerned directly or indirectly with the property or privilege of the religious house from which the books emanate. This is the time that produced the Worcester chartulary, the Rochester chartulary, the Peterborough chronicle which embodies the privileges of the house, and the Winton chartulary. This diplomatic interest was strong and permanent enough to cause Anglo-Saxon studies to be pursued until late in the Middle Age, perhaps even down to the time of the Dissolution by Henry VIII.

But passing from this, which is an artificial continuation of the old literature, we may observe that it had a continuation which was perfectly natural and spontaneous. Examples of this are the late semi-Saxon Homilies, in which we see the gradual decay of the old flectional grammar: but the most

A PRELIMINARY VIEW. 27

signal examples are the two great poetical works of Layamon and Orm. These are full of French influence, though not in the same manner. Layamon's "Brut" is translated (though not without original episodes) from the French of Robert Wace: and the "Ormulum," though drawn as to its matter from Latin comments on the Gospels, yet is in form deeply imbued with the character of French poetry. Indeed, the English language became more and more a vehicle for the reproduction of French literature. This continued to the middle of the fourteenth century, when the plague, which altered so many things, altered also this. The supremacy of the French language was broken, the native language was again heard in legal pleadings, and the poetry of Chaucer laid the permanent foundation of modern English literature.

CHAPTER II.

THE MATERIALS.

THE material of an early Literature is, above all, to be sought in written Books and documents. But, besides these, there are other available sources, which may be called in one word the Antiquities of the nation; and these are of great value as illustrations, that is to say, though the information they severally give may be uncertain and inexplicit, yet when they are put side by side with the literature, they greatly increase its informing power, and often draw, in return, a flow of light upon themselves. Accordingly the present chapter will fall into two parts: 1, of writings; 2, of subsidiary sources.

I.

THERE is a famous book that remains in the place where it was deposited in the Saxon period. Leofric, who was the tenth bishop of Crediton, and the first of Exeter, gave to his new cathedral about sixty books, and the list of these books is extant in contemporary writing. One of them is thus described:—" I. mycel englisc boc be gehwilcum thingum on leoth wisan geworht." = One large English book about various things in lay (song) wise wrought—that is to say, a large volume of miscellaneous poetry in

English. This is the valuable, or rather, invaluable, Exeter Song Book, often quoted as "Codex Exoniensis." It is still where Leofric placed it in or about 1050, and it is in the keeping of his cathedral chapter. The others are dispersed; but many of them are still well known, as the "Leofric Missal," in the Bodleian; and others are at Cambridge. The general break-up of monastic institutions between 1530 and 1540 caused the dispersion of many old libraries, whose forgotten treasures were thus restored to air and light. No doubt many valuable books and records were irrecoverably lost; as it is reasonable to suppose that among the parchments then cast upon the world, there existed material for a continuous and complete history of Anglo-Saxon times. This reflection may make us the more sensible of our penury, but it will not diminish the praise of those who saved something from the wreck.

Matthew Parker, the twentieth archbishop of Canterbury, 1559-1576, has been called a mighty collector of books. He gave commissions for searching after books in England and Wales, and presented the choicest of his miscellaneous collections to his own college at Cambridge, namely, Benet College (now Corpus Christi), where it still rests. In this library are some unique books, such as the oldest Saxon chronicle, which has been thought nearly as old as King Alfred's time. There is also a fine vellum of the laws of King Alfred, with the elder laws of King Ine attached in manner of appendix.

But the most famous book of this great collection is an illuminated manuscript of the Gospels in Latin

(No. 286), which Wanley thought to be probably one of the very books that were sent to Augustine by Gregory. Professor Westwood says that the drawings in this manuscript are the most ancient monuments of Roman pictorial art existing in this country; and he further proceeds to say that, excepting a fourth-century manuscript at Vienna, these are the oldest instances of Roman-Christian iconography of which he can find any notice.[1]

Parker had singular opportunities, by the time in which he lived, by the advantages of his high office and personal character, by his power to command the services of other men, and by their general willingness to serve him. There were three distinguished searchers after books who were of the greatest use to him, viz., Bale, Joscelin, Leland.

John Bale, the antiquary, had been a White Friar in Norwich, then, changing his party, he became bishop of Ossory, but lived at length on a prebend he had in the church of Canterbury, where he followed his studies. Bale, in his preface to Leland's "New Year's Gift,"[2] says that those who purchased the monasteries reserved the books, some to scour their candlesticks, some to rub their boots, some they sold to the grocers and soap-sellers, and some they sent over sea to the book-binders,[3] not in small numbers,

---

[1] "Palæographia Sacra Pictoria."

[2] "Leland's laboryouse journey and serche for Englandes antiquities, given as a newe years gifte to King Henry VIII.; enlarged by John Bale." London. 1549.

[3] This is curiously confirmed by the discovery of Waldhere, described below.

THE MATERIALS.

but at times whole ships full, to the wondering of foreign nations.

John Leland had a commission under Henry VIII. to travel and collect books; his Itinerary is a chief book for English topography. Of Joscelin we shall have occasion to speak below. With all his advantages, however, Parker was weighted with the care of the churches, at a time, too, when that care was unusually heavy; and to this, as in duty bound, he gave his first thought. Though his example could not be exceeded, his collections were surpassed, and that by a gleaner who came after him. Of all book collectors the greatest was Robert Bruce Cotton, the founder of the Cottonian Library. He was born at Denton, in Huntingdonshire, and educated at Trinity College, Cambridge. Cotton's antiquarian tastes declared themselves early; the formation of a library and museum was his life-long pursuit. Not that his interests were all confined to this. He wrote on the revenue, warned King James against the strained exaction of tonnage and poundage, especially in time of peace; and he counselled the creation of an order of baronets, each to pay the Crown £1,000 for the honour. In this way he became a baronet himself in 1611, having been knighted at the king's accession. Under Charles I. he was molested for his opinions, because he dared to disapprove of government without parliaments; and he was touched in his most sensitive part when his own library was sealed against him. He died 6th May, 1631, and was buried in Conington Church, where his monument may still be seen.

His library was further enlarged by his son, Sir Thomas Cotton; and it was sold to the nation by Sir John Cotton, the fourth baronet, in 1700. It was lodged in Ashburnham House, in 1731, when a disastrous fire consumed or damaged many valuable books.[1] Annexed by statute to the British Museum in 1753, it was moved thither in 1757.

Among the books that suffered without being destroyed by the fire of 1731, is the unique copy of the Beowulf.[2] One of the Saxon chronicles was almost consumed; only two or three leaves of it are now extant. But, happily, this particular chronicle had been printed by Wheloc, without curtailment or admixture, and so it was the one that could best be spared. This library also contains the Abingdon and Worcester chronicles, and, indeed, all the known Saxon chronicles except two. This collection is the richest in original Anglo-Saxon deeds and abbey registers.

Among the Cottonian treasures (Vespasian A.I.) is a glossed psalter, which was edited by Mr. Stevenson for the Surtees Society, in two vols., 1843-7, as

---

[1] As this fire is one that the student is only too often reminded of, a few details may be acceptable. A committee was appointed by the House of Commons to view the Cotton Library after this disaster, and we learn from their Report (1732, folio) that "114 volumes are either lost, burnt, or entirely spoiled, and 98 others damaged so as to be defective; so that the said library at present consists of 746 entire volumes and 98 defective ones." The collection when purchased had contained 958 volumes. Of late years great pains have been taken for the preservation of the fragments by careful mounting.

[2] Photographed by the Early English Text Society, 1883.

containing a Northumbrian gloss, which is now, however, supposed to be Kentish.[1] A facsimile of this manuscript by the Palæographical Society, part ii., 18, has a description, from which the following is taken:—"Written about A.D. 700, the gloss at the end of the ninth, or beginning of the tenth, and the later additions in the eleventh century. It formerly belonged to the Monastery of St. Augustine of Canterbury, and corresponds with Thomas of Elmham's description of one of the two psalters stated to have been acquired from Augustine; though the character of the ornamentation clearly shows that it is of English origin." It is sometimes called the Surtees Psalter; Professor Westwood calls it "The Psalter of St. Augustine."

The book which, to the eye of the artist and palæographer, forms the glory of the Cottonian Library, is that which is marked, Nero D. iv., and is commonly called the Lindisfarne Gospels. Other names which it has borne, are:—The Durham Book, because it was long preserved in Durham Cathedral; and the Gospels of St. Cuthbert, as having been written in honour of that saint. It is the most elaborately-ornamented of all Anglo-Saxon manuscripts; it is quite entire, and tells its own origin and date. Two entries enable us to fix the date of the original Latin book about 710; the interlinear Saxon gloss may be of the ninth century.

Locally connected with the Cottonian is the Har-

[1] "Die Sprache des Kentischen Psalters," von Rudolf Zeuner. Halle, 1882. Referring to Mr. Sweet, in Transactions of Philological Society, 1875-6.

leian collection which was formed by Robert Harley (1661-1724), Earl of Oxford; and it was purchased for the British Museum in 1753. It contains, without name of author (Harl. 3,859) the most ancient manuscript (tenth century) of that "History of the Britons" which now bears the name of Nennius; a few originals or good early copies of Saxon charters; some abbey registers, and some Early-English poetry, especially a manuscript of Chaucer's "Canterbury Tales" (Harley, 7,334), which some have thought to be the oldest and best.

A name second only to Cotton is that of Archbishop Laud. He was a collector of old and rare books in many languages, and we are indebted to his care for some of the most valuable monuments of the mother-tongue. He was president of St. John's College, Oxford, and he had been educated there. Some valuable books he gave to his college, but his larger donations were to the library of his university, of which he became vice-chancellor in 1630. These books rest in the Bodleian Library.

THE BODLEIAN LIBRARY

dates from the year 1598; and here we have an admirable guide in the "Annals of the Bodleian Library," by Rev. W. D. Macray, whose annalistic order we will follow.

1601.—The Library bought the copy of the Anglo-Saxon Gospels, from which John Foxe had printed the edition of 1571.[1] It is marked Bod. 441.

---

[1] "The Gospels of the fower Evangelistes, translated in the olde Saxons tyme out of Latin into the vulgare toung of the

1603.—Some manuscripts were given by Sir Robert Cotton, and one of them (Auct. D., ii. 14:—Bod. 857) is an ancient volume of Latin Gospels, written probably in the sixth century, which shares with the illuminated Benet Gospels described above, the traditional reputation of being one of the books that were sent by Gregory to Augustine. It has no miniatures, but it has rubrication, and it is in a similar style of writing with that splendid volume. Thomas Elmham, who was a monk of St. Augustine's at Canterbury, and wrote a history of his monastery, about A.D. 1414, gives a list of the books of his house; and there are two entries of "Textus Evangeliorum," each being particularly described. Humphrey Wanley (p. 172) identified our two books as those known to Elmham; and Westwood pronounces them to be two of the oldest Latin manuscripts written in pure Roman uncials that exist in this country.

1635–1640.—In these years Archbishop Laud gave nearly 1,300 manuscripts, among which there is one (E. 2) that enjoys pre-eminently the title of "Codex Laudianus." This is a famous manuscript of the Acts of the Apostles, which has been variously dated from the sixth to the eighth century. It is the only known manuscript that exhibits certain irregular readings, seventy-four in number, which Bede, in his "Retractations on the Acts," quoted from his copy. Wetstein surmised that this was the very book before

Saxons, newly collected out of Aunciert Monumentes of the sayd Saxons, and now published for testimonie of the same." At London. Printed by Iohn Daye, dwelling ouer Aldersgate, 1571.

Bede when he wrote his "Retractations."[1] At the end is a Latin Creed, written in the same uncial character, though not by the same hand, and Dr. Heurtley says it is one of the earliest, if not the very earliest, of what he calls the "Manuscript Creeds." He has given a facsimile of it.[2]

Another of these was the Peterborough chronicle (No. 636), a celebrated manuscript, containing the most extensive of all the Saxon chronicles.

1675.—Christopher, Lord Hatton, gave four volumes of Saxon Homilies, written shortly after the Conquest. These are now among the Junian MSS. (Nos. 22, 23, 24, 99), simply because Junius had them on loan. Being among his books at the time of his death, they came back to the Bodleian, as if part of the Junian bequest. This explains why Hatton manuscripts, which contain sermons of Ælfric and of Wulfstan, bear the signatures Jun. 22 and Jun. 99.

Other Hatton manuscripts, and very precious ones, have retained the name of their donor, as—

Hatton 20.—King Alfred's Translation of Gregory's "Pastoral Care," of which the king purposed to send a copy to each cathedral church, and this is the copy sent by the king to Werfrith, bishop of Worcester.

Hatton 76.—Translation by Werfrith, bishop of Worcester, of Gregory's "Dialogues," with King Alfred's Preface (in Wanley this is Hatton 100).

Hatton 65.—The Gospels in Saxon, written about the time of Henry II.

[1] See Scrivener, "Introduction to Criticism of New Testament," ed. 2, p. 147.
[2] "Harmonia Symbolica," Oxford, 1858, p. 61.

THE MATERIALS. 37

1678.—Franciscus Junius died at Windsor. He was born at Heidelberg, in 1589, and his vernacular name was Francis Dujon. He lived much in England, as librarian to Howard, Earl of Arundel. He bequeathed to the Bodleian his Anglo-Saxon and Northern collections. Among these is a beautiful Latin Psalter (Jun. 27) of the tenth century, with grotesque initials and interlinear Saxon. This book has been called "Codex Vossianus," because Junius obtained it from his relative, Isaac Voss. Among these also is the unique Cædmon, a MS. of about A.D. 1000, which had been given to Junius by Archbishop Usher, and of which the earlier history is unknown. Usher, a scholar of European celebrity, founded the library of Trinity College, Dublin; and in his enquiries after books for his college he picked up this famous manuscript. It became a favourite with Junius, who edited the Editio Princeps, Amsterdam, 1655. Another book (Jun. 121) is a collection of Canons of the Anglo-Saxon Church, which belonged to Worcester Cathedral. In this book, fol. 101, the writer describes himself: *Me scripsit Wulfgeatus scriptor Wigorniensis*=Me wrote Wulfgeat of Worcester, a writer. This Wulfgeat is said by Wanley (p. 141) to have lived about A.D. 1064. Junius 22 seems to be written by the same hand; so does Junius 99. The former contains writings by Ælfric; the latter, some by Ælfric and some by Wulfstan. Another book of the Junian bequest, hardly less singular and unique, is the "Ormulum," a poetical exposition of the Gospels, a work of the thirteenth century, of singular beauty, as poetry and as English.

1681.—This is probably the year in which John Rushworth, of Lincoln's Inn, the historian of the Long Parliament, presented to the library the book (Auct. D., ii. 19) which is still known as Codex Rushworthianus. It contains the Gospels in Latin, written about A.D. 800, by an Irish scribe, who has recorded his name as Macregol, and it is glossed with an interlinear Anglo-Saxon version by Owun and by Færmen, a priest, at Harewood. It is described by Westwood.

1755.—Richard Rawlinson was born in 1690, son of Sir Thomas Rawlinson, who was lord mayor of London in 1706; was educated at St. John's College, Oxford, of which he always remained an attached member, and to which he left by will the bulk of his estate. Though he passed for a layman, he was a bishop among the Nonjurors, having been ordained deacon and priest by Bishop Jeremy Collier in 1716, and consecrated bishop 25th March, 1728. He was through life an indefatigable collector; he purchased historical materials of all kinds, heraldry, genealogy, biography, topography, and log-books. He was a repeated benefactor to the library during his life, but after his death his books and manuscripts came in overwhelming quantity, so that the staff of the library could not possibly catalogue them; and it was not until Henry Octavius Coxe became Bodley's librarian that the extent of the Rawlinson collection was ascertained. This benefactor founded the Anglo-Saxon professorship which bears his name.

1809.—Richard Gough, the eminent topographer and antiquary, died 20th February; he had bequeathed to the Bodleian all his topographical collections, together with all his books relating to Saxon and Northern literature. The following is from his will:—" Also I give and bequeath to the Chancellor, Masters, and Scholars, of the University of Oxford, my printed Books and Manuscripts on Saxon and Northern Literature, mentioned in a Catalogue of the same, for the Use of the Saxon professor in the said University when he shall have occasion to consult them, with liberty to take them to his Apartments on condition of faithfully returning them."

I close these Bodleian notes with the remark that three of the books above noticed may be easily seen even by the casual visitor. The late librarian, Henry Octavius Coxe, devised the happy plan of exhibiting under a glass case a chronological series of manuscripts written by English scribes, so as to exhibit the progress of the arts of caligraphy and illuminating in England. This case is in the north wing, at the further end from the entrance door. Among the selections for this series occur Alfred's gift-book to Worcester, the " Codex Vossianus," the " Cædmon," and a fourth book, one that has not yet been described. It is a volume of Latin Gospels in Anglo-Saxon writing, of about the end of the tenth century. This book appears, from an entry at the end of it, to have belonged to the abbey of Barking.[1]

[1] Westwood, "Facsimiles," p. 123.

CORPUS CHRISTI COLLEGE, OXFORD,

though not endowed with treasures equal to those of its namesake in Cambridge, has a few books of very high quality and value. Among these a Saxon Bede of the tenth century, wanting at the beginning and end, but otherwise in excellent condition. A remarkably interesting manuscript of the Rule of St. Benedict, Latin and Saxon, which has never yet been published.[1] Mr. H. O. Coxe, in his catalogue of the manuscripts of the colleges, assigned this book to the close of the tenth century. The interest of the volume is greatly increased by some pages of entries, which also tend to fix the date of the book with greater precision. It was written for the monastery of Bury St. Edmunds, and it appears to have been still there in the fourteenth century. It was given by William Fulman, who was a fellow of this college, to the college library. The same donor gave them their "Piers Plowman" and their famous manuscript of the "Canterbury Tales."

ST. JOHN'S COLLEGE, OXFORD,

has an important manuscript containing (1) Ælfric's Grammar, (2) Glossary, and (3) the Colloquy of Ælfric Bata, in usum puerorum (for the boys). On fol. 202, the writer calls himself, "I Ælfric Bata," and says that his master "Ælfric abbot" was the original author. The writing of (1) and (2) is in the round, strong, professional hand of the tenth century; the

[1] It was to have been edited by Professor Buckley for the Ælfric Society, but that society closed its career too soon.

sequel is in later writing. On the first page is written in a hand of the fourteenth century "Liber Sci Cuthberhti de Dunelmo" (a book of St. Cuthbert, of Durham); and next thereto, but in a hand nearly as old as the MS. itself, " de armario precentoris, qui alienaverit de eo anathema sit" (is kept in the precentor's chest; whoever alienates it therefrom, let him be anathema). It was given to the college by Christopher Coles, who took his degree in 1611. The grammar has been recently edited by Dr. Zupitza.

THE UNIVERSITY LIBRARY AT CAMBRIDGE possesses the oldest manuscript of the ecclesiastical history of Bede (K. K. 5. 16). It is supposed to have been written shortly after the death of the venerable author, which happened in 735. This book came into that library in 1715, with the fine collection of 30,000 volumes collected by Dr. More, bishop of Ely. This collection was purchased by George I. for 6,000 guineas, and presented to the University by the king. This invaluable book is distinctively called Bishop More's manuscript.

In the Cathedral Library at Canterbury there are some valuable Saxon charters;[1]—many more whose natural home was there are in the British Museum among the Cottonian collections.

In the library of Lambeth Palace there is an interesting book, which belonged to Archbishop Parker, and has been well scored by him: but it is

[1] They were arranged by Kemble; and have recently been facsimiled by the Ordnance Survey, under the editorship of Mr. W. Basevi Sanders.

not entered either in the Lambeth catalogue of 1812, or in that of Benet College. This is the "Gospels of MacDurnan," in Irish calligraphy of the ninth century, and it contains some valuable Anglo-Saxon entries.[1]

RESEARCH, DISCOVERY, AND RECONSTRUCTION.

Hitherto we have been describing the collection of material; this it was that rescued our early history and literature from hopeless oblivion. The old parchments contained much knowledge that ought to be recovered and diffused; but this would require preparation and labour. Among the labourers, Matthew Parker comes first as he does among the collectors. This prelate was an earnest student in the ancient history of the country and especially in whatever had relation to the Church. He was the first editor of a Saxon Homily. It was printed by John Day, and was entitled, "A Testimony of Antiquity showing the Ancient Faith of the Church of England touching the Sacrament, &c." The interest of this publication as understood at the time, lay in its witness against transubstantiation. It was reprinted at Oxford by Leon Lichfield, 1675.

In 1571 the Saxon Gospels were published by John Fox, who acknowledges obligations to Parker in his preface. This book was reprinted at Dort, in 1665, by Marshall, who was afterwards rector of Lincoln College, in Oxford.

[1] Fully described by Mr. W. B. Sanders in the "Annual Report for 1873 of the Deputy Keeper of Public Records," p. 271 ff.

In 1574 appeared Parker's edition of Asser's Life of Alfred, and we read in Strype that "of this edition of Asserius there had been great expectation among the learned." We can add, that of this edition the interest is not yet extinct.

How far Parker's books were done by himself and how far he was dependent on his literary assistants, is a question of little importance. No doubt, a great deal of it was the work of his secretary, Joscelin. We look at Parker as a master builder, not as a journeyman. The name of Joscelin meets us often when we are following the footsteps of those times. His writing is seen on many a manuscript, and we have to thank him for much valuable information. It is chiefly through his annotations that we know the external and local relations of our several Saxon chronicles.[1] In August, 1565, he was at St. Augustine's, Canterbury; and there he found the old transcript of the first life of St. Dunstan, which is now in the Cotton Library.[2]

But the chief labourers and reconstructors of the first movement were William Camden (b. 1551—d. 1623), and Sir Henry Spelman (b. 1562—d. 1641). The name of Camden's "Britannia" is still alive, and is familiar as a household word with all who explore even a little beyond the beaten track. But it is otherwise with Sir Henry Spelman, whose studies were more recondite, and to whom Abraham Wheloc looked back as to "the hero of Anglo-Saxon literature."

[1] See the particulars in "Two Saxon Chronicles Parallel." Clarendon Press, 1865. Introduction, pp. vii., xxv., xxviii.
[2] Stubbs, "Memorials of Saint Dunstan," p. xxx.

His " Glossary " was a work of vast compass, and for it he corresponded much with learned men abroad; among others with the famous Northern antiquary, Olaus Wormius, the author of " Literatura Runica," of which he sent Spelman a copy in October, 1636.[1] His son, Sir John Spelman, wrote the " Life of King Alfred." Before he died, Sir Henry Spelman founded an Anglo-Saxon chair at Cambridge; and the first occupant of it was Abraham Wheloc, who edited Bede in 1643 and with it that Saxon Chronicle which was burnt in 1731. In 1644 he edited the Anglo-Saxon Laws. His successor was William Somner (b. 1606—d. 1669), who produced the first Anglo-Saxon dictionary. So this foundation was not unfruitful. But the chair fell into abeyance, until it was restored by Dr. Bosworth, and filled by Professor Skeat.

This, the first movement of reconstruction, had its seat in Cambridge, under the shadow of Archbishop Parker's library. The next advance, dating from the middle of the seventeenth century, grew in Oxford, and was connected with the sojourn of Junius in this place. He was much at the Bodleian, and he is said to have lodged opposite Lincoln College. He was a fellow-labourer with Dr. Marshall, the rector of that college, in the Mæso-Gothic and Anglo-Saxon Gospels which they printed at Dordrecht, 1665. This Oxford period may be said to have culminated in the work of George Hickes, Nonjuror and Saxonist (b. 1642—d. 1715), the author of the massive "Thesaurus

[1] "The Englishman and the Scandinavian," by Frederick Metcalfe, M.A., 1880, p. 11.

Linguarum Septentrionalium," Oxford, 1705, a monument of diligence and insight, to which was appended a work of the greatest utility and necessity,—the idea was Hickes's, as was also much of the sustaining energy,—Humphrey Wanley's catalogue of Anglo-Saxon manuscripts. We must not omit Edmund Gibson (b. 1669—d. 1748), who in early life produced his admirable "Chronicon Saxonicum," amplifying the work of Wheloc, and embodying for the first time the Peterborough manuscript. He was afterwards bishop of London. In 1750 Richard Rawlinson gave rents of the yearly value of £87. 16s. 8d. to the University of Oxford, for the maintenance and support of an Anglo-Saxon lecture or professorship for ever.

Up to this time it might still be said of the collections that they were just stored in bulk as goods are stored in great magazines; there was much to explore and to learn. Important discoveries still remained to be made by explorers in these and other collections. Wanley's catalogue had somewhat the effect of running a line of road through a fertile but unfrequented land; and Conybeare's "Illustrations of Anglo-Saxon Poetry," published in 1826, fruit of the Oxford chair, had a great effect in calling the attention of the educated, and more than any other book in the present century has served as the introduction to Saxon studies.

It was not until the close of the eighteenth century that the "Beowulf" was discovered. Wanley had catalogued it, but without any idea of the real nature of the book. Thorkelin was, however, attracted from Denmark; he came and transcribed it, and prepared an edition which was nearly ready in 1808, when his house was burnt in the bombardment of Copenhagen. But he began again, and lived to see his name to the Editio Princeps of "Beowulf," at a time when there were few who knew or cared for his work. He left two transcripts, which are now our highest source in many passages of the poem. The original having been scorched in the fire of 1731, the edges of the leaves went on cracking away, so that many words which were near the margins and which are now gone, passed under the eye of Thorkelin.

In 1832, a learned German, Dr. Blume, discovered at Vercelli, in North Italy, a thick volume containing Anglo-Saxon homilies, and some sacred poems of great beauty. The poems were copied and printed under the care of Mr. Thorpe, by the Record Commission, in a book known as the "Appendix to Mr. Cooper's Report on the Fœdera," a book that became famous through the complaints that were made because of the long years during which it was kept back. A few privileged persons got copies, and when Grimm, in 1840, published the two chief poems of the new find, the Andreas and the Elene, which he had extracted from Lappenberg's copy, he had a little fling at "die Recorders," as if they kept the book to themselves for a rarity to deck their own shelves withal. The poems are six in number: 1. A Legend of St. Andrew; 2. The Fortunes of the Twelve Apostles; 3. The Departed Soul's Address to the Body; 4. A Fragment; 5. A Dream of the Holy Rood; 6. Elene, or The Invention of the Cross.

In 1851 the first notice of a book of homilies

older than Ælfric,—the property of the Marquis of Lothian, and preserved in the library of Blickling Hall, Norfolk,—was made public by Mr. Godwin in the transactions of the Cambridge Antiquarian Society.[1]

In 1860 was discovered the valuable fragment of an epic poem on King Waldhere, and the manner of the find shall be told in the words of Professor George Stephens, which I quote from the Editio Princeps of "Waldhere," published by him in the same year. "On the 12th of January, 1860, Professor E. C. Werlauff, Chief Librarian of the Great National Library, Cheapinghaven [Copenhagen], was engaged in sorting some bundles of papers, parchment leaves, and fragments, mostly taken from books, or bookbacks, which had not hitherto been arranged. While thus occupied, he lighted upon two vellum leaves of great antiquity, and bearing an Old English text. He kindly communicated the discovery to me, and the present work is the result."

II.

INSCRIPTIONS

of the Anglo-Saxon period exist both in the learned and the vernacular language. It is peculiarly interesting, when an inscription is exhumed that gives us back a contemporary monument, however slight, of that Anglian Church which was the first-fruit

[1] In 1880 these Homilies were edited by Dr. Morris, for the Early English Text Society, under the name of "The Blickling Homilies."

of Christianity in our nation. About twenty years ago, a stone was found at Wearmouth which had been buried in the ruins of the monastery ever since the ninth century, and which came up fresh and clear in almost every letter, bearing, " Hic in sepulcro requiescit corpore Hereberecht prb.[1] (Here in this tomb Hereberecht presbiter rests in the body)." A fine inscription from Deerhurst, in Gloucestershire, is now among the Arundel Marbles at Oxford. It is printed in Parker's "Glossary of Architecture," and in my Saxon Chronicles. Often the interest of these Latin inscriptions is enhanced by a strong touch of the vernacular showing through. This is the case on a fine monumental stone in Mortimer Church.

OF VERNACULAR INSCRIPTIONS

there is one at Lincoln, in the tower of St. Mary-le-Wigford Church. Into this tower, which is of early date, a Roman pagan monument (Diis Manibus, &c.) is walled, and, on the triangular gable of the stone, a Saxon inscription has been carved. It is imperfect, but the general sense is clear. It must be read from the lowest and longest line upwards to the apex. It says: " Eirtig caused me to be made and endowed in honour of Christ and St. Mary." Perhaps the tower, or even the church, is the speaker. The founder's name is much defaced: I have adopted the reading of Rev. J. Wordsworth, who has bestowed attention on this stone.

[1] Hübner, 197.

THE MATERIALS. 49

A fragment of a similar inscription, but much more copious, was found at St. Mary's, York, and is described in Hübner, No. 175. But the most characteristic of the vernacular inscriptions are those on sun-dials. There are no less than three of these in the North Riding of Yorkshire; viz., at Old Byland, and at Edstow near Pickering, and at Kirkdale.[1] The last is fullest and most perfect, and is, moreover, dated. It bears: " + Orm Gamalson bought the minster of S. Gregory when it was all to broken and to fallen, and he it let make anew from ground for Christ and S. Gregory in the days of Edward the King and Tosti the Earl.+and Hawarth wrought me and Brand presbiter.+This is day's sun-marker, hour by hour."

The poetical inscription in Runes, on the Ruthwell Cross, is too large a subject for this place.[2]

JEWELLERY.

The Anglo-Saxons retained an old tradition of decorative art, and they had among them skilful jewellers. Several specimens have been found, and are to be seen in museums; but the noblest of all these is that which is known as the Alfred Jewel.

The Alfred Jewel was discovered in Newton Park, near Athelney, in the year 1693, and it found its way to the Ashmolean Museum in Oxford by the

---
[1] Hübner, 179, 180, 181.
[2] Kemble, "Archæologia," Anno 1843; Stephens, "Runic Monuments," p. 405.

E

year 1718, where it still rests. It consists of an enamelled figure enshrined in a golden frame, with a golden back to it, and with a thick piece of rock crystal in front to serve as a glass to the picture. Imagine a longitudinal section of a pigeon's egg, and let the golden plate at the back of our jewel represent the plane of the egg's diameter. From this plane, if we measure three-quarters of an inch in the girth of the egg, and then take another section parallel to the gold plate at the back, we obtain the front surface of the crystal through which the enamelled figure is visible. The smaller end of our oval section is prolonged and is fashioned like the head of a boar. The snout forms a socket, as if to fit on to a peg or dole; a cross-pin, to fix the socket to the dole, is still in place. Around the sloping rim, which remains, the following legend is wrought in the fabric: ÆLFRED MEC HEHT GEWYRCEAN (Alfred me commanded to make). The language of the legend agrees perfectly with the age of King Alfred, and it seems to be the unhesitating opinion of all those who have investigated the subject that it was a personal ornament of the great West Saxon king. As to the manner of wearing it, and as to the signification of the enamelled figure, there has been the greatest diversity of opinion. Sir Francis Palgrave suggested that the figure was older than the setting. Perhaps it was a sacred object, and perhaps one of the presents of Pope Marinus, or some other potentate; and that the mounting was intended to adapt it for fixture in the rim of a helmet or crown over the centre of the royal brow. By its

THE MATERIALS.

side, in the same glass case, there lies a gold ornament of far simpler design, but of like adaptation.

DRAWING AND ILLUMINATION OF BOOKS.

This is the branch of Saxon art which is best represented by extant remains. That the specimens are numerous may be gathered from what has been said above in the description of manuscripts. There are two periods, and the change takes place with the revival of learning in the reign of Edgar. In the earlier period, the drawings and the decorations are of the same general type as the Irish illuminated books, and it has been thought that our artists had learnt their art from the Irish; but now there is a disposition to see in this art a type common to both islands, and to call it British. The Lindisfarne Gospels (A.D. 710) offer the best example of this kind. In the tenth century, Frankish art was much imitated, and the Saxon style was altered. But the Saxons, in their imitations, displayed originality; and they developed a gorgeous form of decoration, which was recognised as a distinct style, and was known on the Continent as English work (*opus Anglicum*). The typical specimen of this kind is the Benedictional of Æthelwold (between 963 and 970). From the same cause, the character of the penmanship also passes through a corresponding change, but more gradually and indistinctly.[1]

[1] Westwood, "Paleographia Sacra Pictoria," and "Facsimiles of Miniatures from Irish and Anglo-Saxon Manuscripts."

ARCHITECTURE.

Of Saxon architecture there are many traces; we will take but a few. The cathedral at Canterbury was an old church, which had been built by Christians under the Romans, and which Augustine, by the king's help, recovered, and consecrated as the Church of St. Saviour;[1] in later times it came to be called Christ Church. This building lasted all through the Saxon period; it was enlarged by Abbot Odo, about 950, and was finally pulled down by Lanfranc, in 1070. But there exists a written description of this old church by a man who had seen it,—namely, Eadmer the Precentor, who was a diligent collector of traditions concerning his cathedral. What makes his description especially valuable to the architectural historian is the fact that he compares it to St. Peter's at Rome, and he had been to Rome in company with Anselm. Now, although the old Basilica at Rome was destroyed in the sixteenth century, yet plans and drawings which were made before its demolition are preserved in the Vatican: and, with all these data before him, Professor Willis reconstructed the plan of the metropolitan church of the Saxon period.[2] In certain features he used, moreover, the evidence of the ancient Saxon church at Brixworth.[3]

[1] Beda, "Church History," i., 33.
[2] "The Architectural History of Canterbury Cathedral," 1845, p. 27.
[3] "The church at Brixworth has plainly had its walls raised, and a clerestory with windows added, even in the Saxon

THE MATERIALS. 53

Not only from models left in Britain by the Romans, but also through the frequent visits of our ecclesiastics to Rome, it naturally happened that the Saxon architecture was imitated from the Roman. Nevertheless, the Anglo-Saxons appear to have developed a style of their own. Sir Gilbert Scott in his posthumous Essays characterises this early church architecture by two features—the square termination of the east end, and the west end position of the tower. This was quite insular, and not to be found in Roman patterns. In Professor Willis's plan of the first cathedral at Canterbury the east and west ends are both apsidal, and the two towers are placed on the north and south sides of the nave.

The great discovery, a few years ago, of the Saxon chapel at Bradford-on-Avon, and the successful way in which it was cleared and detached from other buildings by Canon Jones, has not only given us so complete an example of Saxon church architecture as we had nothing like it before, but it has also improved our faculty of recognising Saxon work in fragmentary relics, and, if I may so speak, of pulling them all together. A remarkable passage in William of Malmesbury records that Aldhelm built a little church (*ecclesiola*) in this place; and the possibility that this may be that very church is not rejected by the best judges. Aldhelm died in 709.

period; assuming that midwall baluster-shafts are to be received as characteristics of this period, for a triple window with such shafts was inserted in the western wall when the walls were so raised." *Ibid.*, p. 30. See also Haddan and Stubbs, i., 38.

Of Saxon construction a chief peculiarity is that which is called "longs and shorts." It occurs in coins of towers, in panelling work, and sometimes in door jambs.[1] Of the latter, a fine example occurs at Laughton, near Maltby, not many miles distant from Sheffield. What makes this latter instance more peculiarly interesting, is the fact that over the churchyard wall on the west, in a small grass field, traditionally called the Castle Field, there is the well-preserved plan of a Saxon lordly mansion. The circuit of the earthwork is almost complete, and at a point in the enceinte there rises the mound on which was pitched the garrison of the little castle. I use the term castle, as the habits of the language now require, and as it is expressed in the name of the spot. But, indeed, castles were little known in England before the Conquest; had it been otherwise, the Conquest would not have been so easy.[2] The name and the thing came in with the Normans. Yet there were ancient places of security, and their great feature was an earthen mound, upon which a wooden building was pitched. The Saxon mounds often became, to borrow a phrase from Mr. Freeman, the kernel of the Norman castle. And there was a traditional method of fortification for the houses of great men of which Laughton is an example.

[1] Some of the churches in which these features may be observed are Deerhurst in Gloucestershire; Earl's Barton, Northants; Benet church in Cambridge; Sompting in Sussex. Figured illustrations may be seen in Parker's "Introduction to Gothic Architecture."

[2] Freeman, N. C., ii., 605; "Reign of Rufus," i., 49.

SCULPTURE.

There are several pieces of Anglo-Saxon sculpture extant; and they are not hard to recognise, because of the peculiar lines of drawing with which we are already familiar in the illuminated manuscripts. In the Saxon chapel at Bradford-on-Avon there are two angels, of life size, or larger, carved in relief on stone. They appear in the wall high above the chancel arch, towards the nave; and it is supposed from the distance between them, and from their facing one another, that there was once a holy rood placed between them, towards which they were in attendance.

In Bristol Cathedral there is a remarkable piece of Saxon sculpture, representing a human figure, life size, apparently the Saviour, delivering a small figure, as it were a soul, out of the mouth of the dragon. This is carved on the upper side of the massive lid of a stone coffin. It was discovered about forty years ago, and it may be seen in the vestry within the Norman chapter-house, where it is masoned into the wall over the chimney-piece.

BURIALS.

The Saxon graves have yielded many illustrative objects, especially weapons and personal ornaments, pottery, and glass.[1]

The Saxon graves were first systematically explored

[1] These are described and figured in Bryan Faussett's "Inventorium Sepulchrale," ed. Roach Smith; Wylie, "Fairford Graves"; Neville, "Saxon Obsequies"; Akerman, "Pagan Saxondom"; Kemble, "Horæ Ferales."

by Bryan Faussett, of Heppington, in Kent (b. 1720 —d. 1776); who was called by his contemporaries "the British Montfaucon." He is unequalled for the extent of his excavations, and the distinctness of his well-kept chronicle. After him, in the next generation, came an interpreter, who was also a great excavator; James Douglas, author of "Nenia Britannica," 1793. The Faussett collection is in Liverpool, the Douglas collection (most of it) in Oxford.

In more recent times the general accuracy of the results has been established by means of comparative researches. The tumuli in the old mother country of the Saxons have been examined, and their affinity with our Saxon graves has been determined beyond question; while a parallel comparison has also been instituted between the Frankish graves in France, and the ancestral Frankish graves in old Franconia over the Rhine. Thus it is well known what interments are really Saxon.

The chronology of the varieties of interment is not, however, so completely ascertained. In the boundaries of property from the tenth century and onwards we find repeated mention of "heathen burial-places," and it has perhaps been too readily inferred that all the Saxon graves in the open country unconnected with churches are older than the Conversion. Mr. Kemble investigated this subject, and he came to the conclusion that the cinerary urns were heathen, but that the whole interments were Christian. His observations were made chiefly in the old mother country, which lies between the Rhine, the Elbe, and the Main. He identified the change from cremation to inhumation with that from heathenism to Christianity.

The tumular relics of different parts of England suggest old tribal distinctions of costume and apparel. In Kent the fibulæ are circular and highly ornamented, but these are sparingly found beyond the area of the earliest settlers. From Suffolk to Leicestershire the fibulæ are mostly bridge-shaped. A third variety, the concave or saucer-shaped, is found in Berkshire, Wiltshire, Oxfordshire, and Gloucestershire. It is, however, possible that these distinctions may be partly chronological.

The most splendid fibula known is of the first kind. It was exhumed by Bryan Faussett, 5th August, 1771, on Kingston Down in Kent, from a deep grave containing numerous relics, and such as indicated a lady of distinction. The Kingston fibula is circular, entirely of gold, richly set with garnets and turquoise; it is $3\frac{1}{2}$ inches in diameter, $\frac{1}{4}$ inch in thickness, and weighs 6 oz. 5 dwt. 18 gr. This is the gem of all Saxon tumular antiquities, and it rests with the other Faussett finds in the Mayer collection at Liverpool. Near it was found a golden neck-ornament, weighing 2 dwt. 7 gr. These and other like examples, though less splendid, from the graves of Saxon ladies, are good illustrations of the poetic epithet "gold-adorned," which is repeatedly applied to women of high degree.

The Saxon pottery is known to us by the burial urns. These are marked by a local character for the various districts, but still with a generic resemblance, which is based upon the comprehensive fact that although they appear like inferior copies from Roman work, yet they are at the same time like the urns found in Old Saxony and Franconia.

The glass drinking-vessels are very peculiar, and they are noticed as such in the poetry.[1] The hooped buckets that have been found in men's graves only, seem also to answer to expressions in convivial descriptions.

Of the tumular remains this general remark may be made, that they richly illustrate the elder poetry. The abundance and variety of the objects which remain after so long a time unperished, give a strong impression of the lavish generosity with which the dead were sent on their way. Answering to these finds there are two descriptions in the "Beowulf," one in the beginning where the mythic hero Scyld Scefing is (not buried but) shipped off to sea; and the other the funeral of Beowulf with which the poem closes.

The graves also afford illustration negative as well as positive. The comparative rarity of swords is a fact that has been particularly remarked. This too agrees with the poetry in which there are swords of fame, which are known by their own proper names, and which have an established pedigree of illustrious owners at the head of which often stands the name of the divine fabricator, Weland. Perhaps it would not be too much to say that affinity with the tumular deposits is one of the notes of the primary poetry.

[1] "The Celt, the Roman, and the Saxon," by T. Wright, p. 424.

CHAPTER III.

THE HEATHEN PERIOD.

> For many a petty king ere Arthur came
> ruled in this isle, and ever waging war
> each upon other, wasted all the land ;
> and still from time to time the heathen host
> swarm'd over seas, and harried what was left.
> And so there grew great tracts of wilderness,
> wherein the beast was ever more and more,
> but man was less and less, till Arthur came.
> For first Aurelius lived and fought and died,
> and after him king Uther fought and died,
> but either fail'd to make the kingdom one.
> And after these king Arthur for a space,
> and thro' the puissance of his Table round,
> drew all their petty princedoms under him,
> their king and head, and made a realm, and reign'd.
> ALFRED TENNYSON, *The Coming of Arthur.*

FOR the first hundred and fifty years of their life in this island our ancestors were heathens. This time has no place in the English memory through any legendary or literary tradition that is associated with the Saxons. The legends of this time which retain a place in literature are not Saxon but British. This is the era of Arthur and the Knights of the Round Table. There is no book or piece of Saxon literature that can in any substantial sense be ascribed to the heathen period; for I cannot go with those who assign this high antiquity to the " Beowulf."

There is a book that claims to be a product of this time, but it is neither Saxon nor heathen. It bears the name of Gildas, a Briton, and it is a fervently Christian book, written in Latin. It has two parts, one being a Lament of the Ruin of Britain, the other a Denunciation of the conduct of her princes. Its genuineness has been questioned, and it has also been ably defended.[1] The strong point in favour of the book is, that it existed and was reputed genuine before the time of Bede, who used it as an authority, and cited it by the author's name, saying that "Gildas, their [the Britons'] historian," describes such and such evils in his "lamentable discourse."[2] Through Bede the information of Gildas has fallen into the stream of English history, and we cease to be aware of the original source. For example, the familiar tradition of the Saxons coming over in "three keels," ordinarily ascribed to Bede, is taken from Gildas. The date of this author and his work, as now generally accepted, is this :—That he was born in 520, the year of the battle of Mons Badonicus, and that he wrote about 564. But this rests on an ill-jointed and uncertain passage, which was misunderstood by Bede, if the modern interpretation is right.

And when we come to look into that Saxon literature which was subsequently developed, the traces of the heathen period are unexpectedly scanty, and the very remembrance of heathenism though not abolished seems already wonderfully remote. But notwithstand-

[1] T. Wright, "Celt, Roman, and Saxon," p. 389; J. R. Green, "Short History," i., 2.
[2] "Ecclesiastical History," i., 22.

ing all this, we cannot treat the subject of Anglo-Saxon literature in any satisfactory manner without some consideration of the heathen period. For, on the one hand, history requires it as a background, and the only appropriate background to our story of the subsequent culture; and, on the other hand, we shall find, by putting the scattered fragments together, that such an impression may be gained as is at least sufficient for a subsidiary purpose.

Among the extant Saxon writings there is one and only one book, in which we detect some possible work of this period. This is in the Chronicles. Between A.D. 450 and 600 we have a sprinkling of curious annals that are naturally calculated to rivet the attention. They are certainly of a very distinct and peculiar cast, and it has been thought that they may possibly represent (through much disguise of transcription) some kind of contemporary records of the heathen period, whether the original shape was that of ballads, or of annals kept in Runes.

These annals are characterised by an occasional touch of poetic fervour, and by several local details which are stimulating to modern curiosity. A few examples may be useful :—

455. Here[1] Hengest and Horsa fought against Wyrtgeorn, the king, in the place that is called Agælesthrep; and his brother Horsa was slain; and after that Hengest took to the kingdom, and Æsc, his son.

457. Here Hengest and Æsc fought against the

[1] It is the manner of the Saxon chronicles to attach each annal to its year-date by an adverb of locality—" Here."

Brettas in the place that is called Crecganford; and there they slew 4,000 men; and the Brets then abandoned Kentland, and in great terror fled to Londonbury.

473. Here Hengest and Æsc fought against the Walas: and they took countless spoil: and the Walas fled the Engles like fire.

491. Here Ælle and Cissa beset Andredescester, and slew all those that therein dwelt: there was not so much as one Bret remaining.

571. Here Cuthwulf fought with the Bretwalas at Bedcanford, and took four towns: Lygeanburg and Ægelesburg (Aylesbury), Bænesingtun (Bensington) and Egonesham (Ensham).

584. Here Ceawlin and Cutha fought against the Brettas, in the place that is named Fethanleag; and Cutha was slain. And Ceawlin took many towns and countless spoils; and in wrath he returned thence to his own.

There is about these entries something remote and primitive, and something, too, of a contemporaneous form, that penetrates even through the folds of a modern dress.

If we would gather an idea of the religious sentiments of that heathen time, two sources are open to us:—1. Classical authors, especially Cæsar and Tacitus; 2. Incidental notices in domestic writings after the establishment of Christianity. In regard to both these sources we must regulate our expectations in accordance with the circumstances.

1. Cæsar and Tacitus wrote of Germany at large, and not of our particular tribes in the north-west;

yet they naturally touch some leading points which are of interest for us here. As to their religion, Cæsar formed a totally different opinion from Tacitus. According to the former, the Germans knew only those visible and palpably useful gods, the Sun and the Moon, and Fire; they had never even heard of any others by report. Tacitus, on the contrary, says, that they worship Hercules and Mars, and, above all, Mercury; that, at the same time, their religious sense is eminently spiritual, for they repudiate the thought of enshrining the celestials within walls, or representing them by the human form; that they venerate groves and forest-glades, and that by the names of their gods they understand mysterious beings visible only to the inward and reverential sight. These estimates are diametrically opposed, and they have been used by an eminent writer to illustrate the difficulty of getting at the truth about the religion of barbarians. But it should be remembered that a long interval had elapsed between Cæsar and Tacitus; an interval, moreover, that was likely to work some, if not all, of the changes required to make these estimates compatible with one another.

Tacitus informs us about the god Tuisco, whose name we still keep in Tuesday;[1] about the supremacy of Mercurius,[2] that is, of Woden; and about the form of the boar as a sacred symbol, which was worn on the person for a charm against danger.[3] He also relates the hideous ceremony of a goddess Nerthus, or Mother Earth, who makes her occasional

[1] "Germania," c. 2.   [2] *Id.*, c. 9.
[3] *Id.*, c. 45.

progresses in a wagon drawn by cows, the attendants being slaves who, when the rite is done, are all drowned in a mysterious lake.[1]

2. From the second source we might have expected more than we find. Knowing that the new religion was not established without struggles and delays and relapses, we might have expected that the traces of the dying superstition would have been numerous in Anglo-Saxon literature. And if we had the domestic writings that were produced in the first Christian ardour, such an expectation might have been partially fulfilled. But in any case we should not expect too much from early and unformed literature. It is the mature fruit of long cultivation to produce a literature that reflects the present. Almost all early literature is conventional, because the spontaneous is not esteemed and is not preserved. But whatever might have happened under other conditions, the fact now is that the literature of our first Christian era is almost entirely lost. It perished in the Danish invasions. The works of Beda are, indeed, preserved, and in one sense they make a large exception to the general statement, yet the exception is not one that is of great import for our immediate purpose. His works, even when he is upon a local subject, breathe little of local curiosity or interest. His was a cloistered life, his view was ever directed through the vista of books and learned correspondence towards the central heart of Christianity, and he deigned but rarely to cast a look behind him at the old superstitions of his people.

[1] "Germania," c. 40.

His writings, which are all in Latin, contribute something, but it is little, towards our knowledge of Saxon heathendom. We are indebted to him for an explicit statement about the meaning of the word "Easter." It is as follows:—"*Rhedmonath* is so called from their goddess *Rheda*, to whom in that month they sacrificed. .... With the people of my nation, the old folk of the Angles, the month of April, which is now styled Paschal Month, had formerly the name of *Esturmonath*, after a goddess of theirs who was called *Eostra*, and whose festival is kept in that month; and they still designate the Paschal Season from her name, by force of old religious habit keeping the same name for the new solemnity."[1] This is a sample of what Beda might have told us about the old heathendom, if he had made it a subject of inquiry. The information is the more valuable because it was not forthcoming from any other source. The Germans have an obscure trace of *Retmonat;* and their *ôstarmânoth*, which remains as a German name for April (Ostermonat) to the present day, is found as early as Eginhard, the biographer of Charlemagne. But of the deities there is no information anywhere but in Beda. The name of Easter appears related to "East" and the growing strength of the sun. In the Edda a male being, a spirit of light, bears the name of *Austri:* the German and Saxon tribes seem to have known only a female divinity in this sense. A being with attributes taken from the Dawn and from the Spring of the year, so full of promise and of blessing, might

[1] "De Temporum Ratione," c. 13.

well be tenaciously remembered and retained for Christian use.

We will now proceed to notice the sources which preserve some relics of the old heathenism.

THE GENEALOGIES

bear the greatest testimony to the former dignity of Woden's name. The royal houses of Kent, Essex, Deira, Bernicia, Wessex, East Anglia, Mercia,—all trace up to Woden.* Some go up far above Woden, who has a series of mythological progenitors, the oldest of whom appears to be Scyld, the name which forms the starting-point of the "Beowulf."

THE LAWS.

In the Kentish code of Wihtræd (d. 725) there are penalties set down for those who sacrifice to devils, meaning heathen gods.

But, on the whole, it is remarkable how little is found on this subject in the codes before Alfred. In the Introduction to Alfred's Laws idolatry is forbidden in two places, not in words of the time, but with the sanction of Scripture texts.

In the Laws of Edward and Guthrum heathenism is denounced with penalties; in the Codes of Æthelred it is forbidden in a hortatory way; but the most explicit prohibition is that of Canute:—

"5. Of Heathenism. And we strictly forbid all heathenism. It is heathenism for a man to worship idols,—that is, to worship heathen gods, and the sun or moon, fire or flood, water-wells or stones, or any kind of wood-trees, or practise witchcraft, or contrive murder by sorcery."

The latter words seem to point to that form of sorcery known as *defixio*, wherein an effigy was maltreated, and incantations were used to direct the injury against the life or health of some private enemy, whom the image was taken to represent.

CANONS ECCLESIASTICAL.

In the Canons of Ælfric, c. 35, priests are not to attend funereal festivities unless they are invited; and if they are invited, they are to forbid the heathen songs of the lewd men, and their loud cachinnations; and they are not to eat or drink where the corpse is deposited (thær thæt lic inne lith), lest they be partakers of the heathen rite which is there celebrated. This seems to be illustrated by a prohibition found in the Capitularies of Charlemagne against eating and drinking over the mounds of the dead; and also by a passage of Boniface (Epist. 71), who says that the Franks immolated bulls and goats to the gods, and ate the sacrifices of the dead. It has been supposed that a number of teeth, of oxen and sheep or goats, which were found among heathen Saxon graves at Harnham, near Salisbury, might be evidence of this practice.[1]

In the "Laws of the Northumbrian Priests," c. 48, it is enacted:—" If there be a sanctuary (frith-geard) in any one's land, about a stone, or a tree, or a wall, or any such vanity, let him that made it pay a fine

[1] "Archæologia," vol. xxxv., p. 259.

(lah-slit), half to Christ, half to the landlord (land-rica); and if the landlord will not aid in executing the law, then let Christ and the king receive the mulct."

THE POETRY

preserves many traces of heathendom. The unconscious relics of old mythology that are imbedded in the recurrent formulæ of the heroic diction is one of our strongest proofs that this diction was already matured in heathen times. A very prominent term is Wyrd = Destiny, Fate; which is the same as the Urðr of the Scandian mythology, one of the three fates, Urðr, Werðandi, Skuld = Past, Present, Future. In Wyrd, the whole of the attributes are included under one name; and it counts among the marks of affinity between the Heliand and our Anglo-Saxon literature, that the same thing is observed there also, though in a less distinct manner. In the "Beowulf" it is said:—"Wyrd often keeps alive the man who is not destined to die, if his courage is equal to the occasion." Wyrd is said to weave, to prescribe, to ordain, to delude, to hurt. In Cædmon she is wælgrim= bloodthirsty. And the heathen association may still be felt, even when the name of Wyrd is displaced by a name of the Christian's God, as in "Beowulf" where we read:—"The Lord gave him webs to speed in war."[1] In the Heliand the attributes are less varied,

[1] Compare with this the "Spaedom of the Norns," in Dasent's "Burnt Njal"; also Gray's "Fatal Sisters," which is another version of the same original, one remove further off, as Gray knew the poem only through the Latin of Torfæus.

THE HEATHEN PERIOD. 69

the vaticination is wanting, and *Wurð* seems almost the same as Death.

But the old tradition of the three mysterious women lived on in this island. It is now best known to us through the German Fairy Tales, where we have the three spinning women. In the Middle Ages there was a remembrance of these mysterious visitants in a certain ceremony of spreading a table for three, whether for protection to the house at night, or to bring good luck to the children born in that house. In the Penitential of Baldwin, Bishop of Exeter (twelfth century), this superstition is noted, and the latter motive assigned.

The monks of Evesham kept up a tradition which traced the origin of their house to a vision of three beautiful maidens, in heavenly garments, sweetly singing. They were seen by a swineherd in the forest, when he was in search of a lost swine, and he went to Bishop Ecgwine and told him. The bishop arrived at the place, was favoured with the same vision, and founded the monastery there. The device on the abbey seal represented this vision.

A less pleasing vision of the Three Sisters is narrated by Wulfstan of Winchester, a poet of the tenth century, who has left us a Latin poem of the Miracles of St. Swithun. In it he tells how, coming back one evening towards Winchester, he was met by two hideous females, who commanded him to stop, but he ran away in terror; he was then met and stopped by a third, who struck him a blow from which he suffered for the remainder of his life; but the three women plunged into the river and disappeared.

The same three appear in *Macbeth* as the Weird Sisters; and it is probably from this connexion that *weird* has become an adjective for all that savours of heathenism.

A frequent word for battle and carnage is *wæl*, and the root idea of this word is choice, which may be illustrated from the German *wählen*—to choose. The heathen idea was that Woden chose those who should fall in battle to dwell with him in Walhalla, the Hall of the chosen. In the exercise of this choice, Woden acted by female messengers, called in the Norse mythology *valkyrja*, pl. *valkyrjor*.[1]

All superior works in metal, as swords, coats of mail, jewels, are the productions of Weland, the smith. His father is called Wudga, and his son is called Wada; and with this child on his shoulder Weland strides through water nine yards deep. This was matter of popular song down to Chaucer's time:—

> He songe, she playede, he told a tale of Wade.
> "Troylus and Crescyde," iii., 615.

He had by Beadohild another son, in German named Witeche, who inherited his father's skill and renown. For his violence to Beadohild, Weland was lamed; but he made for himself a winged garment, wherewith he took his flight through the air. He is

---

[1] The second part of this compound repeats the idea of the first, namely, choice: it is from the verb to choose, for in certain tenses this verb changed *s* to *r*, just as from the verb to *freeze* we have *frore* (Milton), and from *lose* we have a participle *lorn*. The Anglo-Saxon form is *wælcyrige*. Grimm's "Teutonic Mythol." tr. Stallybrass, p. 418. Kemble, "Saxons," i., 402.

at once the Daidalos and the Hephaistos of the
Greeks. The translator of the Boethian Metres has
taken occasion to bring in this heathen god, whose
cult (it seems) was still too active. In Metre ii., 7,
where Boethius has the line—

> Ubi nunc fidelis ossa Fabricii manent?

under colour of *faber* = smith, which the name Fabricius suggests, Weland is made a fruitful text :—

Hwær sind nu thæs wisan
   Welandes ban,
thæs goldsmithes
   the wæs gio mærost?
Forthy ic cwæth thæs wisan
   Welandes ban,
forthy ængum ne mæg
   eorthbuendra,
se craft losian
   the him Crist onlænth.
Ne mæg mon æfre
   thy eth ænne wræccan
his craftes beniman
   the mon oncerran mæg
sunnan on swifan
   and thisne swiftan rodor
of his riht ryne
   rinca ænig.
Hwa wat nu thæs wisan
   Welandes ban,
on hwelcum hi hlæwa
   hrusan theccen?
	Where now are the bones
	   of Weland the wise,
	that goldsmith
	   so glorious of yore?
	Why name I the bones
	   of Weland the wise,
	but to tell you the truth
	   that none upon earth
	can e'er lose the craft
	   that is lent him by Christ?
	Vain were it to try,
	   e'en a vagabond man
	of his craft to bereave;
	   as vain as to turn
	the sun in his course
	   and the swift wheeling sky
	from his stated career—
	   it cannot be done.
	Who now wots of the bones
	   of Weland the wise,
	or which is the barrow
	   that banks them?

One of the most striking points of contact between
our relics of mythology and those of the Edda occurs
in the "Beowulf," where mention is made of the

famous necklace of the Brosings (or, as Grimm would correct, Brisings).

In the Edda the goddess Freyja is the owner of a precious necklace, called *Brîsinga men*. She had acquired this jewel from the dwarfs, and she kept it in an inaccessible chamber, but, nevertheless, it was stolen from her by Loki. Therefore Loki is *Brîsings thiofr*, the thief of the Brising necklace; and Heimdallr fought with Loki for it. When Freyja is angry the heaving of this ornament betrays her emotion. When Thôrr, to get his hammer back, disguises himself as Freyja, he fails not to put on her famous necklace. From its mention in Anglo-Saxon poetry, Grimm would infer the familiarity of the Saxon race with the whole story.[1]

But what adds vastly to the interest of this legend is that we find it in Homer. It is essentially the same with the belt of Aphrodite (Hymn, 1. 88). In Iliad xiv., 214, Aphrodite takes it off and lends it to Hêrê to charm Zeus withal. When we add that just above in the same context (Iliad xiv., 165) Hêrê also has a curiously contrived chamber, made for her by Hephaistos (Vulcan), the parallel is too close to be mistaken.

THE GOSPEL TRANSLATION.

Of the old heathen theogony we have a remarkable document in the names of the days of the week; and

---

[1] The same keen discoverer scents an old heathen reminiscence also when the poet of the Heliand makes that holy thing which is not to be cast before dogs (Matthew vii. 6) a *hêlag halsmeni* = holy necklace.

these names are best preserved to us in the rubrics of the Anglo-Saxon Gospels. These names are supposed to have come from the western shores of Asia, and to have pervaded the nations of Europe, both Roman and barbarian, in the first and second centuries. By a comparison of the sets of names in the two families of nations, we gain certain leading facts about the chief deities of our heathen ancestry, which all the rest of the scattered evidence tends to confirm. Thus our Tuesday, A.-S. Tywes-dæg, compared with the French Mardi and its Latin original Martis dies, teaches us that the old god Tiw (who was also called Tir) was recognised as the analogue of the Roman Mars, the god of war. So Wednesday, A.-S. Wodnes-dæg, compared with the French Mercredi and its Latin form Mercurii dies, gives us proof that the god Woden answered to the Roman Mercurius. So, too, Thursday, A.-S. Thunres-dæg, compared with French Jeudi and Latin Jovis dies, shows that Thunor (whom the Scandinavians call Thor) is the god of thunder, like the Latin Jupiter. So again, Friday, A.-S. Frige-dæg, compared with Vendredi and Veneris dies, gives us the analogy of Frige with Venus.[1] Saturday, A.-S. Satærnes-dæg, seems like a borrowed name from the Latin Saturnus.

Kemble maintained the probability that Sætere was a native divinity, and considered that the local

[1] For the distinct attributes of this goddess, who was the wife of Woden, the reader may consult Grimm's "Teutonic Mythology," who quotes Paulus Diaconus (eighth century), saying that the Langobards called Woden's wife *Frea*, and Saxo, p. 13, saying, " Frigga Othini conjux."

names of Satterthwaite (Lanc.), and Satterleigh (Devon), offered some probable evidence in that direction. More distinct are the local namesakes of Woden. Kemble adduces repeated instances of Wanborough, formerly Wodnesbrook (Surrey, Wilts, Hants), Woodnesborough (Kent), Wanstrow, formerly Wodnestreow = Woden's tree (Somerset), Wansdike, and others.

THE HOMILIES

occasionally denounce and describe the prevalent forms of heathenism still surviving. Thus Ælfric (i., 474):—"It is not allowed to any Christian man, that he should recover his health at any stone, or at any tree." Wulfstan preaches thus :—" From the devil comes every evil, every misery, and no remedy : where he finds incautious men he sends on themselves, or sometimes on their cattle, some terrible ailment, and they proceed to vow alms by the devil's suggestion, either to a well or to a stone, or else to some unlawful things . . ."[1]

In an alliterative homily of the tenth century, the heathen gods that are combated are Danish :—[2]

Thes Jovis is arwurthost ealra thæra goda, The tha hæthenan hæfdon on heora gedwilde, and he hatte Thor betwux sumum theodum ;	This Jove is most worshipped of all the gods that the heathens had in their delusion ; and he hight Thor some nations among ;

---

[1] "Über die Werke des altenglischen Erzbischofs Wulfstan," von Arthur Napier. Weimar, 1882, p. 33.
[2] Printed in Kemble's "Solomon and Saturn," p. 120.

thone tha Deniscan leode lufiath swithost.	him the tribes of the Danes especially love.
. . . . .	. . . . .
Sum man was gehaten Mercurius on life, he was swithe facenful and swicol on dedum, and lufode eac stala and leasbrednysse; thone macodon tha hæthenan him to mæran gode,' and æt wega gelætum him lac offrodon, and to heagum beorgum him on brohton onsegdnysse. Thes god was arwurthra betwux eallum hæthenum, and he is Othon gehaten othrum naman on Denisc.	There once lived a man Mercurius hight; he was vastly deceitful and sly in his deeds, eke stealing he loved and lying device; him the heathens they made their majestical god, and at the cross roads they offered him gifts, and to the high hills brought him victims to slay. This god was main worthy all heathens among, and his name when translated in Danish is Odin.

An interesting example of the methods used to wean our simple forefathers from their old heathen practices may be seen in a "Spell to restore fertility to land."[1] The preamble sets forth:—"Here is the remedy whereby thou mayest restore thy fields, if they will not produce well, or where any uncanny thing has befallen them, like magic or witchcraft." Four turfs are to be cut before dawn from four corners of the land, and these are to be stacked in a heap, and upon them are to be dropped drops of an elaborate preparation whereof one ingredient is holy water; and over them are to be said words of Scripture and Our Father. And then the turfs are taken to church, and prayers are said by the priest while the green of the

[1] Printed in Thorpe's "Analecta" (1846), p. 116.

turfs is turned altarwards ; and then, before sun-down, the turfs are returned to their own original places : but first, four crosses, made of quickbeam, with the names Matthew, Mark, Luke, John, written on their four ends, are to be put, one in the bottom of each pit, and as each turf is restored to its native spot, and laid on its particular cross, say thus :—" Crux, Mattheus ; Crux, Marcus ; Crux, Lucas ; Crux, Joannes."[1] Then the supplicant turns eastward, bows nine times, and says a rhythmic form of prayer, in which some heathen elements are just discernible. Then he turns three times towards the sun in its course, and sings Benedicite, Magnificat, and Pater Noster, and makes a gracious vow, in the friendly comprehension of which all the neighbourhood is included, gentle and simple.

This being done, strange seed must be procured, and this must be got from poor " almsmen " ; and the supplicant must give them a double quantity in return ; and then he must collect together all his plough-gear and tackle, and say over them a poetic formula which has fragments that look very like the real old heathen charm. It begins with untranslatable words :—

>Erce, erce, erce,   Erce, erce, erce,
>eorđan modor.   mother of earth.

---

[1] This recalls the charm that within living memory was used on Dartmoor as an evening prayer :—

>Matthew, Mark, Luke, and John,
>Bless the bed that I lie on ;
>Two to head and two to feet,
>And four to keep me while I sleep.

Then go to work with the plough, and open the first furrow, and say :—

Hál wes thu, folde,	Soil I salute thee,
fira modor ;	mother of souls ;
beo thu growende,	be thou growing
on Godes fæthme ;	by God's grace ;
fodre gefylled,	filled with fodder
firum to nytte.	folks to comfort.

Then a loaf is to be kneaded and baked, and put into the first furrow, with yet another anthem :—

Ful æcer fodres	A full crop of fodder
fira cinne,	may the folks see ;
beorht-blowende	brightly blossoming,
thu gebletsod weorth.	blessed mote thou be.

Then follows a chaplet of three repetitions, twice repeated, and this long day's orison is done.

Here we have a fair example of the artifice used by the clergy in transforming old heathen charms into edifying ceremonies. Men are here led to pray ; to exercise themselves in some of the chief liturgical formularies of the Catholic Church ; to accept Christian versions of their old incantations ; to profess good will to their neighbours, high and low ; and to exercise some bounty towards the poor. Natural means are not neglected ; a change of seed is made a part of the ceremonial.

Such are some of the traces we can gather from the expiring relics of heathenism. They all come from the Christian period, as was natural, seeing that the national profession of heathenism ended before our literature began, unless the annals mentioned at the beginning of this chapter are exceptions. The facilities of writing must have been very limited if the only alphabet in use was the Runic. It is, perhaps, a little too rigid to assume that the use of the Roman alphabet is to be dated strictly from the Conversion. As the use of Runes did not then suddenly terminate, but gradually receded before the superior instrument, so perhaps it is most reasonable to suppose that the adoption of the Roman alphabet was very gradual, and that the Saxons may have begun to use it, at least in Kent, before the reign of Æthelberht.[1]

[1] Some Runic alphabets may be seen in my "Philology of the English Tongue," § 96 (ed. 3, 1879). The best collection of Runic monuments is in the two folio volumes of Professor George Stephens.

CHAPTER IV.

THE SCHOOLS OF KENT.

§ 1.

It is a debatable question whether any Roman culture lived through the Saxon conquest.

The Saxon conquest of Britain was certainly, on the whole, a destructive one, and it has been justly contrasted with the Frankish conquest of Gaul; where the conquerors quickly assimilated with the conquered. The relics of Roman civilisation which the Saxons adopted, were indeed few. This is true, as a general statement. But there is some ground for regarding Kent as a case apart. Here all accounts seem to indicate a gradual and less violent intrusion of the new race, and to suggest the possibility that there was not for that area a complete break in the traditions and customs of life. The capital city itself, Dorobernia (Canterbury), whatever revolution it may have suffered, was at least not destroyed. There is nothing that requires us to assume the extinction of the schools of grammar which existed presumably in Kent as in Gaul.

The foundation of schools by the Roman mission is not recorded, nor does Bede say anything to imply it when thirty years later he describes the foundation of schools in East Anglia. These were founded by king Sigberct because he desired to have good institutions such as he had seen in Gaul, and his wishes were carried into effect by bishop Felix, after the pattern of the schools of Kent.[1] Whether it would be possible to trace the study of Roman law as a scholastic exercise through these obscure times, is very doubtful.[2] But certainly there is something about the Latinity of our earliest legal documents, that has a local and even a vernacular aspect. Slight as these traces may be, they are interesting enough to merit consideration.

In the Kentish laws are preserved our oldest extant relics of ancestral custom. The first code is that of Æthelberht, with this title :—" This be the Dooms that Æthelbriht, king, ordained in Augustine's days." It is much concerned with penalties for personal injuries. These are some of the " Dooms " :—

>   Cap. 40. If an ear be smitten off, 6 shillings amends (bôt).
>   „   41. If the ear be pierced through, 3 shillings.
>   „   43. If an eye is lost, 50 shillings.
>   „   44. If mouth or eye be damaged, 12 shillings.
>   „   45. If the nose be pierced, 9 shillings.
>   „   51. For the four front teeth, 6 shillings each ; the tooth that stands next, 4 shillings ;

---

[1] "Ecclesiastical History," iii., 18.

[2] Aldhelm speaks of the study of Roman law in connexion with other scholastic studies, as Latin verses and music. But then that was after the new start given to education by Theodore and Hadrian. A century later, Alcuin described the studies at York in this order,—grammar, rhetoric, law. — Wharton, "Anglia Sacra," ii. 6 ; Alcuin's poem, " De Pontificibus &c."

THE SCHOOLS OF KENT. 81

the next to that, 3 shillings; and thenceforth, each, 1 shilling.

Penalties for theft are graduated according to the quality of the person injured, *i.e.*, according to the different orders of men in the body politic, each of whom has a separate value: king, noble, freeman, serf, slave. Such we may suppose to have been the primitive institutes of the tribes in the old mother country on the Continent. But the code is headed by a captel, in which the property of the Church is valued beyond that of the king, and the same applies to the higher clergy. "Cap. 1. The property of God and the Church, 12 fold; Bishop's property, 11 fold; Priest's, 9 fold [the same as the King's]; Deacon's, 6 fold; Clerk's, 3 fold." Next follows one that we may well suppose might have been the first of the pre-Christian code: "Cap. 2. If the king summon his people to him, and one there do them evil—double bôt, and 50 shillings to the king." Bede mentions (ii., 5) these laws of Æthelberht, and especially this feature of them, that they began with the protection of Church property. He also says, that the king constituted these laws according to Roman precedent (*juxta exempla Romanorum*), by which some have been led to expect that there would be an element of Roman law in them. The imitation consisted only in committing the laws to writing.

Æthelberht died in 616, and then came a heathen reaction under his son Eadbald; but he was converted to Christianity in 618 by Bishop Laurentius. His son Ercombriht, who succeeded in 640, was the

G

first king who dared to demolish the heathen fanes. Bede informs us that this king made a law for the observance of the Lenten fast; but no law of the kind appears until we come to the laws of Wihtred. Ecgbriht succeeded his father in 664, under whom the waning power of Kent reasserted its former sway. To him succeeded first Hlothære in 673, and then Eadric. These two reigns were short, and the names of both the kings stand at the head of the next Kentish code.

The introductory sentence of this code was this :—
" Hlothhære and Eadric, kings of the men of Kent, enlarged the laws which their predecessors had made aforetime, with these dooms following " :—

Cap. 8. If one man implead another in a matter, and he cite the man to a 'Methel' or a 'Thing', let the man always give security to the other, and do him such right, as the Kentish judges prescribe to them.

This code has a little series of laws concerning offences to the sense of honour, and consequent danger to the king's peace :—

Cap. 11. If in another's house one man calleth another man a perjurer, or assail him offensively with injurious words; let him pay a shilling to the owner of the house, and 6 shillings to the insulted man, and forfeit 12 shillings to the king.

Cap. 12. If a man remove another's stoup where men drink without offence, by old right he pays a shilling to him who owns the house, and 6 shillings to him whose stoup was taken away, and 12 shillings to the king.

Cap. 13. If weapon be drawn where men drink, and no harm be done; a shilling to the owner of the house, and 12 shillings to the king.

After a troublous time of encroachment from the side of Wessex, the kingdom of Kent had again a time of honour, if not of absolute independence, under king Wihtred (691—725), who, in the preamble to his laws, is called the most gracious king of the Kentish folk (*se mildesta cyning Cantwara*). His laws are mostly ecclesiastical. The rights of the Church and of her ministers, the keeping of the Sunday, manumission of slaves at the altar, penalties for heathen rites, these subjects make the bulk of a code of 28 captels, of which the last four are about theft. The closing provision is characteristic of the state of society:

Cap. 28. If a man from a distance, or a stranger, go off the road, and he neither shout nor blow a horn, as a thief he is liable to be examined, or slain, or redeemed.

In the preamble this code is precisely dated on the 6th day of August in Wihtred's fifth year, which is 696. Also it mentions Berghamstyde, which seems to mean Berkhamstead (Herts), as the place of enactment, and Gybmund, bishop of Rochester, as having been present. Doubts have been cast upon the genuineness of this code, but it is defended in Schmid's introduction. This is the last of the laws of Kent.

The Kentish laws are found in a register of the twelfth century, which has a high character for fidelity. No doubt the substance of them is faithfully preserved.

But they are not in the original Kentish dialect; they have been translated into West Saxon. The translation has not, however, obliterated all traces of the original; there are some peculiarities which survive, and which enable us to see through the present form those traces of a higher antiquity, which strengthen that confidence which the contents are calculated to inspire.

The Kentish dialect was the first literary form of the language of our Saxon ancestors. It has been thought that in the Epinal Gloss, of which a specimen will be given below, we have the best extant representation of this ancient dialect. Early in the ninth century we have some original documents in the Kentish dialect, and these are our surest guides in judging of other specimens.[1]

The following extract is from a legal document of the year 832. Luba had made a deed of gift from her estate to the fraternity of Christ Church at Canterbury, and the following sanction was appended:

☦ Ic luba eaðmod godes ðiwen ðas forecwedenan god ꝫ ðas elmessan gesette ꝫ gefestnie ob minem erfelande et mundlingham ðem hiium to cristes cirican ꝫ ic bidde ꝫ an godes libgendes naman bebiade ðæm men ðe ðis land ꝫ ðis erbe hebbe et mundlingham ðet he ðas god forðleste oð wiaralde

I, Luba, the humble handmaid of God, appoint and establish these foresaid benefactions and alms from my heritable land at Mundlingham to the brethren at Christ Church; and I entreat, and in the name of the living God I command, the man who may have this land and this inherit-

---

[1] They are in Kemble, "Codex Diplomaticus," Nos. 226, 228, 229, 231, 235, 238.

ende se man se ðis healdan wille ⁊ lestan ðet ic beboden hebbe an ðisem gewrite se him seald ⁊ gehealden sia hiabenlice bledsung se his ferwerne oððe hit agele se him seald ⁊ gehealden helle wite bute he to fulre bote gecerran wille gode ⁊ mannum uene ualete.

ance at Mundlingham, that he continue these benefactions to the world's end. The man who will keep and discharge this that I have commanded in this writing, to him be given and kept the heavenly blessing; he who hinders or neglects it, to him be given and kept the punishment of hell, unless he will repent with full amends to God and to men. Fare ye well.

§ 2.

The middle of the seventh century was a very dark period throughout the West. The lingering rays of ancient culture had grown very faint in France, Italy, and Spain. Literary production had ceased in France since Gregory of Tours and his friend Venantius Fortunatus, the poet; in Spain, soon after Isidore of Seville, the Christian area had been narrowed by the Moslem invasion; in Italy, though the tradition of learning was never extinguished, yet no writer of eminence appeared for a long time after Gregory the Great. At such a time it was that the seed of learning found a new and fruitful soil among the Anglo-Saxon people; and they who had been the latest receivers of the civilising element, quickly took the lead in religion and learning.

In the year 668 three remarkable men came into Britain. These were Theodore, a Greek of Tarsus, who came as Archbishop of Canterbury; Hadrian, an African monk who had deprecated his own appointment to that office; and Biscop Baducing (called

Benedict Biscop), an Angle of Northumbria, who had left his retreat in the monastery of Lerins, to guide and accompany the travellers into his native country.

This had risen out of an unforeseen event, and had almost the appearance of accident. But the consequences were great and far-reaching. Theodore organised the English Church upon lines that proved permanent. A new era was also inaugurated for literature and art. Literature was represented by Hadrian, who set up education at St. Augustine's upon an improved plan ; and art, especially in relation to religious and educational institutions—books, buildings, ritual—was the province of Benedict Biscop.

Up to this time education and literature had two rival sources, the old schools of Kent, and the schools of the Irish teachers. But from Hadrian's coming a new literary era commences. For more than a hundred years our island was the seat of learning beyond any other country in the world of the West. Even Greek learning, extinct elsewhere, was revived for a time ; and Bede, whose childhood had corresponded to the opening of this new activity, looked back on it when he was old as a glorious time, and he put it on record that he had known many scholars to whom both the Latin and Greek languages were as their mother tongue.

Of those who were formed in the school of Hadrian, the first and most conspicuous is Aldhelm. His rudimentary education must have been over before he knew Hadrian. The school of Maidulf gave him his boyish training at the monastery which was called after the Irish founder, and which has given name to the town of Malmesbury (Maidulfes burh). So Aldhelm stands between the two systems, the old Irish and the new Kentish. His preference was for the latter, but his works retain the characteristics of both. He has a love of grandiloquence which is both Keltic and Saxon, and a delight in alliteration which is more especially Saxon. His familiarity with the national poetry looms often through his Latin. But his proper characteristics, those whereby he fills a position altogether his own, are apart from these peculiarities. He is the scholar of the age, the type of that set whom Bede delighted to recall, who knew Latin and Greek like their mother tongue. He is the father of Anglo-Latin poetry. He made a zealous study of the Latin metres, and he commended the pursuit to other scholars. His Greek knowledge manifests itself everywhere: not always with a good effect, according to present taste; but in a manner which is of historical value as demonstrating his real familiarity with the Greek language.

Aldhelm's great work, and the work which most conveys his interpretation of the spiritual conditions of his time, is his book, " De Laude Virginitatis," in praise of Celibacy. But for the purposes of literary history, his artistic studies are of more importance than those which are strictly religious and ecclesiastical. Of the greatest interest for us are his Riddles. These are short Latin poems somewhat after the model of Symphosius, whose work he describes,[1] and whom

[1] Aldhelm's "Works," ed. Giles, p. 228.

he seems ambitious to outstrip. The riddles of Symphosius are uniformly of three hexameter lines, those of Aldhelm vary in length from four lines to sixteen; rarely more. The external structure is that of the Epigram, with the object speaking in the first person. The riddles both of Symphosius and Aldhelm are so closely identified with the vernacular riddles of the famous Exeter Song Book, that the reader may be glad of a specimen from each author. It should be premised that in each collection the subject stands as a title at the head of each piece. The subject of the sixteenth in Symphosius is the book-moth:—

DE TINEA.

Litera me pavit, nec quid sit litera novi,
In libris vixi nec sum studiosior inde,
Exedi musas nec adhuc tamen ipse profeci.

I have fed upon literature, yet know not what it is; I have lived among books, yet am not the more studious for it; I have devoured the Muses, yet up to the present time I have made no progress.

One of Aldhelm's riddles is on the Alphabet; and this will be a fit specimen here, as containing something that is germane to the history of literature:—

Nos denæ et septem genitæ sine voce sorores,
Sex alias nothas non dicimus adnumerandas,
Nascimur ex ferro rursus ferro moribundæ,
Necnon et volucris pennâ volitantis ad æthram;
Terni nos fratres incertâ matre crearunt;
Qui cupit instanter sitiens audire, docemus,
Tum cito prompta damus rogitanti verba silenter.

We are seventeen sisters voiceless born; six others, half-sisters, we exclude from our set; children of iron by iron we die, but children too of the bird's wing that flies so high; three brethren our sires, be our mother as may; if any one is very eager to hear, we tell him, and quickly give answer without any sound.[1]

Aldhelm is the first of the Anglo-Latin poets, and he was a classical scholar at a time when to be so was a great distinction. Both in prose and verse, his style has the faults which belong to an age of revived study. His love of learning, his keen appreciation of its beauty and its value, have tended to inflate his sentences with an appearance of display. His poetic diction is simpler than that of his prose; but here, too, he is habitually over-elevated, whence he becomes sometimes stilted, and oftentimes he drops below pitch with an inadequate and disappointing close. But we must honour him in the position which he holds. He is the leader of that noble series of English scholars who represent the first endeavouring stage of recovery after the great eclipse of European culture.

There is nothing of his remaining in the vernacular; but that he was an English poet we have testimony which, though late, is not to be disregarded. William of Malmesbury quotes a book of King Alfred's, which said that Aldhelm had been a peerless writer of English poetry: and he adds, moreover, that a popular

---

[1] Seventeen consonants and six vowels; made with iron style and erased with the same, or else made with a bird's quill; whatever the instrument, three fingers are the agents; and we can convey answer without delay even in situations where it would be inconvenient to speak.

song, which had been mentioned by Alfred as Aldhelm's, was still commonly sung in his own time —that is, in the twelfth century.

Attempts have been made to identify some of our extant Anglo-Saxon literature with a name so eminent. In 1835 the Anglo-Saxon Psalter of the Paris manuscript was first printed at Oxford, and as this book gives a hundred of the Psalms in vernacular poetry, the suggestion that they might be Aldhelm's, though modernised, had rhetorical attractions for the editor (Thorpe), and supplied him with material for a few rather idle sentences of his Latin preface. In 1840 Jacob Grimm edited (from Thorpe's editio princeps) two poems of the Vercelli book, the "Andreas" and the "Elene;" and in his preface he sought to fix this poetry upon Aldhelm by a line of argument altogether fallacious, as was afterwards shown by Mr. Kemble in his edition of the "Andreas" for the Ælfric Society.

That which we have to show for this period in the native Kentish dialect is less ambitious, but it will not be despised by the considerate reader. In the beginnings of learning, when students had not the apparatus of grammars and dictionaries, which now, being common, are almost as much a matter of course as any gift of nature, it was necessary for students to make lists of words and phrases for themselves, and after a while a few of these would be thrown together, and would be reduced to alphabetical order for facility of reference. It is to such a process as this that we owe the Glossaries which form an interesting branch of Anglo-Saxon literature. The Epinal

Gloss is the oldest of these, and it is very valuable because of the archaic forms of many of the words. A selection is here given by way of specimen :—[1]

EPINAL GLOSS.

(Cooper, Appendix B, p. 153.)

Alba spina, haegu thorn (hawthorn).
Aesculus, boecae (beech).
Achalantis, luscina netigalæ (nightingale).
Acrifolus, holegn (holly).
Alnus, alaer (alder).
Abies, saeppae (fir).
Argella, laam (loam).
Accitulium, geacaes surae (sorrel).
Absintium, uuermod (wormwood).
Alacris, snel (swift, German *schnell*).
Alveus, stream rad (stream-road = channel).
Aquilæ, segnas (military standards).
Anser, goos (goose).
Beta, berc, *arbor* (birch).
Ballena, hran (whale).
Buculus, rand beag (buckler).
Berruca, uueartæ (wart).
Cados, ambras (casks).

---

[1] I have given the *th*, or þ, or ð, as in the manuscript. This is done in the present instance because a peculiar interest attaches to it in the earliest specimens of writing. The frequency of *th*, and the rarity of the monograms, is itself a distinguishing feature. Speaking in general terms of Anglo-Saxon literature, as it appears in manuscripts, it might be fairly said that there is no *th* ; this sound is represented by ð or þ. And of these two, the modified Roman character, Ð ð, is found to prevail over the native Rune (þ) in the oldest extant writings. Throughout this little book the *th* is commonly used, as being most convenient for the general reader.

Chaos, duolma (confusion, error).
Cicuta, hymblicae (hemlock).
Cofinus, mand (hamper).
Fulix, ganot, dop aenid (gannet, dip-chick).
Filix, fearn (fern).
Fasianus, uuor hana (pheasant).
Fungus, suamm (German *schwamm*).
Fragor, suoeg (swough, sough).
Finiculus, finugl (fennel).
Follis, blest baeelg (blast-bellows).
Glarea, cisil (pebble, cf. Chesil Bank).
Hibiscum, biscop uuyrt (marsh mallow).
Horodius, uualh hebuc (foreign hawk).
Hirundo, sualuuae (swallow).
Intestinum, thearm (German *Darm*).
Jungetum, risc thyfil (jungle).
Inprobus, gimach (troublesome).
Iners, asolcaen (lazy).
Inter primores, bituien aeldrum (among the chief men).
Juris periti, red boran (counsellors).
Invisus, laath (loath).
Iuuar (= *jubar*), leoma, earendil (gleam, beacon, crest).
Ignarium, al giuueorc (fire-work).
Ibices, firgen gaett (mountain goats, chamois).
Lunules, mene scillingas (coins or bracteates on a necklace).
Lucius, haecid (hake, German *Hecht*).
Lolium, atae (oats).
Limax, snel (snail).
Ligustrum, hunaeg sugae (honeysuckle).
Manipulatim, threatmelum (in bands).
Manica, gloob (glove).
Mascus, grima (mask).
Malva, cotuc, geormant lab (mallow).
Mars, Tiig (cf. Tuesday).
Ninguit, hsniuuith (snoweth).
Nigra spina, slach thorn (sloe-thorn).
Nanus, duerg (dwarf).
Olor, aelbitu (the elk, wild swan).

Piraticum, uuicing sceadan (pirates).
Parcæ, uuyrdae (Fates).
Perna, flicci (flitch).
Pictus acu, mið naeðlae sasiuuid (embroidered).
Pronus, nihol (perpendicular).
Pollux, thuma (thumb).
Quoquomodo, aengiþinga (anyhow).
Rumex, edroc.
Ramnus, theban (thorn).
Salix, salch (sallow).
Sturnus, staer (starling).
Titio, brand (firebrand).
Tignarius, hrofuuyrcta (roofwright).
Vadimonium, borg (pledge, security).

In this glossary we see the preparation for our modern Latin-English dictionaries. Already, as early as the reign of Augustus, the foundation of the Latin dictionary was laid by Verrius Flaccus, but his dictionary would naturally consist of Latin words with Latin explanations. But in the seventh century there was a demand for Latin vocabularies, with equivalents in the vernacular languages; and here, in the Epinal Glossary, we have the earliest known example of such a work. At first such glossaries would be merely lists of words formed in the course of studying some one or two Latin texts, and in process of time would follow the compilation of several such glossaries into one, until, in the tenth and eleventh centuries, we find vocabularies of some compass (as Ælfric's), and by the fifteenth century we have such bulky dictionaries as the "Catholicon" and the "Promptorium Parvulorum."

We will close this chapter with specimens of the "Psalter of St. Augustine," which received an Anglo-

Saxon gloss (dialect Kentish[1]) at the end of the ninth, or early in the tenth century. The book has been already described above, p. 33.

PSALM XLIX. (L.), 7 :—" Hear, O my people," &c.

    geher   folc   min ond sprecu to israhela folce ond
7. Audi populus meus et loquar   Israhel   et
ic cythu   the   thætte   god   god   thin ic eam
testificabor tibi quoniam Deus Deus tuus ego sum
        na les ofer onsegdnisse thine ic dregu the onsegdnisse
8. Non super sacrificia tua arguam te holocausta
soth thine in gesihthe   minre sind   aa
autem tua in conspectu meo sunt semper
      ic ne   on foo   of   huse thinum calferu   ne   of
9. Non accipiam de domo tua vitulos neque de
eowdum thinum buccan
gregibus tuis hircos
      for thon   min   sind   all   wildeor   wuda
10. Quoniam meæ sunt omnes feræ silvarum
neat   in   muntum ond oexen
jumenta in montibus et boves
      ic on cneow all tha flegendan heofenes ond hiow
11. Cognovi omnia volatilia   cæli et species
londes mid mec is
agri mecum est
      gif ic hyngriu ne cweothu ic to the min is sothlice
12. Si esuriero non dicam   tibi, meus est   enim
ymb hwerft eorthan ond   fylnis   his
    orbis   terræ et plenitudo ejus
        ah   ic eotu   flæsc   ferra   oththe
13. Numquid manducabo carnes taurorum   aut
    blod   buccena ic drinco
sanguinem hircorum potabo

---

[1] Transactions of the Philological Society for 1875–6.

THE SCHOOLS OF KENT. 95

       ageld   gode onsegdnisse   lofes ond geld   tham
14. Immola Deo sacrificium laudis et redde Altis-
hestan gehat thin
simo vota tua
          gece   mec in dege geswinces thines thæt ic genere
15. Invoca me in die tribulationis tuæ ut eripiam
thec ond   thu miclas mec
te et magnificabis me
           D I A P S A L M A.
   to thæm synfullan sothlice cweth   god   for hwon thu
16. Peccatori   autem dixit Deus   Quare tu
asagas rehtwisnisse mine ond genimes   cythnisse   mine
enarras justitias meas et adsumes testamentum meum
thorh muth thinne
per os tuum
        thu sothlice thu fiodes theodscipe ond thu awurpe
17. Tu vero   odisti disciplinam et projecisti
word   min efter the
sermones meos post te
      gif thu gesege theof somud thu urne mid hine ond
18. Si videbas furem simul currebas cum eo et
mid unreht hæmderum   dæl   thinne thu settes
cum   adulteris   portionem tuam ponebas
      muth. thin genihtsumath mid nithe ond tunge thin
19. Os tuum abundavit nequitia et lingua tua
hleothrade   facen
concinnavit dolum
       sittende   with   broether thinum thu teldes ond
20. Sedens adversus fratrem tuum detrahebas et
with   suna moeder thinre thu settes   eswic
adversus filium matris tuæ ponebas scandalum
        thas thu dydes ond ic swigade thu gewoendes   on
21. Hæc fecisti et   tacui   existimasti iniqui-
unrehtwisnisse thæt ic wære the   gelic
   tatem   quod ero tibi similis

                    ic threu thec ond   ic setto   tha   ongegn onsiene
              Arguam te   et statuam   illa contra faciem
thinre   Ongeotath thas   alle   tha   ofer geoteliath
tuam (22.) intelligite hæc omnes qui obliviscimini
    dryhten   ne hwonne gereafie ond ne   sie   se generge
Dominum ne quando rapiat et non sit qui eripiat
          onsegdnis   lofes   gearath   mec ond ther
23. Sacrificium laudis honorificabit me et illic
sithfet is   thider   ic oteawu him   haelu   godes
iter est in quo ostendam illi salutare Dei

PSALM LXXVI. (LXXVII.)

        Ond smegende ic eam in   allum   wercum thinum
13. Et meditatus sum in omnibus operibus tuis
ond in   gehaeldum   thinum   ic bieode
et in observationibus tuis exercebor
          god   in halgum weg thin hwelc god   micel
14. Deus in sancto via tua quis Deus magnus
swe swe god   ur   thu earth god   thu the doest
sicut Deus noster (15.) tu es Deus qui facis
 wundur   ana   cuthe   thu dydes in   folcum   megen
mirabilia solus notam fecisti in populis virtutem
 thin   gefreodes in   earme   thinum   folc   thin
tuam (16.) liberasti in brachio tuo populum tuum
bearn
filios Israhel et Joseph
          gesegun thec weter   god   gesegun thec weter ond
    17. Viderunt te aquæ Deus viderunt te aquæ et
on dreordun gedroefde werun niolnisse   mengu
timuerunt turbati sunt abyssi (18.) multitudo
 swoeges   wetre   stefne   saldun   wolcen ond sothlice
sonitus aquarum Vocem dederunt nubes et enim

strelas thine thorh leordun   stefn thunurrade thinre
sagittæ tuæ pertransierunt   (19.)   vox   tonitrui   tui
in hweole
in rota
        in lihton   bliccetunge   thine eorthan ymbhwyrfte
    Inluxerunt coruscationes   tuæ   orbi   terræ
gesaeh ond   onstyred   wes eorthe
vidit et commota est terra
        in   sae   wegas thine ond   stige   thine in wetrum
  20. In mari viæ   tuæ   et semitæ tuæ   in   aquis
miclum ond   swethe   thine   ne   bioth oncnawen
multis et vestigia tua non cognoscentur
        thu gelaeddes swe swe scep   folc   thin in honda
  21. Deduxisti   sicut oves populum tuum in manu
mosi ond aaron
Moysi et Aaron

These specimens of the Kentish dialect (with the exception of the Epinal Gloss) are of much later date than the times which our narrative has yet reached; and they are only offered as a proximate representation of that which was the first of English dialects to receive literary culture. This dialect is peculiarly interesting as being that from which the West Saxon was developed; in other words, it is the earliest form of that imperial dialect in which the great body of extant Saxon literature is preserved. But the Kentish did not ripen into the maturer outlines of the West Saxon without the intervention of a third dialect; and in order to appreciate this it is necessary for us to review that more spacious culture of which the scene was laid in the country of the Northern Angles.

CHAPTER V.

THE ANGLIAN PERIOD.

WHILE Canterbury was so important a seminary of learning, there was, in the Anglian region of Northumbria, a development of religious and intellectual life which makes it natural to regard the whole brilliant era from the later seventh to the early ninth century as "The Anglian Period." Not only did the greatest school of the whole island grow up at York, but also one that, with its important library, was for the time the most active and useful in the whole of Western Europe.

The importance of the Anglian period consists in the fact that it belongs not merely to one nation, but that Anglia became for a century the light-spot of European history; and that here we recognise the first great stage in the revival of learning, and the first movement towards the establishment of public order in things temporal and spiritual. Happily, the period stands out in a good historical light, and the chief elements of its influence are finely exhibited in the persons of representative men or representative groups.

There is Paulinus, the fugitive missionary from Kent, who made the first rapid evangelisation of the northern country; King Edwin and his court form a well-displayed group between the old darkness and the coming light, as they consult and compare the two; Oswald, returning from exile to be king, and bringing with him the Scotian type of Christianity; Aidan, the first Scotian bishop of Lindisfarne, and the model of pastors; Wilfrid, the champion of Roman unity, confronting Colman at the synod of Whitby before Oswy, the presiding king, on the absorbing question of the time; Wilfrid appealing to Rome against Theodore; and yet again, Wilfrid, the first Anglo-Saxon missionary; Biscop Baducing (Benedict Biscop), the founder of abbeys, the traveller, the introducer of arts from abroad; Cædmon, the cowherd, the divinely-inspired singer and the father of a school of English poetry; Cuthberht, the shepherd-boy, abbot, bishop, hermit, and finally the national saint of Northumbria; Willebrord and the two Hewalds, and all the glorious band of missionaries and martyrs; Winfrid (Boniface), the crown of them all, apostle of Germany, and martyr; Beda, the teacher and historian; Ecgberct and Alberct, successively archbishops of York, acknowledged presidents of Western learning; Alcuin, the bearer of Anglian learning to the Franks, and the organiser of schools for the future ages.

After Aldhelm, the first Englishman who appeared as an author was Æddi, better known as Eddius Stephanus. He was the friend and companion of Wilfrid in his contentions and troubles, and, after his death, he wrote a biography of him in Latin. This book is of great value as an authority, and as illustrating the history of the later seventh and early eighth century. Wilfrid died in 709, the same year as Aldhelm.

Wilfrid was the master-spirit of this age. He represented the best aims of his nation; he understood the needs of the time; he worked for them, and he suffered for them. With an overbearing spirit, fantastic too often in his conduct, he saw what was needed—he saw the necessity for unity with Rome. This was a necessity, not for one country alone, but for the whole West at that time. Protestant writers have looked at Wilfrid through a distorting medium. Nowhere, perhaps, is there more need to allow for difference of times than in estimating Wilfrid. He had great faults; he quarrelled with the best men; but, on the other hand, Theodore, the most important of all his adversaries, sought reconciliation at last, and accused himself of injustice. Wilfrid initiated the German missions; he impressed on that great field of Saxon activity the policy of his agitated life, and that policy was ever militant in Boniface, the chief apostle of Germany, and may be said to have triumphed when the Roman Empire was renewed in harmony with the Holy See, and Charles was crowned in 800. Wilfrid, more than any other man, appears as the ideal representative of that varied influence, religious, literary, political, which the Anglo-Saxon Church exercised upon the Western world.

The beginning of our vernacular literature, so far as it can be treated chronologically, lies between the years 658 and 680. For these are the years of the abbacy of Hild at Whitby, and it was in her time that Cædmon appeared, who had received the gift of divine song in a vision of the night. When this heavenly call was recognised, the herdsman became a brother of the religious fraternity, and devoted his life to the pursuit of sacred poetry. To the lover of the mother tongue it must appear a singular felicity that Cædmon's first hymn is preserved in a book that was written not much more than half-a-century after his death.[1]

Nu scylun hergan	Now shall we glorify
hefaenricaes uard,	the guardian of heaven's realm,
metudæs maecti	the Maker's might
end his modgidanc;	and the thought of his mind;
uerc uuldurfadur;	the work of the glory-father,
sue he uundra gihuaes,	how He of every wonder,
eci dryctin,	He the Lord eternal
or astelidæ.	laid the foundation.
He aerist scop	He shapèd erst
aelda barnum	for the sons of men,
heben til hrofe,	heaven their roof,
halig scepen;	holy Creator;
tha middungeard	the middle world he,
moncynnæs uard,	mankind's sovereign,
eci dryctin,	eternal captain,
æfter tiadæ	afterwards created,
firum foldan	the land for men
frea allmectig.	Lord Almighty.[2]

[1] In the famous manuscript of the "Ecclesiastical History" of Bede, which is commonly known as the Moore manuscript, because it passed with the library of Bishop Moore (Ely) to the University of Cambridge, is in a hand which is thought to be as old as the time of Bede, who died in 735.

[2] Bede gives the "sense" of this first hymn as follows:—"Nunc laudare debemus auctorem regni caelestis, potentiam creatoris et consilium illius, facta patris gloriae; quomodo ille, cum sit

BEDA was born in 672, in the neighbourhood of Wearmouth, two years before Biscop founded an abbey there. Of this abbey Beda became an inmate in his seventh year, under Abbot Biscop. He was afterwards moved to the sister foundation at Jarrow, under Abbot Ceolfrid, and there he lived, with rare absences, the remainder of his life. He was ordained deacon at the early age of nineteen ; in his thirtieth year he was ordained priest; he died in his sixty-third year, A.D. 735. He was a very prolific author, and he has left us, at the end of his most considerable work, a sketch of his life, and a list of his writings, down to the fifty-ninth year of his age, A.D. 731. The bulk of his works are theological, chiefly in the form of commentaries, and they are little more than extracts from the best known of the Fathers. This was adapted to the needs of the time, and Bede's commentaries were held in great esteem during the whole period. Ælfric, in the tenth century, used them largely for his " Homilies."

Of all Bede's works, the chronological made the greatest immediate impression, and was of most general use at the time and for some centuries afterwards. The computation of Easter was the groundwork of the ecclesiastical year, and every church felt the benefit of his services. Chronology was then in its early maturity, and the Christian era was not yet a familiar method of reckoning. Bede

aeternus deus, omnium miraculorum auctor extitit, qui primo filiis hominum caelum pro culmine tecti, dehinc terram custos humani generis omnipotens creavit."—" Ecclesiastical History." iv. 24.

was the first historian who arranged his materials according to the years from the Incarnation. He had made himself completely master of this subject, and he left it in such order that nothing more had to be done to it, or could be improved upon it, for many centuries.

His fullest and most detailed work on chronology is entitled "De Temporum Ratione," and to this is added a chronicle of the world. On this elaborate work he was working down to A.D. 726. We have the authority of Ideler for saying that this is a complete guide to the calculation of times and festivals. He treats of the several divisions of time; and under the months, he speaks of the moon's orbit (c. xvii.), and its importance for the calendar, and the relation of the moon to the tides (c. xxix.); then of the equinoxes and solstices, the varying length of the days, the seasons of the year, the intercalary day, the cycle of nineteen years, the reckoning Anno Domini (c. xlvii.), indictions, epacts, the determination of Easter. All these things are taught with theoretical thoroughness, as well as also in their practical application. He also (c. lxv.) made a table for Easter from A.D. 532, "when Dionysius began the first cycle," to A.D. 1063.[1] This is followed by the "Chronicle or Six Ages of this World," altogether a work that was a growing nucleus, and went

---

[1] Adolf Ebert's account of Bede in "History of Christian-Latin Literature," translated by Mayor and Lumby in their admirable edition of the third and fourth books of Bede's "Church History" (Pitt Press Series), 1878, p. 11.

on expanding down to the invention of printing and the revival of classical literature.

But the works on which his eminence permanently rests, and by which he made all posterity indebted to him, are his historical and biographical writings. He wrote a poem on the miracles of St. Cuthbert, and afterwards he wrote a prose narrative " Of the Life and Miracles of St. Cuthbert, Bishop of Lindisfarne ;" and in this, though a new and independent work, something of the poem is reproduced. It is in this prose work that we find the call of Cuthbert on the night of Aidan's death, the details of his hermit life on the rocky islet of Farne, to which he had retired for greater rigour of devotion, from which he was called back to be bishop at Lindisfarne, and to which after two years' episcopate he again retired for the remnant of his life.

He wrote also a prose life of St. Felix, drawing his materials from the metrical life of that saint in hexameters by Paulinus.

His greatest biographical work is " Lives of the Abbots of Wearmouth and Jarrow, namely, Benedict, Ceolfrid, Easterwini, Sigfrid, and Hwetbert." These were the heads of the two sister foundations with which his career was identified ; and some of them had been his own teachers. The Life of Benedict is the most interesting, as might be expected, and it fills the largest part of the book.

Finally, his greatest work, the work which is a gift for all time, is his " Church History of the Anglian People." This was the work of the author's mature powers, and some of his earlier writings are made use of in it. In this history, which is divided into five books, there is, first, a summary of the history of Britain, from the time of Julius Cæsar down to the time of Gregory the Great. This part occupies twenty-two chapters, and is drawn from Orosius and Gildas and Constantius. The proper narrative of Bede begins at chap. xxiii., and there the conversion and early history of Saxon Christianity is given down to the time of the restoration of the old church of St. Saviour (Canterbury Cathedral), and the institution of the monastery of SS. Peter and Paul (St. Augustine's). The last chapter is of the decisive battle of Degsastan, which determined the superiority of the Angles over the Scotti. The second book begins with the death of Gregory and goes down to the death of Æduini, King of Northumbria, A.D. 633. In this book occurs a remarkable speech made by one of Æduini's nobles, in the debate about a change of religion :—

"The present life of man in the world, O. king, is, by comparison with that time which is unknown, like as when you are sitting at table with your aldermen and thanes in the winter season, the fire blazing in the midst, and the hall cheerfully warm, while the whirlwinds rage everywhere outside and drive the rain or the snow; one of the sparrows comes in and flies swiftly through the house, entering at one door and out at the other. So long as it is inside, it is sheltered from the storm, but when the brief momentary calm is past, the bird is in the cold as before, and is no more seen. So this human life is visible for a time: but of what follows or what went before we are utterly ignorant. Wherefore, if this new doctrine should offer anything surer, it seems worthy to be followed." (ii., 13.)

The third book goes down to the appointment of Theodore to be Archbishop of Canterbury, A.D. 665.

This book contains the decision for Roman unity, and the defeat and departure of Colman and his Scotian clergy. Bede was a hearty adherent of the Roman obedience, and his affectionate tribute to the work of the Irish is all the more remarkable. He pauses upon the record of their departure as upon the close of a good time that had been, and to which he looks wistfully back.

"The great frugality and content of him and his predecessors was witnessed by the very place they ruled; for at their departure there were very few buildings besides the church; just what civilised life absolutely requires, and no more. Their only capital was their cattle; for if rich men gave them money, they presently gave it to the poor. Of funds and halls for entertaining the worldly great they had no need, as such personages never came but to pray and hear the word of God. The King himself, when occasion required, would come with just five or six thanes, and after prayer in church would depart; and if it chanced they took refreshment there, they were content with just the simple every-day fare of the brothers, and wanted nothing better. For at that time those teachers made it their entire business to serve not the world but God, and their whole care to cherish not the belly but the heart. And consequently the religious garb was at that time in great veneration; so much so that, wherever a cleric or a monk arrived, he was joyfully received by all as the servant of God. Even upon the road, if one were found travelling, they would run to him, and bend the head, and rejoice if he signed them with the cross, or uttered a blessing; at the same time they gave careful attention to their words of exhortation. Moreover, on Sundays they would race to the church or the monasteries, not to refresh the body, but to hear God's word; and if one of the priests happened to come to a village, the villagers were quickly assembled, and were wanting to hear from him the word of life. And, indeed, the priests on their part or the clerics had no other object in going to the villages but for preaching, baptising, visiting the sick, and in a word for the care of souls; being so entirely purged from all infection of avarice, that none accepted lands and possessions for building monasteries unless compelled to do so by secular lords. Such conduct was maintained in the Northumbrian churches for some time after this date. But I have said enough." (iii., 26.)

The fourth book goes down to the death, A.D. 687, of the saint of whom Bede had previously written, both in verse and in prose, the Saint of Northumbria, St. Cuthbert.

This book contains another passage to show that Bede looked wistfully back to a blessed time that had been, and for which he was born too late. He has been speaking of Theodore and Hadrian, and he is about to speak of Wilfrid and Æddi, when he thus breaks out:—"Never, never, since the Angles came to Britain, were there happier times; brave and Christian kings held all barbarians in awe; the universal ambition was for those heavenly joys of which men had recently heard; and all who desired to be instructed in sacred learning had masters ready to teach them." (iv., 2.)

This book also contains the history of Cædmon, which is perhaps the most frequently quoted piece of all Bede's writings :—

"In the monastery of this abbess [Hild], there was a certain brother, eminently distinguished by divine grace, for he was wont to make songs fit for religion and piety, so that, whatever he learnt out of Scripture by means of interpreters, this he would after a time produce in his own, that is to say, the Angles' tongue, with poetical words, composed with perfect sweetness and feeling. By this man's songs often the minds of many were kindled to contempt of the world and desire for the celestial life. Moreover, others after him in the nation of the Angles tried to make religious poems, but no one was able to equal him. For he learnt the art of singing not from men, nor through any man's instructions, but he received the gift of singing unacquired and by divine help. Wherefore he could never make any frivolous or unprofitable poem, but those things only which pertain to religion were fit themes for his religious tongue. During his secular life, which continued up to the time of advanced age, he had never learnt any songs. And, therefore, sometimes at a feast, when for merriment sake it was agreed that all should sing in turn, he, when he saw that the harp was nearing him, would rise from his unfinished supper and go quietly away to his own home." (iv., 24.)

On one occasion, when this had happened, he went, not to his home, but to the cattle sheds, to rest, because it was his turn to do so that night. In his sleep one appeared to him and bade him sing. He pleaded inability, but the command was repeated. "What then," he asked, "must I sing?" He was told he must sing of the beginning of created things. Then he sang a Hymn of Creation, and this hymn he remembered when he was risen from sleep, and it was the proof of his divine vocation. The hymn was preserved in Latin as well as in the original; and both have been quoted above. The poems which he subsequently wrote are thus described :—

"He sang of the creation of the world and the origin of the human race, and the whole story of Genesis, of Israel's departure out of Egypt and entrance into the land of promise, of many other parts of the sacred history, of the Lord's Incarnation, Passion, Resurrection, and Ascension into Heaven, of the coming of the Holy Spirit, and the doctrine of the Apostles. Likewise of the terror of judgment to come, and the awful punishment of hell, and the bliss of the heavenly kingdom, he made many poems; many others also concerning divine benefits and judgments, in all which he sought to wean men from the love of sin, and stimulate them to the enjoyment and pursuit of good action."

The fifth and last book contains a survey of the condition of the national Church down to 731, within about four years of the author's death.

Books of his on the technicalities of literature are a tract on "Orthography," another "On the Metric

Art," also a book "On Figures and Tropes of Holy Scripture." Least esteemed have been his poetical compositions, some of which have been suffered to perish. The poem on the " Miracles of St. Cuthberht " is extant, but the " Book of Hymns in Various Metre or Rhythm " is lost, and so also is his " Book of Epigrams in Heroic or Elegiac Metre." But we are not left without an authentic specimen of his hymnody, as he has incorporated in his history the Hymn of Virginity in praise of Queen Ethelthryð, the foundress of Ely. His extant poetry proves him to have been an accomplished scholar and a man of cultivated taste rather than of poetic genius. But we could afford to lose many Latin poems in consideration of the slightest vernacular effort of such a man.

Many manuscripts of the "Ecclesiastical History" contain a letter by one Cuthbert to his fellow-student Cuthwine, describing the manner of Bede's death. In this letter is contained a pious ditty in the vernacular, which Bede, who was "learned in our native songs," composed at the time when he was contemplating the approach of his own dissolution.

Fore there neidfarae	Before the need-journey
nænig ni uurthit	no one is ever
thonc snoturra	more wise in thought
than him tharf sie	than he ought,
to ymbhycggannae,	to contemplate
aer his hin iongae,	ere his going hence
huaet his gastae	what to his soul
godaes aeththa yflaes	of good or of evil
aefter deothdaege	after death-day
doemid uueorthae.	deemed will be.[1]

---

[1] The general correctness of our translation is assured by the

Other remains in the Northumbrian dialect are the Runic inscription on the Ruthwell Cross, for which the reader is referred to Professor Stephens's "Old Northern Runic Monuments of Scandinavia and England," vol. i., p. 405; also the interlinear glosses in the Lindisfarne Gospels, and in the Durham Ritual. For fuller information on these glosses I must refer the reader to Professor Skeat's Gospels "in Anglo-Saxon and Northumbrian Versions Synoptically Arranged;" and more especially to his preface in the concluding volume, which contains the fourth Gospel. The Psalter, which was published by the Surtees Society as Northumbrian, is now judged to be Kentish; but that volume contains, besides, an "Early English Psalter," which presents a later phase of the Northumbrian dialect.

The poetical works which now bear Cædmon's name received that name from Junius, the first editor, in 1655, on the ground of the general agreement of the subjects with Bede's description of Cædmon's works. In this book we find a first part containing the most prominent narratives from the books of Genesis, Exodus, and Daniel; and a second part containing the Descent of Christ into Hades and the delivery of the patriarchs from their captivity, according to the apocryphal Gospel of Nicodemus

---

fact that the Latin text in which it is embodied supplies a Latin translation, thus:—"quod ita latine sonat : 'ante necessarium exitum prudentior quam opus fuerit nemo existit, ad cogitandum videlicet antequam hinc proficiscatur anima, quid boni vel mali egerit, qualiter post exitum judicanda fuerit."—"Bedæ Hist. Eccl.," iii., iv. (Mayor and Lumby), p. 177.

and the constant legend of the Middle Ages. This comprises a kind of Paradise Lost and Paradise Regained. Of all this, the part which has attracted most notice is a part of which the materials are found neither in Scripture nor in any known Apocrypha. The nearest approximation yet indicated is in the hexameters of Avitus, described above.[1] This problematical part describes the Fall of Man as the sequel of the Fall of the Angels, substantially running on the same lines as Milton's famous treatment of the same subject. It has often been surmised that Milton may have known of Cædmon through Junius, and that this knowledge may have affected the cast of his great poem as well as suggested some of his most famous touches.[2]

The precipitation is thus described :—

329 wæron tha befeallene	So were they felled
fyre to botme	to the fiery abyss
on tha hatan hell	into the hot hell
thurh hygeleaste	through heedlessness
and thurh ofermetto.	and through arrogance.
Sohten other land	They arrived at another land
thæt wæs leohtes leas	that was void of light
and wæs liges full	and was full of flame
fyres fær micel.	fire's horror huge.[3]

---

[1] Page 14.

[2] There has been a recent discussion of this question by Professor Wülcker in "Anglia," with a negative result. But the conclusion rests on too slight a basis.

[3] "Milton has the same idea in a kindred passage, but it is not so terse, so condensed, as Cædmon's :—

When the fallen angel speaks, he begins thus:—

355 Is thes ænga stede	This confined place
ungelic swithe	is terribly unlike
tham othrum	that other one
the we ær cuthon	that we knew before
heah on heofenrice	high in heaven's realm
the me min hearra	which my lord conferred
onlag.	on me.

Having thus begun with a lamentable cry, he gradually recovers composure and propounds a policy. He observes that God has created a new and happy being, who is destined to inherit the glory which he and his have lost:—

>394 He hæfth nu gemearcod anne middangeard
>   thær he hæfth mon geworhtne
> æfter his onlicnesse;
>   mid tham he wile eft gesettan
> heofena rice, mid hluttrum saulum.
>   We thæs sculon hycgan georne,
> thæt we on Adame
>   gif we æfre mægen,
> and on his eafrum swa some
>   andan gebetan.

>'Yet from those flames
>No light, but rather darkness visible
>Served only to discover sights of woe.'

"In Job x. 22 we also find a similar idea:—'A land of darkness, as darkness itself; and of the shadow of death without any order, and where the light is as darkness.' They are all powerful, all dreadful, but Cædmon's 'without light, and full of flame,' is much the strongest. It is an Inferno in a line."—ROBERT SPENCE WATSON, "Cædmon," p. 44.

> He hath now designed a middle world
>   where He man hath made,
> after His likeness :—
>   with which He will repeoplè
> heaven's realm, with stainless souls.
>   We must thereto give careful heed
> that we on Adam
>   if we ever may
> and on his offspring likewise
>   our harm redress.

The way proposed is by inducing them to displease their Maker, and then they will be banished to the same place and become the slaves of Satan and his angels. A messenger is required :—

409. Gif ic ænigum thegne	If I to any thane
theoden madmas	lordly treasures
geara forgeafe	in former times have given,
thenden we on than	while we in the good realm
godan rice	
gesælige sæton	all blissful sate,
and hæfdon ure setla	and had sway of our man-
geweald,	sions :—
thonne heme na on leofrantid	at no more acceptable time
leanum ne meahte	could he ever with value
mine gife gyldan.	my bounty requite.
Gif his gien wolde	If now for this purpose
minra thegna hwilc	any one of my thanes
gethafa wurthan	would himself volunteer
thæt he up heonon	that he from here upward
ute mihte	and outward might go,
cuman thurh thas clustro	might come through these barriers
and hæfde cræft mid him	and strength in him had
thæt he mid fetherhoman	that with raiment of feather
fleogan meahte	his flight he could take
windan on wolcne	to whirl on the welkin
thær geworht stondath	where the new work is
	standing

Adam and Eve	Adam and Eve
on eorth rice	in the earthly realm
mid welan bewunden.	with wealth surrounded—
and we synd aworpene hider	and we are cast away hither
on thas deopan dalo.	into these deep dales!

Satan rages not so much on account of his own loss as for their gain. If they could only be ruined by the wrath of God, he declares he could be at ease even in the midst of woes; and whoever would achieve this he will reward to his utmost, and give him a seat by his side. Presently we come to the accoutring of the emissary:—

442. Angan hine tha gyrwan Godes andsaca	Began him then t' equip th' antagonist of God,
fus on frætwum:	prompt in harness:—
hæfde fræcne hyge.	he had a guileful mind.
Hæleth helm on heafod asette	A magic helm on head he set,
and thone full hearde geband,	he bound it hard and tight,
spenn mid spangum.	braced it with buckles.
Wiste him spræca fela vora worda.	Speeches many wist he well, crooked words.

He takes wing and rises in air; and then comes a passage like Milton:—

Swang thæt fyr on twa feondes cræfte.	he dashed the fire in two with fiendish craft.[1]

Arrived at the garden he takes the shape of a serpent, and winds himself round the forbidden tree. The description recalls the familiar picture so vividly

[1] "Paradise Lost," i., 221:—
"Forthwith upright he rears from off the pool
His mighty stature; on each hand the flames,
Driv'n backward, slope their pointing spires, and roll'd
In billows, leave i' th' midst a horrid vale."

that we cannot doubt the same picture was before the eyes of children in the Saxon period as now. He takes some of the fruit and finds Adam, and addresses him in a speech. He gives a naïve reason why he is sent :—

507. Brade synd on worulde	Broad are in the world
grene geardas,	the green plains,
and God siteth	and God sitteth
on tham hehstan	in the highest
heofna rice	heavenly realm
ufan. Alwalda	above. The Almighty
nele tha earfethu	will not the trouble
sylfa habban	himself have,
that he on thisne sith fare,	that He should on this journey fare,
gumena drihten :—	the Lord of men :—
ac he his gingran sent	but He sends his deputy
to thinre spræce.	to speak with thee.

These poems are surrounded by interesting questions which it is barely possible here to indicate. Upon the top of the discussion about Milton, which is not by any means exhausted, there comes a much larger and wider field of inquiry as to the relation existing between this Miltonic part (if I may so speak) and the Old Saxon poem of the "Heliand." The investigation has been admirably started by Mr. Edouard Sievers in a little book containing this portion of the text, and exhibiting in detail the peculiar intimacy of relation between it and the "Heliand," in regard to vocabulary, phraseology, and versification. This part of Mr. Sievers' work is complete. Probably no one who has gone through his proofs will be found to question his conclusion, that there is between the "Heliand" and the Saxon "Paradise Lost" such an identity as isolates those two works from all other literature, and makes it necessary to trace them to one source. What remains is only to determine the order of their affiliation. His theory is that our "Cædmon" contains a large insertion which has been borrowed, not, of course, from the "Heliand," because the "Heliand" is a poem solely on the Gospel history, but from a sister poem to the "Heliand," a corresponding poem on the Old Testament. Professor George Stephens, of Copenhagen, offered a simpler explanation. He supposed that our piece is a purely domestic remnant of that school of English poetry which Bede described, and that the "Heliand" is a continental offspring of the same school, being a monument of the poetic culture which was planted along the borders of the Rhine by the Anglo-Saxon missionaries.

ALCUIN'S name connects the Anglian period with the great Frankish revival of literature under Charlemagne. And as he bears a prominent part in the establishment of literature in its next European seat, so also he had the grief of witnessing the earlier stages of that devastation which extinguished the light in his own country. This is how he writes on hearing of the invasion of Lindisfarne by the northern rovers in 793, to Bishop Hugibald and the monks of Lindisfarne :—

"As your beloved society was wont to delight me when I was with you, so does the report of your tribulation sadden me continually now that I am absent from you. How have the heathen defiled the sanctuaries of God, and shed the blood of the saints round about the altar. They have laid waste the dwelling-place of our hope; they have trodden down the bodies of the saints in the temple of God like mire in the street. What can I say? I can only lament in my heart with you before the altar of Christ, and say: Spare, Lord, spare Thy people, and give not Thy heritage to the heathen, lest the pagans say, Where is the God of the Christians? What confidence is there for the churches of Britain if Saint Cuthbert, with so great a company of saints, defends not his own? Either this is the beginning of a greater sorrow, or the sins of the people have brought this upon them."[1]

Thus we have arrived at the verge of that catastrophe which closes for ever the singular greatness of Anglia. Charles brought learning to France by drawing from Anglia and from Italy the best plants for his new field; he inherited the civilising labours of the Saxon missionaries in his dominions beyond the Rhine; he founded a centre of power and a centre of education together; and France remained the chief seat of learning throughout the Middle Ages.[2] The glory of a European position in literature can no longer be claimed for England. Through the remainder of our narrative we must be content with a provincial sphere; and our compensation must be found in the fact that the vernacular element is all the more freely developed.

[1] Wright, "Biographia Literaria," Anglo-Saxon Period, p. 353.
[2] The new start of literature under Charles is briefly and brilliantly stated in the first paragraph of Adolf Ebert's second volume.

CHAPTER VI.

THE PRIMARY POETRY.

WE have now seen something of a culture that was introduced from abroad, and guided by foreign models. But our people had a native gift of song, and a tradition of poetic lore, which lived in memory, and was sustained by the profession of minstrelsy. The Christian and literary culture obtained through the Latin tended strongly to the suppression and extinction of this ancient and national vein of poetry. But happily it has not all been lost, and it will be the aim of this chapter to present some specimens of that poetry which is rooted in the native genius of the race, and which we may call the primary poetry. The poetry which is manifestly of Latin material we will call the secondary poetry. It is not asserted that we have two sorts of poetry so entirely separate and distinct the one from the other, that the one is purely native and untinged with foreign influence, while the other springs from mere imitation. The two sorts are not so utterly contrasted as that. Even the secondary poetry is not without originality. On the other hand the primary poetry betrays here and there the Latin culture and the Christian sentiment; and yet it is quite sufficiently distinct and characterised to justify the plan of grouping it apart from the general body of the poetical remains.

The chief features of the Saxon poetry may conveniently be arranged under three heads: 1. The mechanical formation. 2. The rhetorical characteristics. 3. The imaginative elements.

1. Of these the first turns on Alliteration, Accent, and Rhythm; and this part, which is generally held to belong rather to grammar than to literature, I have described elsewhere.[1]

2. The Rhetorical characteristic of Anglo-Saxon poetry which is most prominent, is a certain repetition of the thought with a variation of epithet or phrase, in a manner which distinctly resembles the parallelism of Hebrew poetry.

3. The Imaginative element resides chiefly in the metaphor, which is very pervading and seems to be almost unconscious. It seldom rises to that conscious form of metaphor which we call the Simile, and when it does it is laconically brief, as in the comparison of a ship with a bird (fugle gelicost). The later poetry begins to expand the similes somewhat after the manner of the Latin poets. In Beowulf we have four brief similes and only one that is expanded; namely, that of the sword-hilt melting like ice in the warm season of spring (line 1,608).

We will begin with the "Beowulf," the largest and in every sense the most important of the remaining Anglo-Saxon poems. It has much in it that seems

[1] In "A Book for the Beginner in Anglo-Saxon," Clarendon Press Series; ed. 2 (1879), p. 70.

THE PRIMARY POETRY. 121

like anticipation of the age of chivalry. The story of the "Beowulf" is as follows:[1]—

Hroðgar, king of the Danes, ruled over many nations with imperial sway. It came into his mind to add to his Burg a spacious hall for the greater splendour of his hospitality and the dispensing of his bounty. This hall was named Heorot. But all his glory was undone by the nightly visits of a devouring fiend; Hroðgar's people were either killed, or gone to safer quarters. Heorot, though habitable by day, was abandoned at night; no faithful band kept watch around the seat of Danish royalty; Hroðgar, the aged king, was in dejection and despair.

Higelac was king in the neighbouring land of the Geatas, and he had about him a young nephew, a sister's son, Beowulf, son of Ecgtheow. Beowulf had great bodily strength, but was otherwise little accounted of. The young man loved adventure, and hearing of Hroðgar's misery, he determined to help him. He embarked with fourteen companions, and reached the coast of the Danes, where he was challenged by the coast-warden in a tone of mistrust. After a parley, that officer sped him on his way, and Beowulf's company stood before Hroðgar's gate. Asked the meaning of this armed visit, the leader answers:

[1] The editions and translations are by Thorkelin, Copenhagen, 1815; Kemble, ed. 1, London, 1833; ed. 2, London, 1835; translation, 1837; Ettmüller, German translation, Zürich, 1840; Schaldemose, with Danish translation, Copenhagen, 1851; Thorpe, with English translation, Oxford, 1855; Grundtvig, Copenhagen, 1861; Moritz Heyne, German translation, Paderborn, 1863; Grein, 1867; Arnold, Oxford, 1876; Moritz Heyne, Text, ed. 4, 1879.

"We sit at Higelac's table: my name is Beowulf. I will tell mine errand to thy master, if he will deign that we may greet him." Hroðgar knew Beowulf's name, remembered his father Ecgtheow,[1] had the visitor to his presence, heard his high resolve, was ready to hope for deliverance, and prompt to see in Beowulf a deliverer. Festivity is renewed in the deserted hall, and tales of old achievements revive forgotten mirth—mirth broken only by the gibes of the eloquent Hunferth, which give Beowulf occasion to tell the tale of an old swimming-match when he slew sea-monsters; and all is harmony again. But night descends, and with it the fears that were now habitual. Beowulf shrinks not from his adventure; the guests depart, and the king, retiring

[1] Wulfgar then spoke to his own dear lord:
"Here are arrived, come from afar
Over the sea-waves, men of the Geats;
The one most distinguished the warriors brave
Beowulf name. They are thy suppliants
That they, my prince, may with thee now
Greetings exchange; do not thou refuse them
Thy converse in turn, friendly Hrothgar!
They in their war-weeds seem very worthy
Contenders with earls; the chief is renowned
Who these war-heroes hither has led."
Hrothgar then spoke, defence of the Scyldings;
"I knew him of old when he was a child;
His agèd father was Ecgtheow named;
To him at home gave Hrethel the Geat
His only daughter: his son has now
Boldly come here, a trusty friend sought."

This is from Mr. Garnett's translation, which is made line for line. Published by Ginn, Heath, & Co., Boston, 1882.

to his castle, commits to his visitor the night-watch of Heorot.

Næfre ic ænegum men
    ær alyfde,
siðð an ic hond and rond
    hebban mihte,
thryth ærn Dena :—
    buton the nu tha !
Hafa nu and geheald
    husa selest ;
gemyne mærtho,
    mægen ellen cyth ;
waca with wrathum !
    ne bith the wilna gad,
gif thu thæt ellen weorc
    aldre gedigest.
	Never I to any man
	    ere now entrusted,
	(since hand and shield
	    I first could heave)
	the Guardhouse of the Danes :—
	    never but now to thee !
	Have now and hold
	    the sacred house ;
	of glory mindful
	    main and valour prove ;
	watch for the foe !
	    no wish of thine shall fail,
	if thou the daring work
	    with life canst do.

Beowulf and his companions have their beds in the hall.

They sleep; but he watches. It was not long before the depredator of the night was there, and a lurid gleam stood out of his eyes. While Beowulf cautiously held himself on the alert, the fiend had quickly clutched and devoured one of the sleepers. But now Grendel—such was the demon's name—found himself in a grasp unknown before. Long and dire was the strife. The timbers cracked, the iron-bound benches plied, and work deemed proof against all but fire was now a wreck. Grendel finding the foe too strong, thought only of escape. He did escape, and got away to the moor, but he left an arm in Beowulf's grip.

Early in the morning men came from far and near to see the hideous trophy on the gable of the hall:

men came to rejoice in the great deliverance; for Heorot, they said, was now purged. Great was their joy. Mounted men rode over the moor, tracking Grendel's retreat by his blood; they followed his path to the dismal pool where he had his habitation; then they turn homewards, riding together and conversing as they go. They talk of Beowulf, they liken him with Sigemund, that hero of greatest name. When they come to galloping ground, they break away from the tales, and race over the turf. In another tale they talk of Heremod; but he was proud and cold, not like Beowulf, who is as genial as he is valiant. The early riders are back to Heorot in time to see the king and the queen moving from bower to hall, the king with his guard, the queen with her maidens. Then follows a noble scene. Hroðgar sees the hideous trophy on the gable; he stands on the terrace, and utters a thanksgiving to God as stately as it is simple. He reviews the woe and the grief, the disgrace, the helplessness, and the utter despondency of himself and of his people; "and now a boy hath done the deed which we all with our united powers could not compass! Verily that woman is blessed that bare him; and if she yet lives, she may well say that God was very gracious to her in her childbearing. Beowulf, I will love thee as a son, and thou shalt lack nothing that it is in my power to give."

Beowulf spake: "We did our best in a risky tussle; would I could have brought you the fiend a captive. I could not hold him; he gave me the slip: but he left a limb behind; *that* will be his death." Next

Heorot is restored and beautified anew. Marvellous gold-embroidered hangings drape the walls, the admiration of those who have an eye for such things. The whole interior had been a wreck, the roof alone remained entire. Now, it was straight and fair once more; and now it was to be the scene of such a profusion of gifts as poet had never sung.

In honour of his victory Beowulf received a golden banner of quaint device, a helmet, and a coat of mail; but what drew all eyes was the ancient famous sword now brought forth from the treasure house, and borne up to the hero. Furthermore, at the king's word, eight splendid horses, cheek-adorned, were led into the hall; and on one of them was seen the saddle, the well-known saddle of Hroðgar, wherein he, never aloof in battle-hour, sate when he mingled in the fray of war. "Take them," said the king, "take them, Beowulf, both horses and armour; and my blessing with them."

The companions of Beowulf were not forgotten: they all received appropriate gifts. The festivities proceed, and we have a picture of the course of the banquet. The minstrel's tale on that occasion was the Fearful Fray in the Castle of Finn, when Danes were there on a visit. The song being ended, Waltheow the queen bears the cup to the king, and bids him be merry and bountiful. Her queenly counsel stops not here. The king had sons of his own; he should give no hint of any other succession to his seat; while he occupied the throne, he should be large in bounty and encircle himself with grateful champions. Next, with like ceremony she honours

Beowulf, and hands the cup to him. She also presents her own special gifts to the deliverer :—bracelets, and a rich garment, and a collar surpassing all most famed in story since Hama captured the collar of the Brosings. The queen addresses Beowulf, wishes him joy of her gifts, exalts his merits, bids him befriend her son and be loyal to the king. She took her seat, and the revelry grew. Little deemed they, what next would happen, when the night should be dark, and Hroðgar asleep in his bower!

The hall is made ready as a dormitory for the men-at-arms; the benches are slewed round, and the floor is spread from end to end with beds and bolsters. Every warrior's shield is set upright at his head, and by the bench-posts stands his spear, supporting helmet and mail. Such was their custom; they slept as ever ready to rise and do service to their king. Horror is renewed in the night; Grendel's fiendish dam visits the hall and kills one of the sleepers, Æschere by name.

In the morning the king is in great distress. He sends for Beowulf, who, after the purging of Heorot, had occupied a separate bower, like the king. Beowulf arrives, and hopes all is well. Hroðgar spake :—
" Ask not of welfare ; sorrow is renewed for the Danish folk ! My trusty friend Æschere is dead; my comrade tried in battle when the tug was for life, when the fight was foot to foot and helmets kissed :—oh ! Æschere was what a thane should be ! The cruel hag has wreaked on him her vengeance. The country folk said there were two of them, one the semblance of a woman, the other the spectre of a man. Their

haunt is in the remote land, in the crags of the wolf, the wind-beaten cliffs, and untrodden bogs, where the dismal stream plunges into the drear abyss of an awful lake, overhung with a dark and grisly wood rooted down to the water's edge, where a lurid flame plays nightly on the surface of the flood—and there lives not the man who knows its depth! So dreadful is the place that the hunted stag, hard driven by the hounds, will rather die on the bank than find a shelter there. A place of terror! When the wind rises, the waves mingle hurly-burly with the clouds, the air is stifling and rumbles with thunder. To thee alone we look for relief; darest thou explore the monster's lair, I will reward the adventure with ancient treasures, with coils of gold if thou return alive!"

Said Beowulf, the son of Ecgtheow:—"Sorrow not, experienced sire! Better avenge a friend than idly deplore him:—each must wait the end of life, and should work while he may to make him a name— the best thing after life! Bestir thee, guardian of the folk! let us be quick upon the track of Grendel's housemate. I make thee a promise:—not highest cliff, not widest field, not darkest wood, nor deepest flood—go where he will—shall be his refuge! Bear up for one day, and may thy troubles end according to my wish!" The king mounts, and with his retinue conducts Beowulf to the charmed lake: the wildness of the way, and the strange nature of the scenes, are all in keeping. The armed followers sit them down in a place where they command a view of the dismal water. Monstrous creatures writhe about the crags; the men shoot some of them.

Beowulf equips for his adventure. His sword was the famous Hrunting, lent to him by Hunferth, the boastful orator, he who had gibed at Beowulf on the day of his arrival. It was a sword of high repute; a hoarded treasure; its edge was iron; it was damascened with device of coiled twigs; it had never failed in fight the hand that dared to wield it. Now Beowulf spoke, ready for action: "Remember, noble Hroðgar, how thou and I talked together, that if I lost life in thy service thou wouldest be as a father to me departed:—protect my comrades if I am taken; and the gifts thou gavest me, beloved Hroðgar, send home to Higelac. When he looks on the treasures he will know that I found a bounteous master, and enjoyed life while it lasted. And let Hunferð have his old sword again: I will conquer fame with Hrunting, or die fighting." Act followed word: he was gone, and the wave had covered him. He was most of the day before he reached the depths of the abyss. While yet on the downward way, he was met by the old water-wolf that had dwelt there a hundred years, who had perceived the approach of a human visitor. She clutched him and bore him off, till he found himself with his enemy in a vast chamber which excluded the water and was lighted by some strange fire-glow. At once the fight began, and Hrunting rang about the demon's head; but against such a being the sword was useless, the edge turned that never had failed before: he flung it from him and trusted to strength of arm. In his rage he charged so deadly that he felled the monster to the ground; but she recovered and Beowulf fell. And now the furious wight thought to revenge Grendel; she plunged her knife at Beowulf's breast, and his life had ended there but for the good service of his ringed mail-serk. Protected by this armour, and helped by Him who giveth victory, he passed the perilous moment, and was on his feet again. And now he espied among the armour in that place an old elfin sword, such as no other man might carry; this he seized, and with the force of despair he so smote that the fell hag lay dead:—the sword was gory, and the boy was fain of his work. With rage unsated, he ranged through the place till he came to where Grendel lay lifeless: he smote the head from the hateful carcase.

To Hroðgar's men watching on the height the lake appeared as if mingled with blood, and this seemed to confirm their fears. The day was waning: the old men about Hroðgar took counsel, and, concluding they should see Beowulf no more, they moved homeward. But Beowulf's followers, though sick at heart and with little hope, yet sate on in spite of dejection.

Meanwhile the huge, gigantic blade had melted marvellously away "likest unto ice, when the Father (he who hath power over times and seasons, that is, the true ruler) looseneth the chain of frost and unwindeth the wave-ropes":—so venomous was the gore of the fiend that had been slain therewith. Beowulf took the gigantic hilt and the monster's head, and, soaring up through the waters, he stood on the shore to the surprise and joy of his faithful comrades, who came eagerly about him to ease him

K

of his dripping harness. Exulting they return to Heorot, Grendel's head carried by four men on a pole; they march straight up the hall to greet the king, and the guests are startled with the ghastly evidence of Beowulf's complete success. Beowulf tells his story and presents the hilt to Hroðgar. The aged king extols the unparalleled achievements of Beowulf, and warns him against excessive exaltation of mind by the example of Heremod.

Soon after this we have the parting between the old king and the young hero, who declares his readiness to come with a thousand thanes at any time of Hroðgar's need; while Hroðgar's words are of love and admiration and confidence in his discretion: and so he lets him go not without large addition of gifts, and embraces, and kisses, and tears. "Thence Beowulf the warrior, elate with gold, trod the grassy plain, exulting in treasure; the sea-goer that rode at anchor awaited its lord; then as they went was Hroðgar's liberality often praised." At the coast they are met by the coast-warden with an altered and respectful mien: they are soon afloat, and we hear the whistle of the wind through the rigging as the gallant craft bears away before the breeze to carry them all merrily homewards after well-sped adventure. The welcome is worthy of the work:—Higelac's reception of Beowulf, the joy of getting him back; Beowulf presenting to his liege lord the wealth he had won; old reminiscences called up and couched in song; an ancient sword brought out and presented to Beowulf, and with the sword a spacious lordship, a noble mansion, and all seigneurial rights.

And so he dwelt until such time as he went forth with Higelac on his fatal expedition against the Frisians, who were backed by a strong alliance of Chauci, and Chattuarii, and Franks; and there Higelac fell, and his army perished. Beowulf, by prodigious swimming, reached his home again, where now was a young widowed queen and her infant son. She offered herself and her kingdom to Beowulf; he preferred the office of the faithful guardian. At a later time the young king fell in battle, and then Beowulf succeeded. He reigned fifty years a good king, and ended life with a supreme act of heroism. He fought and slew a fiery dragon which desolated his country, and was himself mortally wounded in the conflict. One single follower, Wiglaf by name, bolder or more faithful than the rest, was at his side in danger, though not to help; and he received the hero's dying words :—" I should have given my armour to my son if I had heir of my body. I have held this people fifty years; no neighbour has dared to challenge or molest me. I have lived with men on fair and equal terms; I have done no violence, caused no friends to perish, and that is a comfort to one deadly wounded who is soon to appear before the Ruler of men. Now, beloved Wiglaf, go thou quickly in under the hoary stone of the dragon's vault, and bring the treasures out into the daylight, that I may behold the splendour of ancient wealth, and death may be the softer for the sight." When it was done, and the wondrous heap was before his eyes, the victorious warrior spake :—" For the riches on which I look I thank the Lord of all, the king of glory, the everlasting ruler, that I have been able before my death-day to acquire such for my people. Well spent is the remnant of my life to earn such a treasure; I charge thee with the care of the people; I can be no longer here. Order my warriors after the bale-fire to rear a mighty mound on the headland over the sea: it shall tower aloft on Hronesness for a memorial to my people: that sea-going men in time to come may call it Beowulf's Barrow, when foam-prowed ships drive over the scowling flood on their distant courses." Then he removed a golden coil from his neck and gave it to the young thane; the same he did with his helmet inlaid with gold, the collar, and the mail-coat: he bade him use them as his own.

"Thou art the last of our race of the Wægmundings: fate has swept all my kindred off into Eternity; I must follow them." That was his latest word; his soul went out of his breast into the lot of the just. Reflections and discourses proper to the occasion are spoken by Wiglaf, such as chiding of the timorous who stood aloof, and gloomy anticipations of the future.

3,000. Thæt is sio fæhtho	This is the feud
and se feondscipe,	and this the foeman's hate
wæl nith wera,	the vengeful spite
thæs the ic wen hafo,	that I expect
the us seceath to	against us now will bring
Sweona leode	the Swedish bands;
syððan hie gefricgeath	soon as they hear
frean userne,	our chieftain high
ealdorleasne	of life bereft—
thone the ær geheold	who held till now

with hettendum	'gainst haters all
hord and rice ;	the hoard and realm ;
folc ræd fremede,	peace framed at home ;
oððe furthur gen	and further off
eorlscipe efnde.	respect inspired.
Nu is ofost betost	Now speed is best
thæt we theod cyning	that we our liege and king
thær sceawian	go look upon,
and thone gebringan,	and him escort,
the us beagas geaf,	who us adorned,
on âd fære.	the pile towards.
Ne scal anes hwæt	Not things of petty worth
meltan mid tham modigan,	shall with the mighty melt,
ac thær is mathma hord,	but there a treasure main,
gold unrime	uncounted gold
grimme geceapod	costly procured
and nu æt sithestan	and now at length
sylfes feore	with his great life
beagas gebohte.	jewels dear-bought ;
Tha sceal brond gretan	them shall flame devour,
æled theccean,	burning shall bury :—
nalles eorl wegan	never a warrior bear
maððum to gemyndum,	jewel of dear memory,
ne mægth scyne	nor maiden sheen
habban on healse	have on her neck
hring weorthunge,	ring-decoration ;
ac sceal geomor mod	nay, shall disconsolate
golde bereafod	gold-unadorned
oft nalles æne	not once but oft
el land tredan ;	tread strangers' land ;
nu se here wisa	now the leader in war
hleahtor alegde,	laughter hath quenched
gamen and gleo dream.	game and all sound of glee.

And so this noble poem moves on to its close, ending, like the "Iliad," with a great bale-fire. Two closing lines record like an epitaph the praise of the dead in superlatives ; not as a warrior, but as a man and a ruler: how that he was towards men the mildest and most affable, towards his people he was most gracious and most yearning for their esteem.

About the structure of this poem the same sort of questions are debated as those which Wolff raised about Homer—whether it is the work of a single poet, or a patchwork of older poems. Ludwig Ettmüller, of Zürich, who first gave the study of the "Beowulf" a German basis, regarded the poem as originally a purely heathen work, or a compilation of smaller heathen poems, upon which the editorial hands of later and Christian poets had left their manifest traces. In his translation, one of the most vigorous efforts in the whole of Beowulf literature, he has distinguished, by a typographical arrangement, the later additions from what he regards as the original poetry. He is guided, however, by considerations different from those that affect the Homeric debate. He is chiefly guided by the relative shades of the heathen and Christian elements. Wherever the touch of the Christian hand is manifest, he arranges such parts as additions and interpolations.[1]

[1] Dr. Karl Müllenhof (papers in Haupt's "Zeitschrift") follows the same line. His treatment is thus described by Mr. Henry Morley:—"The work was formed, he thinks, by the combination of several old songs—(1) 'The Fight with Grendel,' complete in itself, and the oldest of the pieces; (2) 'The Fight with Grendel's Mother,' next added; then (3) the genealogical introduction to the mention of Hrothgar, forming what is now the opening of the poem. Then came, according to this theory, a poet, A, who worked over the poem thus produced, interpolated many passages with skill, and added a continuation, setting forth Beowulf's return home.

Grein saw in the poem the unity of a single work, and he thought the motive allegorical. He interpreted the assaults of the water-fiend as the night attacks of sea-robbers. I cannot see any such allegory as this, but I agree with him as to the unity of the poem, so far as unity is compatible with the traces of older materials. And I see allegory too, but in a different sense.

The material is mythical and heathen; but it is clarified by natural filtration through the Christian mind of the poet. Not only are the heathen myths inoffensive, but they are positively favourable to a train of Christian thought. Beowulf's descent into the abyss to extirpate the scourge is suggestive of that Article in the Apostles' Creed which had a peculiar fascination for the mind of the Dark and Middle Ages; the fight with the dragon; the victory that cost the victor his life; the one faithful friend while the rest are fearful—these incidents seem almost like reflections of evangelical history. Without seeing in the poem an allegorical design, we may imagine that, with the progress of Christianity, those parts of the old mythology which were most in harmony with Christian doctrines had the best chance of survival; and that, as a poet puts a new physiognomy

Last came a theoretical interloper, B, a monk, who interspersed religious sayings of his own, and added the ancient song of the fight with the dragon and the death of Beowulf. The positive critic not only finds all this, but proceeds to point out which passages are old, older, and oldest, where a few lines are from poet A, and where other interpolation is from poet B."— "English Verse and Prose" in "Cassell's Library of English Literature," p. 11.

on an old story without distorting the tradition, as we have seen in our own day the story of Arthur told again, not with the elaborate allegory of Spenser, but with a spiritual transfiguration which makes the "Idylls of the King" truly an epic of the nineteenth century, so I conceive that Beowulf was a genuine growth of that junction in time (define it where we may) when the heathen tales still kept their traditional interest, and yet the spirit of Christianity had taken full possession of the Saxon mind—at least, so much of it as was represented by this poetical literature.

We may not dismiss the "Beowulf" without hazarding an opinion as to the date of its production. It has been said to be older than the Saxon Conquest, and some of the materials are doubtless of this antiquity. But for the poem, as we have it, Kemble assigned it to the seventh century; then Ettmüller thought it belonged to the ninth; then Grein went back halfway to the eighth, and this has been adopted by Mr. Arnold, and most generally followed. I think Ettmüller is the nearest to the mark; and I would rather go forward to the tenth than back to the eighth. A pardonable fancy might see the date conveyed in the poem itself. The dragon watches over an old hoard of gold, and it is distinctly a heathen hoard (hæðnum horde, 2,217) of heathen gold (hæðen gold, 2,277). In the same context we find that the monster had watched over this earth-hidden treasure for 300 years; and if this may be something more than a poetical number, it may possibly indicate the time elapsed since the heathen age. Three hundred years would bring us to the close of the ninth or the beginning of the tenth century, a date which, on every consideration, I incline to think the most probable.[1]

All the traces of affinity with, or consciousness of, the "Beowulf" that we can discover—and they are very few—are such as to favour this date. The only complete parallel to the fable is found in the Icelandic Saga of Grettir, who is a kind of northern Hercules. This hero performs many great feats, but there are three which belong to the supernatural. In one of these he wrestles with a fiend called Glam, and kills him; and though Glam is not the same as Grendel, yet the circumstances of the encounter are so full of parallels as to establish, at least, the literary affinity of the two stories. The other two supernatural feats are coupled, just in the same way as two of the feats of Beowulf are. It is two fights, one in a hall and one under a waterfall, with two monsters of one family. The fight with the troll-wife in the hall is a true parallel to Beowulf's fight with Grendel; but the fight with the troll in the cavern under the force is in great essentials and in minute details so identical with Beowulf's under-water adventure, that one may call it a prose version

[1] No one needs to be told that the dragon story is of high antiquity. But even of the elements which have most the appearance of history some may be traced so far back till they seem to fade into legend. Thus Higelac can hardly be any other than that Chochilaicus of whom Gregory of Tours records that he invaded the Frisian coast from the north, and was slain in the attempt. In our poem, this recurs with variations no less than four times as a well-known passage in the adventures of Higelac. But it affords a doubtful basis for argument about the date of our poem.

of the same thing under different names. A certain house was haunted. Men that were there alone by night were missing, and nothing more was heard of them. Grettir came and lay in that hall. The troll-wife came and he vanquished her. This he had done under an assumed name, but the priest of the district knows he can be no other than Grettir, and he asks Grettir what had become of the men who were lost. Grettir bids the priest come with him to the river. There was a waterfall, and a sheer cliff of fifty fathom down to the water, and under the force was seen the mouth of a cavern. They had a rope with them. The priest drives down a stake into a cleft of the rock and secured it with stones, and he sate by it. Grettir said, "I will search what there is in the force, but thou shalt watch the rope." He put a stone in the bight of the rope, and let it sink down in the water. He made ready, girt him with a short sword, and had no other weapon. He leaped off the cliff, and the priest saw the soles of his feet. Grettir dived under the force, and the eddy was so strong that he had to get to the very bottom before he could get inside the force, where the river stood off from the cliff. By a jutting rock he reached the cavern's mouth. In the cave there was a fire burning on the hearth. A giant sate there, who at once leaped up and struck at the intruder with a pike made equally to cut and to thrust. This weapon had a wooden shaft, and men called it a hepti-sax.[1] Grettir's sword demolishes

[1] See Dr. Vigfusson's remarks in the Prolegomena to his edition of the "Sturlinga Saga," Oxford, Clarendon Press, 1878.

this weapon, and the giant stretched after a sword that hung there in the cave. Then Grettir smote him and killed him, and his blood ran down with the stream past the rope where the priest sate to watch. The priest concluded that Grettir was dead, and it being now evening he went home. But Grettir explored the cave. He found the bones of two men, and put them into a skin. He swam to the rope and climbed up by it to the top of the cliff. When the priest came to church next morning he found the bones in the bag, and a rune-stick whereon the event was carved; but Grettir was gone.

The identity is so manifest that we have only to ask which people (if either) was the borrower, the English or the Danes. And here comes in the consideration that the geography of the "Beowulf" is Scandinavian. There is no consciousness of Britain or England throughout the poem. If this raises a presumption that the Saxon poet got his story from a Dane, we naturally ask, When is this likely to have happened? and the answer must be that the earliest probable time begins after the Peace of Wedmore in 878.

In the "Blickling Homilies" there is a passage which recalls the description of the mere in "Beowulf."[1] So far as this coincidence affects the question, it makes for the date here assigned.

Beyond the "Beowulf" we have but small and fragmentary remains of the old heroic poetry. The most important pieces are "The Battle of Finn's Burgh,"

---

[1] See Dr. Morris's Preface to the Blickling Homilies.

and "The Lay of King Waldhere." These are now often printed in the editions of the "Beowulf."

Ettmüller conjectured that the "Invitation from a True Lover Settled Abroad," was not a single lyric, but a beautiful incident taken from some epic poem.[1] A messenger comes with a token to a lady at home, by which she may credit his message; he bids her take ship as soon as she hears the voice of the cuckoo, and go out to him who has all things ready about him to give her a suitable reception.

Next we will consider

"THE RUINED CITY."[2]

The subject of this piece is a city in ruins. There is massive masonry: the place was once handsomely built and decorated and held by warriors, but now all tumbled about; works of art exposed to view and forming a strange contrast with the desolation around; there is a wide pool of water, hot without fire; and there are the once-frequented baths. This is no vague poetic composition, but the portrait of a definite spot. It suits the old Brito-Roman ruin of Akeman after 577; and it suits no other place that I can think of in the habitable world. The old view that it was a fortress or castle seems misplaced in time, as well as incompatible with the expressions in the text.[3]

[1] Cod. Exon., ed. Thorpe, p. 473.
[2] Cod. Exon., ed. Thorpe, p. 476; Grein, i., 248.
[3] Years ago I discussed this little poem before the Bath Field Club; and my arguments were subsequently printed in the "Proceedings" of that society (1872). Professor Wülcker

The poem begins:—

Wrætlic is thes weal stan wyrde gebræcon,	Stupendous is this wall of stone, strange the ruin!

The strongholds are bursten, the work of giants decaying, the roofs are fallen, the towers tottering, dwellings unroofed and mouldering, masonry weather-marked, shattered the places of shelter, time-scarred, tempest-marred, undermined of eld.

Eorth grap hafath waldend wyrhtan forweorene geleorene heard gripe hrusan oth hund cnea wer theoda gewitan. Oft thes wag gebad ræg har and read fah rice æfter othrum ofstonden under stormum . . .	Earth's grasp holdeth the mighty workmen worn away lorn away in the hard grip of the grave till a hundred ages of men-folk do pass. Oft this wall witnessed (weed-grown and lichen-spotted) one great man after another take shelter out of storms. . .

* * * * * * *

How did the swift sledge-hammer flash and furiously come down upon the rings when the sturdy artizan was rivetting the wall with clamps so wondrously together. Bright were the buildings, the bath-houses many, high-towered the pinnacles, frequent the war-clang, many the mead-halls, of merriment full, till all was overturned by Fate the violent. The walls crumbled widely; dismal days came on; death swept off the valiant men; the arsenals became ruinous foundations; decay sapped the burgh. Pitifully

has since agreed with me that the subject of the poem is a city, and not a fortress. My identification of the ruin with Aceman-ceaster (Bath) has been approved by Mr. Freeman in his volume on "Rufus."

crouched armies to earth. Therefore these halls are a dreary ruin, and these pictured gables;[1] the rafter-framed roof sheddeth its tiles; the pavement is crushed with the ruin, it is broken up in heaps; where erewhile many a baron—

glædmod and goldbeorht	joyous and gold-bright
gleoma gefrætwed	gaudily jewelled
wlonc and wingal	haughty and wine-hot
wig hyrstum scan ;	shone in his harness ;
seah on sinc on sylfor	looked on treasure, on silver,
on searo gimmas ;	on gems of device ;
on ead, on æht,	on wealth, on stores,
on eorcan stan :	on precious stones ;
on thas beorhtan burg	on this bright borough
bradan rices.	of broad dominion.
Stan hofu stodan ;	There stood courts of stone !
stream hate wearp	The stream hotly rushed
widan wylme,	with eddy wide,
weal eal befeng	(wall all enclosed)
beorhtan bosme ;	with bosom bright,
thær tha bathu wæron,	(There the baths were !)
hat on hrethre ;	hot in its nature !
thæt wes hythelic !	That was a boon indeed !

---

[1] The feeling which pervades this remarkable fragment was strangely recalled by the following passage in a recent book that has interested many :—"Masses of strange, nameless masonry, of an antiquity dateless and undefined, bedded themselves in the rocks, or overhung the clefts of the hills ; and out of a great tomb by the wayside, near the arch, a forest of laurel forced its way, amid delicate and graceful frieze-work, moss-covered and stained with age. In this strangely desolate and ruinous spot, where the fantastic shapes of nature seem to mourn in weird fellowship with the shattered strength and beauty of the old Pagan art-life, there appeared unexpectedly signs of modern dwelling."—"John Inglesant," by J. H. Shorthouse, new edition, 1881, vol. ii., p. 320.

"THE WANDERER" (EARDSTAPA).[1]

In patriarchal or sub-patriarchal times social life was still confined within the family pale; and the man who belonged to no household was a wanderer and a vagabond on the face of the earth. Through invasion or war or other accidents a man who had been the honoured member of a well-found home might live to see that home broken up or pass into strange hands, and he might be thus like a plant uprooted when he was too old to get planted in a fresh connexion. His only chance of any share in social life was to wander from house to house, getting perhaps a brief lodging in each; and such a homeless condition might be well expressed by the compound eardstapa, one who tramps (*stapa*) from one habitation (*eard*) to another. In such an outcast plight the speaker in this piece went to sea, and there he often thought of the old happy days that were gone. He would dream of the pleasure of his old access to the giefstol of his lord, whom he saluted with kiss and head on knee, and then he would wake a friendless man in the wintry ocean, and his grief would be the sorer at his heart for the recollections of lost kindred that the dream had revived. Such a lot is in ready sympathy with old-world ruins, of which there were many in England at that time, and they raise the anticipation of a time when a like ruin will be the end of all! "It becomes a wise man to know how awful it will be when all this world's wealth

[1] Cod. Exon., ed. Thorpe, p. 286.

stands waste, as now up and down in the world there are wind-buffeted walls standing in mouldering decay "—and the description which follows is either a reminiscence of "The Ruined City," or else it shows that the subject of ruins was familiar with the Scōpas.[1]

"THE MINSTREL'S CONSOLATION."[2]

Ettmüller reckoned this the oldest of the Saxon lyrics; influenced, perhaps, by the mythical nature of the contents. But, if we regard the form rather than the material, there is a refinement about the versification which does not look archaic. The poem is cast in irregular stanzas, and it has a refrain. The poet, whose name is Deor, has experienced the fallaciousness of early success. His prospects are clouded; once the favourite minstrel of his patron, he is now superseded by a newer Scōp. His consolation is a well-known one; perhaps the oldest and commonest of all the formulæ of consolation. Others have been in trouble before him, and have somehow got over it. This is not conveyed as a mere generalisation; it is done poetically through striking examples, of which Weland is the first, and Beadohild the second. After each example comes the refrain :—

| thæs ofereode | That [distress] he overwent, |
| thisses swa mæg! | So . I . can . this ! |

---

[1] A translation of this poem in Alexandrines appeared in the *Academy*, May 14, 1881, by E. H. Hickey.

[2] Cod. Exon., ed. Thorpe, p. 377. His title is "Deor the Scald's Complaint." I have adopted the title from Professor Wülcker, "Des Sängers Trost."

THE PRIMARY POETRY. 145

The failures of life's hopes and ambitions have been so often lamented, that the subject is rather hackneyed and conventional. Here is a piece out of the beaten track; fresh, though ingenious and artistic. Such a poem is all the more welcome as the subject belongs to an extinct career—the career of a court minstrel.

The Ballads have a peculiar value of their own. There is a sense in which they are the best representatives of the native muse. There are several extant specimens of various merit, but two are preeminent, and these are, beyond all doubt, preserved in their original and unaltered form. They were manifestly produced in the moment when the sensation of a great event was yet fresh. They are impassioned and effusive, and they bear good witness to the characteristics of primitive poetry. One spontaneous element they preserve, which has been quite discarded from modern poetry, and of which the other traces are few. I mean the poetry of derision. The light and shade of the ballad is glory and scorn. The most popular subject of this species of poetry is a battle. Whether your ballad is of victory or of disaster, these two elements, not indeed with the same intensity or the same proportions, but still these two, are the constituents required. Our best examples are the "Victory of Brunanburh" (937), and the "Disaster of Maldon" (991).

The battle of Brunanburh was fought by King Athelstan and his brother Edmund (children of Edward), against the alliance of the Scots under Constantinus with the Danes under Anlaf.

L

Various attempts have been made to present in modern English the Ballad of Brunanburh, the most successful being that by the Poet Laureate. Our language is rather out of practice for kindling a poetic fervour around the sentiment of flinging scorn at a vanquished foe; but the following will serve to illustrate this heathenish element, or such relics of it as survived in the tenth century. The person first railed at is Constantinus:—

X.

Slender reason had
He to be proud of
The welcome of war-knives—
He that was reft of his
Folk and his friends that had
Fallen in conflict,
Leaving his son, too,
Lost in the carnage,
Mangled to morsels,
A youngster in war!

XI.

Slender reason had
He to be glad of
The clash of the war-glaive—
Traitor and trickster
And spurner of treaties—
He nor had Anlaf,
With armies so broken,
A reason for bragging
That they had the better
In perils of battle
On places of slaughter—
The struggle of standards,
The rush of the javelins,

> The crash of the charges,
> The wielding of weapons—
> The play that they played with
> The children of Edward.
>
> ALFRED TENNYSON, "Ballads and Other Poems,"
> 1880, p. 174.

The longest of our ballads, though it is imperfect, is that of the "Battle of Maldon." In the year 991 the Northmen landed in Essex, and expected to be bought off with great ransom; but Brithnoth, the alderman of the East Saxons, met them with all his force, and, after fighting bravely, was killed. The lines here quoted occur after the alderman's death:—

Leofsunu gemælde,	Then up spake Leveson
and his linde ahof,	and his shield uphove,
bord to gebeorge;	buckler in ward;
he tham beorne oncwæth;	he the warrior addressed:
Ic thæt gehate,	I make the vow,
thæt ic heonon nelle	that I will not hence
fleon fotes trym,	flee a foot's pace,
ac wille furthor gan,	but will go forward;
wrecan on gewinne	wreak in the battle
mine wine drihten!	my friend and my lord!
Ne thurfon me embe Sturmere	Never shall about Stourmere,
stede fæste hæleth,	the stalwart fellows,
wordum ætwitan,	with words me twit
nu min wine gecranc,	now my chief is down,
thæt ic hlafordleas	that I lordless
ham sithie	homeward go march,
wende from wige!	turning from war!
ac me sceal wæpen niman,	Nay, weapon shall take me,
ord and iren!	point and iron.

Other ballads, or something like ballads, that are embodied in the Saxon chronicles are:—"The

Conquest of Mercia" (942); "The Coronation of Eadgar at Bath" (973); "Eadgar's Demise" (975); "The Good Times of King Eadgar" (975); "The Martyr of Corf Gate" (979); "Alfred the Innocent Ætheling" (1036); "The Son of Ironside" (1057); "The Dirge of King Eadward" (1065).

Others there are of which only brief scraps remain, almost embedded in the prose of the chronicles:—"The Sack of Canterbury" (1011); "The Wooing of Margaret" (1067); "The Baleful Bride Ale" (1076); "The High-handed Conqueror" (1086).[1]

Our last piece shall be "Widsith, or the Gleeman's Song."[2] This is a string of reminiscences of travel in the profession of minstrelsy; some part of which has a genuine air of high antiquity.[3] In the course of a long tradition it has undergone many changes which cannot now be distinguished. But, besides these, there are some glaring patches of literary interpolation, chiefly from Scriptural sources. I quote the concluding lines:—

[1] Sometimes a prose passage of unusual energy raises the apprehension that it may be a ballad toned down. Dr. Grubitz has suggested this view of the Annal of 755, in which there is a fight in a Saxon castle (burh). The graphic description of the place, the dramatic order of the incidents, and the life-like dialogue of the parley, might well be the work of a poet.

[2] Kemble called it "The Traveller's Song;" Thorpe, Cod. Exon., p. 318, "The Scop or Scald's Tale."

[3] A valuable testimony is borne to the substantial antiquity of this poem, by the fact that Schäfarik, who is the chief ethnographer for Sclavonic literature, regards it as a valuable source on account of the Sclavonic names contained in it. I am indebted to Mr. Morfil, of Oriel College, for this information.

Swa scrithende	So wandering on
gesceapum hweorfath,	the world about,
gleo men gumena	glee-men do roam
geond grunda fela ;	through many lands;
thearfe secgath	they say their needs,
thonc word sprecath,	they speak their thanks,
simle suth oththe north	sure south or north
sumne gemetath,	some one to meet,
gydda gleawne	of songs to judge
geofum unhneawne,	and gifts not grudge,
se the fore duguthe	one who by merit hath a mind
wile dom aræran	renown to make
eorlscipe æfnan ;	earlship to earn ;
oth thæt eal scaceth	till all goes out
leoht and lif somod :	light and life together.
Lof se gewyrceth	Laud who attains
hafath under heofenum	hath under heaven
heahfæstne dom.	high built renown.

CHAPTER VII.

THE WEST SAXON LAWS.

"No other Germanic nation has bequeathed to us out of its earliest experience so rich a treasure of original legal documents as the Anglo-Saxon nation has." Such is the sentence of Dr. Reinhold Schmid, who upon the basis of former labours, and particularly those of Mr. Benjamin Thorpe, has given us the most compact and complete edition yet produced of the Anglo-Saxon laws.[1]

It might seem as if laws were too far removed from the idea of literature, to merit more than a passing notice here. Writers on modern English literature generally leave the lawyer's work altogether out of their field. But these are among the things that alter with age. Laws become literary matter just as they become old and obsolete. Then the traces they have left in words and phrases and figures of speech, their very contrasts with the laws of the present, makes them material eminently literary. We know what effective literary use Sir Walter Scott has made of the antiquities and curiosities of law.

---

[1] The Anglo-Saxon laws have been edited by William Lombarde, London, 1568, 4to.; Abraham Whelock, Cambridge, 1644; Wilkins, London, 1721, folio; Dr. Reinhold Schmid, Leipzig, 1832; Thorpe, 1840; Schmid, ed. 2, 1858. It is Schmid's second edition that is spoken of above.

And to this may be added another remark. When we are engaged in reconstructing an ancient, we might almost say a lost literature, we need above all things some leading ideas concerning the conditions of social life and opinion and mental development at the period in question. Nothing supplies these things so safely as the laws of the time.

INE'S LAWS.

The oldest extant West Saxon laws are those of King Ine,[1] who reigned thirty-eight years, A.D. 688–726. As the West Saxon power gradually absorbed all other rule in this island, we here find ourselves entering the central stream of history. In the preamble to Ine's Laws the name of Erconwald, bishop of London, who died in 693, is among the persons present at the Gemôt. Consequently these laws must be referred to the first years of Ine's reign, and they must be older than the date of the Kentish laws of Wihtred.

The laws of Ine are preserved to us as an appendix of the laws of Alfred. This is the case in all the manuscripts. Not only does the elder code follow the younger, but the numbering is continuous as if welding the two codes into one. Thorpe follows the manuscripts in this arrangement, though not in the numbering of the sections, and the student who consults his edition is apt to be confused with this chronological inversion, unless he has taken note of the cause. Ine reigned over a mixed population of

---

[1] Ine is to be pronounced as a word of two syllables.

Saxons and Britons, and his code is of a more comprehensive character than that of the Kentish kings. His enactments became, through subsequent re-enactments, the basis of the laws not only of Wessex, but also of all England. Accordingly they seem more intelligible to the modern reader.[1]

9. If any one take revenge before he sue for justice, let him give up what he has seized, and pay for the damage done, and make amends with thirty shillings.

12. If a thief be taken, let him die, or let his life be redeemed according to his "wer." .... Thieves we call them up to seven men; from seven to thirty-five a band (*hloth*); after that it is a troop (*here*).

32. If a Wylisc-man have a hide of land, his "wer" is 120 shillings; if he have half a hide, eighty shillings; if he have none, sixty shillings.

36. He who takes a thief, or has a captured thief given over to him, and then lets him go or conceals the theft, let him pay for the thief according to his "wer." If he be an ealdorman, let him forfeit his shire, unless the king be pleased to show him mercy.

39. If any one go from his lord without leave, or steal himself away into another shire, and word is brought; let him go where he before was, and pay his lord sixty shillings.

40. A ceorl's close should be fenced winter and summer. If it be unfenced, and his neighbour's cattle get in through his own gap, he hath no claim on the cattle; let him drive it out and bear the damage.

---

[1] Palgrave, "English Commonwealth," i., 46.

THE WEST SAXON LAWS.

43. In case any one burn a tree in a wood, and it come to light who did it, let him pay the full penalty, and give sixty shillings, because fire is a thief. If one fell in a wood ever so many trees, and it be found out afterwards, let him pay for three trees, each with thirty shillings. He is not required to pay for more of them, however many they might be, because the axe is a reporter and not a thief (*forthon seo æsc bith melda, nalles theof*).[1]

44. But if a man cut down a tree that thirty swine may stand under, and it is found out, let him pay sixty shillings.

52. Let him who is accused of secret compositions clear himself of those compositions with 120 hides, or pay 120 shillings.[2]

---

[1] Grimm, "Legal Antiquities," § 10, quotes some widely-scattered parallels: from Rügen he produces the proverb, "Mit der exe stelt men nicht" (with the axe men steal not); and from Wetterau, "Wan einer hauet, so ruft er" (when one hews, he shouts). He dubs the Anglo-Saxon formula the more poetical (*poetischer*).

[2] "These secret compositions are forbidden by nearly every early code of Europe; for by such a proceeding both the judge and the Crown lost their profits. The "Capitulary" of 593 puts the receiver of a secret composition on a level with the thief: 'Qui furtum vult celare, et occulte sine judice compositionem acceperit, latroni similis est.' And even now in common law, the rule is to obtain the sanction of the Court for permission 'to speak with the prosecutor,' and thus terminate the suit by compounding the affair in private."—THORPE. The reason assigned is, however, not the whole reason.

ALFRED'S LAWS.

Here I will quote from the introductory portion a piece which illustrates the subject generally, and which is rendered interesting by the wide diversity of comment which it has elicited from Mr. Kemble and Sir H. Maine. The former is almost outrageously angry at Alfred for attributing the system of bôts or compensations to the influence of Christianity; while in the strong terms wherewith treason against the lord is branded, he can only see " these despotic tendencies of a great prince, nurtured probably by his exaggerated love for foreign literature."[1] It is positively refreshing to come out of this heat and dust into the orderly and consecutive demonstration of Sir H. Maine, who concludes a course of systematic exposition on the History of Criminal Law, and indeed concludes his entire book on Ancient Law, with an appreciative quotation of this passage from the Laws of Alfred. It is thus introduced:—

"There is a passage in the writings of King Alfred which brings out into remarkable clearness the struggle of the various ideas that prevailed in his day as to the origin of criminal jurisdiction. It will be seen that Alfred attributes it partly to the authority of the Church and partly to that of the Witan, while he expressly claims for treason against the lord the same immunity from ordinary rules which the Roman Law of Majestas had assigned to treason against the Cæsar."

[1] "Saxons in England," vol. ii., p. 208.

Siththan thæt tha gelamp, thæt monega theoda Cristes geleafan onfengon, tha wurdon monega seonothas geond ealne middan geard gegaderode, and eac swa geond Angel cyn, siththan hie Cristes geleafan onfengon, haligra biscepa and eac otherra gethungenra witena. Hie tha gesetton for thære mildheortnesse, the Crist lærde, æt mæstra hwelcre misdæde, thæt tha woruld hlafordas moston mid hiora leafan buton synne æt tham forman gylte thære fioh-bote onfon, the hie tha gesettan ; buton æt hlaford searwe, tham hie nane mildheortnesse ne dorston gecwæthan, fortham the God Ælmihtig tham nane ne gedemde the hine oferhogodon, ne Crist, Godes sunu, tham nane ne gedemde, the hyne sealde to deathe ; and he bebead thone hlaford lufian swa hine selfne.

Hie tha on monegum senothum monegra menniscra misdæda bote gesetton, and on monega senoth bec hy writon hwær anne dom hwær otherne.

Ic tha Ælfred cyning thas togædere gegaderode and awritan het monege thara, the ure foregengan heoldon, tha the me licodon ; and manege

After that it happened that many nations received the faith of Christ, and there were many synods assembled through all parts of the world, and likewise throughout the Angle race after they had received the faith of Christ, of holy bishops and also of other distinguished Witan. They then ordained, out of that compassion which Christ had taught, in the case of almost every misdeed, that the secular lords might, with their leave and without sin, for the first offence accept the money penalty which they then ordained ; excepting in the case of treason against a lord, to which they dared not assign any mercy, because God Almighty adjudged none to them that despised Him, nor did Christ, the Son of God, adjudge any to them that sold Him to death ; and He commanded that the lord should be loved as Himself.

They then in many synods ordained a "bot" for many human misdeeds, and in many a synod-book they wrote, here one decision, there another.

I then, Afred, king, gathered these together, and I ordered to write out many of those that our forefathers held which to me seemed good ; and many of

thara the me ne licodon, ic awearp mid minra witena getheahte, and on othre wisan bebead to healdenne, fortham ic ne dorste gethristlæcan thara minra awuht feala on gewrit settan, fortham me wæs uncuth, hwæt thæs tham lician wolde, the æfter us wæren. Ac tha the ic gemette, awther oththe on Ines dæge, mines mæges, oththe on Offan, Myrcena cyninges, oththe on Æthelbryhtes, the ærest fulluht onfeng on Angel cynne, tha the me ryhtoste thuhton, ic tha her on gegaderode and tha othre forlet.

Ic tha Ælfred, West seaxna cyning, eallum minum witum thas geeowde, and hie tha cwædon, thæt him thæt licode eallum to healdenne.

those that to me seemed not good I rejected, with the counsel of my Witan, and in other wise commanded to hold; forasmuch as I durst not venture to set any great quantity of my own in writing, because it was unknown to me what would please those who should be after us. But those things that I found established, either in the days of Ine my kinsman, or in Offa's, king of the Mercians, or in Æthelbryht's, who first received baptism in the Angle race, those which seemed to me rightest, those I have here gathered together, and the others I have rejected.

I then, Alfred, king of the West Saxons, to all my Witan showed these; and they then said, that it seemed good to them all that they should be holden.

ALFRED AND GUTHRUM'S PEACE.

This is a little code which marks a crisis in Alfred's life, and, it may be added, a crisis also in the life of the nation. When Alfred by his victory over the Danes in 878 had brought them to sue for peace, the treaty was made at Wedmore in Somersetshire. The original text of the peace between Alfred and Guthrum is among the Anglo-Saxon laws, and we present it to the reader in its entire form. The first item is about the frontier line between the two races which was drawn diagonally through the heart of England, cutting Mercia in two, and leaving half of it under the Danes. The two parts into which the country was thus divided, were designated severally as the "Engla lagu" and the "Dena lagu."

Ælfredes and Guthrumes frith.

This is thæt frith, thæt Ælfred cynincg and Gythrum cyning and ealles Angel cynnes witan, and eal seo theod the on East Englum beoth, ealle gecweden habbath, and mid athum gefeostnod, for hy sylfe and for heora gingran, ge for geborene, ge for ungeborene, the Godes miltse recce oththe ure.

Cap. I. Ærest ymb ure landgemæra: up on Temese and thonne up on Ligan, and andlang Ligan oth hire æ wylm, thonne on gerihte to Bedan forda, thonne up on Usan oth Wætlinga stræt.

2. Thæt is thonne, gif man ofslagen weorthe, ealle we lætath efen dyrne Engliscne and Deniscne, to VIII healfmarcum asodenes goldes, buton tham ceorle the on gafol lande sit, and heora liesingum, tha syndan eac efen dyre, ægther to CC scill.

3. And gif mon cyninges thegn beteo manslihtes, gif he hine ladian dyrre, do he thæt mid XII cininges thegnum. Gif

Alfred and Guthrum's Peace.

This is the peace that king Alfred and king Guthrum and the counsellors of all Angel-kin, and all the people that are in East Anglia, have all decreed and with oaths confirmed for themselves and for their children, both for the born and for the unborn, all who value God's favour or ours.

Cap. I. First about our land-boundaries:—Up the Thames, and then up the Lea, and along the Lea to her source, then straight to Bedford, then up the Ouse to Watling Street.

2. Videlicet, if a person be slain, we all estimate of equal value, the Englishman and the Dane, at eight half-marks of pure gold; except the ceorl who resides on gafol-land, and their [*i.e.* the Danish] liesings, those also are equally dear, either at two hundred shillings.

3. And if a king's thane be charged with killing a man, if he dare to clear himself, let him do it with twelve king's

man thone man betyhth, the bith læssa maga thonne se cyninges thegn, ladige he hine mid XI his gelicena and mid anum cyninges thægne. And swa ægehwilcere spræce, the mare sy thonne IIII mancussas. And gyf he ne dyrre, gylde hit thry gylde, swa hit man gewyrthe.

Be getymum.

4. And thæt ælc man wite his getyman be mannum and be horsum and be oxum.

5. And ealle we cwædon on tham dæge the mon tha athas swor, thæt ne theowe ne freo ne moton in thone here faran butan leafe, ne heora nan the ma to us. Gif thonne gebyrige, thæt for neode heora hwilc with ure bige habban wille, oththe we with heora, mid yrfe and mid æhtum, thæt is to thafianne on tha wisan, thæt man gislas sylle frithe to wedde, and to swutelunge, thæt man wite thæt man clæne bæc hæbbe.

thanes. If the accused man be of less degree than the king's thane, let him clear himself with eleven of his equals, and with one king's thane. And so in every suit that may be for more than four mancuses. And if he dare not, let him pay threefold, according as it may be valued.

Of Warrantors.

4. And that every man know his warrantor for men and for horses and for oxen.

5. And we all said on that day when the oaths were sworn, that neither bond nor free should be at liberty to go to the host[1] without leave, nor of them any one by the same rule (come) to us. If, however, it happen, that for business any one of them desires to have dealings with us or we with them, about cattle and about goods, that is to be granted on this wise, that hostages be given for a pledge of peace, and for evidence whereby it may be known that the party has a clean back [*i.e.*, that he has not carried off on his back what is not his own].

---

[1] *I.e.*, go to the Danish camp in East Anglia.

THE WEST SAXON LAWS.

EADWARD AND GUTHRUM'S LAWS.

Besides two codes of laws of Eadward, the son of Alfred, we have also a code entitled as above. Of these laws it is said that they were first made between Alfred and Guthrum, and afterwards between Eadward and Guthrum.[1] Many of the enactments of this code were transmitted to later ordinances.

This syndon tha domas the Ælfred cyneg and Guthrum cyneg gecuran.	These are the dooms that king Alfred and king Guthrum chose.
And this is seo gerædnis eac the Ælfred cyng and Guthrum cyng. and eft Eadward cyng and Guthrum cyng. gecuran and gecwædon. Tha tha Engle and Dene to frithe and to freondscipe fullice fengen. and tha witan eac the syththan wæron eft and unseldan thæt seolfe geniwodon and mid gode gehihtan.	And this is the ordinance, also, which king Alfred and king Guthrum, and afterwards king Eadward and king Guthrum, chose and ordained, when the English and Danes fully took to peace and to friendship; and the Witan also, who were afterward, often and repeatedly renewed the same and increased it with good.

ATHELSTAN'S LAWS.

Under the name of Athelstan we have five codes, of which the second and third are mere abstracts in Latin; but the others are in Saxon; and besides these a substantive ordinance bearing the special title of "The Judgments of the City of London." This has been described as follows:—"The rules of the guild composed of thanes and ceorls (gentlemen and

[1] Here we have to understand two distinct kings of the name of Guthrum.

yeomen), under the perpetual presidency of the bishop and portreeve of London."[1] They combine to protect themselves against robbery, and this in two ways : (1) by promoting the action of the laws against robbers ; (2) by mutual insurance.

The determination of this code to the reign of Athelstan is guided by the mention of the places of enactment, which are Greatley (near Andover, Hants) ; Exeter ; and Thundersfield (near Horley, Surrey), with which places all the previous laws of Athelstan are associated.

From the fourth of the above-mentioned ordinances I will quote the law about the tracking of cattle lost, stolen, or strayed :—

2. "And if any one track cattle within another's land, the owner of that land is to track it out, if he can ; if he cannot, that track is to count as the fore-oath," *i.e.*, the first legal step in an action to recover.

A more explicit description of the method of tracking cattle occurs in the Ordinance of the Dunsæte.

This ordinance is placed by Thorpe between the laws of Æthelred and those of Cnut. This little code of nine sections is intended to rule the relations of a border country which, on its home side, is continuous with Wessex, and on its outer side is next the Welsh. Sir Francis Palgrave, misled perhaps by a questionable reading in Lambarde (1568), who has the form Deunsætas, took this to be a treaty between the English and British inha-

---

[1] Coote, "The Romans of Britain," p. 397.

bitants of Devon, and bestowed on it the succinct title of the Devonian Compact. But Mr. Thorpe objected to the form "Deun" as groundless, and he also quoted the text of the code against it; for the last section speaks thus:—"Formerly the Wentsæte belonged to the Dunsæte, but that district more strictly belongs to Wessex, for they have to send thither tribute and hostages." This admits of no explanation in Devonshire, but in South Wales it does, and we learn from William of Malmesbury that the river Wye was fixed by King Athelstan as the boundary between the English and Welsh. On this basis the Wentsæte will be the people of Gwent, and the Dunsæte will be the Welsh of the upland or hill-country.

One of the most remarkable sections of this Code is the first, which prescribes the method for tracking stolen cattle.

The laws concerning theft relate almost entirely to the protection of cattle, and naturally so, because the chief wealth of the time consisted in flocks and herds. Stolen cattle were tracked by fixed rules. If the track led into a given district, the men of that district were bound to show the track out of their boundary or to be responsible for the lost property. We have just seen this in Athelstan's laws; but in the previous reign a law of Edward, the son of Alfred, directs that every proprietor of land is to have men ready to dispatch in aid of those who are following the track of cattle, and that they are not to be diverted from this duty by bribes, or inclination, or violence. But the most explicit text on this subject is in the first chapter of the Ordinance respecting the Dunset folk, as above said. It runs thus:—

"If the track of stolen cattle be followed from station to station, the further tracking shall be committed to the people of the land, and proof shall be given that the pursuit is genuine. The proprietor of the land shall then take up the pursuit, and he shall have the responsibility, and he shall pay for the cattle by nine days therefrom, or deposit a pledge by that date, which is worth half more, and in a further nine days discharge the pledge with actual payment. If objection be made that the track was wrongly pursued, then the tracker must lead to the station, and there with six unchosen men, who are true men, make oath that he by folk-right makes claim on the land that the cattle passed up that way."

We cannot follow the laws in detail, but must now conclude this subject with one or two observations of a general kind. In the above I have repeatedly used the word "Code"; but this is not to be understood with technical exactness. Of late years we have heard much of "codifying" our laws; and this expression suggests the idea of a compact and consistent body of law, which should take the place of partial, occasional, anomalous, and often conflicting legislation. Of "codes" in this sense, there is very little to be found in the whole record of English law. Our Kentish and West Saxon laws are little more than statements of custom or amendments of custom; and while Professor Stubbs claims for the laws of Alfred, Æthelred, Cnut, and those described as Edward the Confessor's, that they aspire to the character of codes, yet "English law (he adds) from its first to its latest phase, has never possessed an authoritative, constructive, systematic, or approximately exhaustive statement, such as was attempted by the great compilers of the civil and canon laws, by Alfonso the Wise or Napoleon Bonaparte."[1]

There is a prominent characteristic of our laws which they have in common with all primitive codes. These all differ from maturer collections of laws in their very large proportion of criminal to civil law. Sir Henry Maine says that, on the whole, all the known collections of ancient law are distinguished from systems of mature jurisprudence by this feature,—that the civil part of the law has trifling dimensions as compared with the criminal.[2] This is strikingly seen in the Kentish laws; and even in the West Saxon laws a very little study will enable the reader to verify this characteristic.

Our next and last observation shall be based on the absence of something which the reader might possibly expect to find in the Saxon laws.

Of all the legal institutions that have claimed a Saxon origin, none compares for importance with that of trial by jury. This has been called the bulwark of English liberty, and it has been assigned to King Alfred as the general founder of great institutions. But this is only a popular opinion.

Perhaps there is no single matter in legal antiquities that has been so much debated as the origin of trial by jury. In the vast literature which the

[1] "Documents Illustrative of English History," p. 60.
[2] "Ancient Law," chap. x. init.

subject has called forth, the most various accounts have been proposed. It is an English institution, but whence did the English get it? From which of the various sources that have contributed to the composite life of the English nation? Was it Anglo-Saxon, or was it Anglo-Norman, or was it Keltic? Was it a process common to all the Germanic family? If it was Norman, from which source—from their Scandinavian ancestors or from their Frankish neighbours? All these origins have been maintained, and others besides these. According to some writers, it is a relic of Roman law; some trace it to the Canon law; and champions have not been wanting to vindicate it as originally a Slavonic institution which the Angles borrowed from the Werini ere they had left their old mother country.[1]

In all this diversity of view there is one fixed point of common agreement. It is allowed on all hands that England is the arena of its historical career, and the question therefore always takes this start,—How did the English acquire it?

The Anglo-Saxon laws have been diligently scanned to see if the practice or the germ of it could be discovered there. In Æthelred iii., 3, there is an ordinance that runs thus:—

| And gan ut tha yldestan XII thegnas, and se gerefa mid, and swerian on tham halig- | Let the XII senior thanes go out, and the reeve with them, and swear on the halidom that |

---

[1] Palgrave, "Anglo-Saxon Commonwealth;" Stubbs, "Constitutional History;" Heinrich Brunner, "Die Entstehung der Schwurgerichte," Berlin, 1872.

dome, the heom man on hand sylle, thæt hig nellan nænne sacleasan man forsecgan, ne nænne sacne forhelan.	is put in their hand, that they will not calumniate any sackless man, nor conceal any guilty one (? suppress any suit).

This looks like the grand jury examining the bills of indictment before trial, and determining *primâ facie* whether they are true bills which ought to be tried in court. But the progress of modern inquiry has led to the conclusion, that though there may be rudiments of the principle in Anglo-Saxon and in all Germanic customs, still it was among the Franks in the Carling era that a definite beginning can first be recognised. The Frankish capitularies had a process called Inquisitio, which was adopted into Norman law, and was there called Enquête; this, having passed with the Normans into England, was finally shaped and embodied in the common law among the legal reforms of Henry II.

Under the Saxon laws, the true men who were sworn to do justice had a very different part to act from that which falls to the lot of our English jury. The duty of the latter is to deliver a verdict on matter of fact as proved by evidence given in court. The judge charges them to put aside what they may have heard out of court, and let it have no influence on their verdict, but to let that verdict be strictly based upon the evidence of witnesses before the court.

In Æthelred's time it was different. The sworn men were not to judge testimony truly, but to bear witness truly. They were to bring into court their own knowledge of the case, and of any circumstances that threw light upon it, including the general opinion and persuasion of the neighbourhood. There was no attempt to collect evidence piecemeal, and to rise above the level of local rumour, by a patient judicial investigation. This provides us with something like a measure of the intellectual stage of the public mind in Saxon times, and will perhaps justify these remarks if they have seemed like drifting away from our proper subject. The notion of weighing evidence had not taken its place among the institutions of public life. This has now become with us almost a popular habit. Proficiency and soundness in it may be rare, but the appreciation of it, the perception of its power and beauty, and withal a pride and glory in it, is almost universal. How wide a distance does this seem to put between us and our Saxon forefathers, only to say that they had but the most rudimentary notions about the nature of evidence!

Witnesses came into court, not to speak, one by one, to a matter of fact, but to pronounce in a body what they all believed and held. They came to testify and uphold the popular opinion. Such testimony is like nothing known to us now, except when witnesses are called to speak to general character. These witnesses gave their evidence on oath; but it would naturally happen sometimes that such sworn testimony was to be had on both sides of the question. When this was the case, there was but one resource left, and that was the Ordeal—the appeal to the judgment of God. Such are the devices of inexperienced nations, who have no skill in sifting out the truth, and are baffled by contending testimony.

Nothing can better illustrate the stage of our national progress in the times which produced the literature which we are now surveying.

But, withal, it was in such a rude age that the foundations of English law were laid, and those customs took a definite form which are the groundwork of our jurisprudence, and in which consists the distinction between our English law and the law of the other nations of Western Europe, who have all (Scotland included) formed their legal system upon the civil law of Rome.

LEGAL DOCUMENTS.

From the seventh century down to the end of our period we have a series of legal documents, such as grants of land, purchases, memorials, written wills, memoranda of nuncupatory wills, royal writs, family arrangements, interchanges of land. The first thing to be noticed about this whole body of writings is that they, at the beginning of the series, are entirely in Latin; then a few words of the vulgar tongue creep in, and then this native element goes on increasing until we have entire documents in Saxon. Nevertheless, it remained a prevalent habit in the case of transfer of land to have the grant written in Latin, and the boundaries and other details expressed in Anglo-Saxon. This is a large body of literature, and it fills six octavo volumes in Kemble's "Codex Diplomaticus." Being of very various degrees of genuineness—some absolute originals, some faulty copies, some too carefully amended, down to the veriest forgeries— there is here a good field for the exercise of critical discrimination. And there are many curious and interesting details to reward the patient student. The following extract is from a memorial addressed to Edward, the son of Alfred, touching matters that had mostly fallen in his father's time; and it opens a glimpse of Alfred in his bed-chamber receiving a committee that came to report progress.

Tha bær mon tha boc forth and rædde hie; tha stod seo hondseten eal thæron. Tha thuhte us eallan the æt thære some wæran thet Helmstan wære athe thæs the near. Tha næs Æthelm na fullice gethafa ær we eodan in to cinge and rædan eall hu we hit reahtan and be hwy we hit reahtan: and Æthelm stod self thær inne mid; and cing stod thwoh his honda æt Weardoran innan thon bure. Tha he thæt gedon hæfde tha ascade he Æthelm hwy hit him ryht ne thuhte thæt we him gereaht hæfdan; cwæth thæt he nan ryhtre gethencan ne meahte thonne he thone ath agifan moste gif he meahte.

Then they brought forward the conveyance and read it; there stood the signatures all thereon. Then seemed it to all of us who were at the arbitration, that Helmstan was all the nearer to the oath. Then was not Æthelm fully convinced before we went in to the king and explained everything—how we reported it, and on what grounds we had so reported it: and Æthelm himself stood there in the room with us; and the king stood and washed his hands at Wardour in the chamber. When he had done that, then he asked Æthelm why it seemed to him not right what we had reported to him; he said that he could think of nothing more just than that he might be allowed to discharge the oath if he were able.

CHAPTER VIII.

THE CHRONICLES.

OF the historical writings that remain from the Anglian period—namely, those of Æddi and Bede, we have already spoken; the subject of the present chapter will be the Saxon Chronicles and the Latin histories which are more or less related to these Chronicles.

The habit of putting together annals began to be formed very early. In our Chronicles there are some entries that may perhaps be older than the conversion of our people. The contributors to Bede's "History" would appear to have sent in their parts more or less in the annalistic form. That form is even now but slightly veiled in the grouped arrangement into which the venerable historian has, with little reconstruction but considerable skill, cast his materials. Annal-writing, we may venture to say, had by his time become a recognised habit in literature, and there is extant a brief Northumbrian Chronicle which ends soon after Bede's death.[1] Continuous

---

[1] Lappenberg, "Geschichte," Introduction, p. xlviii.; referring to Hickes' "Thesaurus," iii., 288; and the preface to Smith's edition of Bede. That lover of English history, Dr. Reinhold Pauli, in the Göttingen "Gelehrt. Anzeig." for 1866, p. 1407, suggested that the whole mediæval institution

with this we have a series of annals which were produced in the north, and which are now imbedded in the West Saxon Chronicles; but the traces of their birth are not obliterated. Such vernacular annals were probably at first designed as little more than notes and memoranda to serve for a Latin history to be written another day; but the Danish wars broke the tradition of Latin learning, and made a wide opening which gave opportunity for the elevation of a vernacular literature. There is no part of Anglo-Saxon literature more characterised by spontaneity than are the Saxon Chronicles. Nowhere can we better see how the mother-tongue received the devolution of the literary office in an unexpected way when the learned literature was suddenly and violently displaced.

One of the strong features of these Chronicles is the genealogies of the kings, ascending mostly to Woden as their mythical ancestor. The most complete of these is that of the West Saxon kings, which is prefixed to the Parker manuscript in manner of a preface. This genealogy was originally made for Ecgbryht, who reigned from 800 to 836,—it was made at his death, and it comprised the accession of his son, Æthelwulf. Subsequently an addition was made, which continued the line of kings down to Alfred, and closed with the date of his accession. This, when combined with the fact that the first hand in this book ends with 891, seems to fix the

of annal-writing came from Northumbria, and was carried on the mission-path of the Saxons into Frankland and Germany, and there produced the fine Carlovingian series.

date of the Winchester Chronicle. This interesting appendix is as follows:—

Ond tha feng Æthelbald his sunu to rice and heold v gear. Tha feng Æthelbryht his brother to and heold v gear. Tha feng Æthered hiera brothur to rice and heold v gear. Tha feng Ælfred hiera brothur to rice and tha wæs agan his ielde xxiii wintra, and ccc and xcvi wintra thæs the his cyn ærest Wessexana lond on Wealum geodon.	And then Æthelbald his son took to the realm and held it 5 years. Then succeeded Æthelbryht his brother, and held 5 years. Then Æthered their brother took to the realm, and held 5 years. Then took Alfred their brother to the realm, and then was agone of his age 23 years; and 396 years from that his race erst took Wessex from the Welsh.

These Chronicles are remarkable for a certain unconscious ease and homeliness. Even when, in the course of their progress, they grow more copious and mature, they hardly discover any consciousness of literary dignity. Of the Latin writings of the Anglo-Saxon period this could not be said. This *naïveté* is naturally more observable in the earlier parts, which seem like rescued antiquities, which might have been built into their place when, in the latter end of the eighth or beginning of the ninth century, the importance of the national and vernacular chronicle began to be realised.

Some of the brief entries concerning the various settlements on the coasts and the early contests with the Britons have the appearance of traditional reminiscences that had been preserved in popular songs. Such is that of 473, that the Welsh flew the English like fire; 491, that Ælle and Cissa besieged Andredescester, and slew all those that therein dwelt—there was not so much as one Bret left; 584, how that Ceawlin, in his expedition up the Vale of Severn, where his brother fell, took many towns and untold spoils, and, angry, he turned away to his own.

Mingled with these are entries which, though ingenious, are hardly less spontaneous. Such are those in which there is a manifest rationalising upon the names of historical sites, and a fanciful discovery of their heroes or founders. Thus, in 501, we read that Port landed in Britain at the place called Portsmouth. Now, we know that the first syllable in Portsmouth is the Latin *portus*, a harbour, and it seems plain that here we have a name made into a personage. In 534 we read how Cynric gave the Isle of Wight to Stuf and Wihtgar, and how Wihtgar died in 544, and was buried at Wihtgaraburg, also called Wihtgaræsburh. Here the person of Wihtgar has been made out of the name of the place, because that name was understood as meaning Castle of Wihtgar. But it meant the Burgh " of " Wihtgar only in the sense of the Burgh which was called Wihtgar. The last syllable, *gar*, is the British word for burg, fortress, castle, which the Welsh call *Caer* to this day. And the Saxons, having often to use the word *gar* in this sense—much as our reporters of New Zealand affairs have to speak of a *pa*—distinguished the *gar* that was in Wiht, as Wihtgar, and then they added their own word, *burh*, as the interpretation of *gar*, and after a time the historian, finding the name of Wihtgarburh, took Wihtgar for a man, and called it Wihtgar's Burg, Wihtgaresburh, a genitive form which still lives in " Carisbrooke."

THE CHRONICLES.   173

The originals of the Chronicles are preserved in seven different books. They are known by the signatures A, B, C, D, E, F, G.

A, the famous book in Archbishop Parker's library, preserved in Corpus Christi College, Cambridge. The structure of this book indicates that it was made in 891, and, indeed, the penmanship of this copy—at least, of the compilation—may possibly be as old as the lifetime of King Alfred. It bears the local impress of Winchester, except in the latest continuation, 1005–1070, which appears to belong to Canterbury. It seems to have passed from Canterbury to the place where it is now deposited; but that it was a Winchester book in its basis seems indicated by the regular notices of the bishops of Wessex from 634 to 754, by the diction of the compilation to 891, and especially by that of the remarkable continuation, 893–897.

B, British Museum, Cotton Library, Tiberius A. vi. Closes with the year 977, and was probably written at St. Augustine's, Canterbury.

C, British Museum, Cotton Library, Tiberius B. i. The first handwriting stops at 1046, and is probably of that date. Closes with 1066. Apparently a work of the monks of Abingdon.

D, British Museum, Cotton Library, Tiberius B. iv. The first hand, which stops at 1016, may well be of that date. Closes with 1079. This book contains strong internal evidence of being a product of Worcester Abbey.

E, Bodleian Library, Laud, 636. This is the fullest of all extant Chronicles; it embodies most of the contents of the others, and it adds the largest quantity of new and original history. It gives seventy-five years' history beyond any of the others, and closes with the death of Stephen in 1154. The local relations of this book are unmistakable. The first hand ends with 1121, and all the evidence goes to prove that this book was prepared at that date in the abbey of Peterborough. On Friday, August 3, 1116, a great fire had occurred at Peterborough which had destroyed the town and a large part of the abbey, and this book was apparently undertaken among the acts of restoration. The varying shades of Saxon which this book contains, both in the compilation and in the several continuations, render it of great value for the history of the English language, especially in the obscure period of the twelfth century.

F, British Museum, Cotton Library, Domitian A. viij. A bilingual Chronicle, Latin and Saxon, which, by internal evidence, is assigned to Christ Church, Canterbury. The abrupt ending at 1058 is no indication of the book's date: it was written late in the twelfth century.

G, British Museum, Cotton Library, Otho B. xi. A late copy of A, made probably in the twelfth century. It nearly perished in the fire of 1731, and only three leaves have been rescued; but happily the book had, before this disaster, been published entire and without intermixture by Wheloc; and, consequently, his edition is now the chief representative of this authority.

Of these books there are three which are distin-

THE CHRONICLES. 175

guished above the rest by individuality of character. These are the Parker book (A); the Worcester book (D); and the Peterborough book (E). A Chronicle may have a marked individuality in two ways—that is to say, either in its compilation or in its continuation. I will give an example of each kind. The first shall be from the Worcester Chronicle, which combines with the former stock of southern history a valuable body of northern history between the years 737 and 806. The following are selected as being annals which, either wholly or in part, are derived from a northern source. The new matter is indicated by inverted commas:—

737. Her Forthhere biscop. and Freothogith cwen ferdon to Rome . "and Ceolwulf cyning feng to Petres scære . and sealde his rice Eadberhte his fæderan sunu . se ricsade xxi wintra . And Æthelwold biscop . and Acca forthferdon . and Cynwulf man gehalgode to biscop . And thy ilcan gære Æthelbald cyning hergode Northhymbra land."

757. "Her Eadberht Northhymbra cyning feng to scære . and Oswulf his sunu feng to tham rice . and ricsade an gær . and hine ofslogon his hiwan . on viii Kl. Augustus."

762. Her Ianbryht was

737. Here Forthere bishop (of Sherborne) and Freothogith queen (of Wessex) went to Rome; "and Ceolwulf, king (of Northumbria) received St. Peter's tonsure, and gave his realm to Eadberht, his father's brother's son; who reigned 21 years. And Æthelwold, bishop (of Lindisfarne) and Acca died, and Cynwulf was consecrated bishop. And that same year Æthelbald, king (of Mercia) ravaged the Northumbrians' land."

757. "Here Eadberht, king of the Northumbrians, became a monk; and Oswulf, his son, took to the realm, and reigned one year, and him his domestics slew, on July 25."

762. Here Ianbryht was

gehadod to arcebiscop . on thone XL dæg ofer midne winter . "and Frithuweald biscop æt Hwiterne forthferde . on Nonas Maius . se wæs gehalgod on Ceastre on xviii Kl. September . tham vi Ceolwulfes rices . and he wæs biscop xxix wintra. Tha man halgode Pehtwine to biscop æt Ælfet ee on xvi Kl. Agustus . to Hwiterne."

777. Her Cynewulf and Offa gefliton ymb Benesingtun . and Offa genom thone tun . "and tha ilcan geare man gehalgode Æthelberht to biscop to Hwiterne in Eoforwic . on xvii Kl. Jul'."

779. Her Ealdseaxe and Francan gefuhton. "and Northhymbra heahgerefan forbærndon Beorn ealdorman on Seletune . on viii Kl. Janr. and Æthelberht arcebiscop forthferde in Cæstre . in thæs steal Eanbald wæs ær gehalgod . and Cynewulf biscop gesæt in Lindisfarna ee."

782. "Her forthferde Werburh . Ceolredes cwen . and Cynewulf biscop on Lindisfarna ee . and seonoth wæs æt Aclæ."

788. "Her wæs sinoth gegaderad on Northhymbra lande

ordained archbishop (of Canterbury) on the fortieth day after Midwinter (Christmas). "And Frithuweald, bishop of Whitehorne, died on May 7th. He was consecrated at York, on the 15th of August, in the sixth year of Ceolwulf's reign ; and he was bishop 29 years. Then was Pehtwine consecrated to be bishop of Whitehorne at Ælfet Island on the 17th of July."

777. Here Cynewulf and Offa fought about Bensington (Benson, Oxf.), and Offa took the town. "And that same year was Æthelberht hallowed for bishop of Whitehorne, at York on the 15th of June."

779. Here the Old Saxons and the Franks fought. "And Northumbrian high-reeves burned Beorn the alderman at Silton on the 25th of December. And Æthelberht, the archbishop, died at York, into whose place Eanbald had been previously consecrated ; and bishop Cynewulf sate on Lindisfarne island."

782. "Here died Werburh, queen of Ceolred (king of Mercia) : and Cynewulf, bishop of Lindisfarne Island. And synod was at Aclea."

788. "Here was a synod gathered in the land of the

æt Pincanheale . on iiii Non. Septemb . and Aldberht abb . forthferde in Hripum."

793. "Her wæron rethe forebecna cumene ofer Northymbra land . and thæt folc earmlice bregdon . thæt wæron ormete thodenas . and ligræscas . and fyrenne dracan wæron gesewene on tham lifte fleogende. Tham tacnum sona fyligde mycel hunger . and litel æfter tham . thæs ilcan geares . on vi Id. Janv. earmlice hæthenra manna hergung adilegode Godes cyrican in Lindisfarna ee . thurh hreaflac and mansliht . and Sicga forthferde on viii Kl. Martius."

806. "Her se mona athystrode on Kl. Septemb. and Eardwulf Northhymbra cyning wæs of his rice adrifen . and Eanberht Hagestaldes biscop forthferde."

Northumbrians at Finchale, on 2nd September. And abbot Aldberht died at Ripon."

793. "Here came dire portents over the land of the Northumbrians, and miserably terrified the people ; these were tremendous whirlwinds, and lightning-strokes ; and fiery dragons were seen flying in the air. Upon these tokens quickly followed a great famine :—and a little thereafter, in that same year, on January 8, pitifully did the invasion of heathen men devastate God's church in Lindisfarne Island, with plundering and manslaughter. And Sicga died on Feb. 22."

806. "Here the moon eclipsed on Sept. 1 ; and Eardwulf, king of the Northumbrians, was driven from his realm : and Eanberht, bishop of Hexham, died."

In these few selections the orthography shows occasional relics of the northern dialect; and an expression here and there, such as "Ceaster" for York, indicates the writer's locality. Apart, however, from such traces, the contents and the domestic interest would sufficiently declare the home of these annals. They are specimens of the vernacular annals of the north, which are now best seen in bulk in Simeon of Durham's Latin Chronicle.

Our next example will serve to illustrate the free

writing of an original continuation. It is taken from the Winchester Chronicle (A). This Chronicle exhibits, in the annals of 893-897, the first considerable piece of original historical composition that we have in the vernacular. Indeed, we may say that these pages, on the whole, contain the finest effort of early prose writing that we possess. The quotation relates how Alfred set to work to construct a navy :—

Thy ilcan geare drehton tha hergas on East Englum and on Northhymbrum West Seaxna lond swithe be thæm suth stæthe . mid stæl hergum . ealra swithust mid thæm æscum the hie fela geara ær timbredon. Tha het Alfred cyng timbran lang scipu ongen tha æscas[1] . tha wæron fulneah tu swa lange swa tha othru . sume hæfdon lx ara . sume ma. Tha wæron ægther ge swiftran ge unwealtran . ge eac hieran thonne tha othru. Næron nawther ne on Fresisc gescæpene . ne on Denisc . bute swa him selfum thuhte thæt hie nytwyrthoste beon meahten.	That same year the armies in East Anglia and in Northhymbria distressed the land of the West Saxons very much about the south coast with marauding invasions; most of all with the "æscas" that they had built many years before. Then king Alfred gave orders to build long ships against the "æscas;" those were well-nigh twice as long as the others; some had 60 oars, some more. Those were both swifter and steadier, and also higher than the others. They were not shaped either on the Frisic or on the Danish model, but as he himself considered that they might be most serviceable.

The most extensive original continuations are in the Peterborough Chronicle (E). From one of these I quote the character of the Conqueror, which accompanies the record of his death in 1086. The passage is remarkable as containing the nearest approach to

[1] The "æscas" were the light and speedy galleys of the Danes.

a discovery of authorship that anywhere occurs in these Chronicles :—

Gif hwa gewilnigeth to gewitane hu gedon mann he wæs. oththe hwilcne wurthscipe he hæfde . oththe hu fela lande he wære hlaford . Thonne wille we be him awritan swa swa we hine ageaton . the him onlocodan . and othre hwile on his hirede wunedon. Se cyng Willelm the we embe specath wæs swithe wis man . and swithe rice . and wurthfulre and strengere thonne ænig his foregengra wære . He wæs milde tham godum mannum the God lufedon . and ofer eall gemett stearc tham mannum the withewædon his willan . On tham ilcan steode the God him geuthe thæt he moste Engleland gegan . he arerde mære mynster . and munecas thær gesætte . and hit wæll gegodade . On his dagan wæs thæt mære mynster on Cantwarbyrig getymbrad . and eac swithe manig other ofer eall Englaland . Eac this land wæs swithe afylled mid munecan . and tha leofodan heora lif æfter sc̄s Benedictus regule . and se Cristendom wæs swilc on his dæge thæt ælc man hwæt his hade to belumpe . folgade se the wolde . Eac he wæs swythe

If any one wishes to know what manner of man he was, or what dignity he had, or how many lands he was lord of; then will we write of him as we apprehended him, who were wont to behold him, and at one time were resident at his court. The king William about whom we speak was a very wise man, and very powerful; and more dignified and more authoritative than any one of his predecessors was. He was gentle to those good men who loved God; and beyond all description stern to those men who contradicted his will. On that selfsame spot where God granted him that he might conquer England, he reared a noble monastery, and monks he there enstalled, and well endowed the place. In his days was the splendid minster in Canterbury built, and also a great many others over all England. Also this land was abundantly supplied with monks; and they lived their life after St. Benedict's rule; and the state of Christianity was such in his time, that each man who was so disposed might follow that which appertained

wurthful . thriwa he bær his cyne helm ælce geare . swa oft swa he wæs on Englelande . on Eastron he hine bær on Winceastre . on Pentecosten on Westmynstre . on mide wintre on Gleaweceastre . And thænne wæron mid him ealle tha rice men ofer eall Englaland . arcebiscopas . and leodbiscopas . abbodas and eorlas . thegnas and cnihtas . Swilce he wæs eac swythe stearc man and ræthe . swa thæt man ne dorste nan thing ongean his willan don . He hæfde eorlas on his bendum the dydan ongean his willan. Biscopas he sætte of heora biscoprice . and abbodas of heora abbodrice . and thægnas on cweartern . and æt nextan he ne sparode his agenne brothor Odo het . he wæs swithe rice biscop on Normandige . on Baius wæs his biscopstol . and wæs manna fyrmest to eacan tham cynge.

to his order. Likewise he was very ceremonious:—three times he wore his crown every year (as often as he was in England); at Easter he wore it in Winchester, at Pentecost in Westminster, at Christmas in Gloucester. And then there were with him all the mighty men over all England; archbishops and suffragan bishops, abbots and earls, thanes and knights. Withal he was moreover a very severe man and a violent; so that any one dared not to do anything against his will. He had earls in his chains who acted against his will. Bishops he put out of their bishoprick, and abbots from their abbacy, and thanes into prison; and at last he spared not his own brother, who was named Odo; who was a very mighty bishop in Normandy; at Baieux was his see, and he was the first of men next to the king.

These annals being all anonymous, every indication of the date of writing excites interest. Under 643 the chronicler of B added a single word to what he had before him (as we may presume) in his copy. That copy said that the church at Winchester was built by order of King Cenwalh. The chronicler of B says that the "old" church was built by Cenwalh. This harmonises excellently with other indications of this

Chronicle, by which it is made probable that it was compiled in or about 977, when Bishop Æthelwold had built a new church at Winchester.

In the Peterborough Chronicle, under 1041, the accession of Eadward is accompanied by a benediction which indicates that the writer wrote near the time, or at least before 1065. He says :—Healde tha hwile the him God unne = May he continue so long as God may be pleased to grant to him! And the half legible closing sentence of this Chronicle, in 1154, is a prayer of the same kind for a new abbot of Peterborough, of whom it is said that "he hath made a fair beginning."

The Saxon Chronicles offer one of the best examples of history which has grown proximately near to the events, of history written while the impression made by the events was still fresh. It would be difficult to point to any texts through which the taste for living history—history in immediate contact with the events—can better be cultivated.

The Chronicles stretch over a long period of time. As to their contents, they extend as a body of history from A.D. 449 to 1154—that is, exclusive of the book-made annals that form a long avenue at the beginning, and start from Julius Cæsar. The period covered by the age of the extant manuscripts is hardly less than 300 years, from about A.D. 900 to about A.D. 1200. A large number of hands must have wrought from time to time at their production, and, as the work is wholly anonymous and void of all external marks of authorship, the various and several contributions can only be determined by internal evidence, and this offers a fine arena for the exercise and culture of the critical faculty.

It is no small addition to the charm and value of these Chronicles that they are in the mother tongue at several stages of its growth, and for the most part in the best Anglo-Saxon diction. We have, moreover, the very soil of the history under our feet, and this study would tend to invest our native land with all the charm of classic ground.

The Chronicle form is the foundation of the structure of historical literature. We are no longer content to study history now in one or two admirable specimens of mature perfection, but rather we seek to know history as a subject. All who have this aim must study Chronicles, and nowhere can this kind of documentary record be found in a form preferable to that of the Saxon Chronicles.

The Saxon Chronicles are sometimes said to be meagre; indeed, it has almost become usual to speak of them as meagre. When such a term is used, it makes all the difference whether it is made vaguely and at random, or with meaning and discrimination. The Saxon Chronicles stretch over seven centuries, from the middle of the fifth to the middle of the twelfth; and it would indeed be wonderful if in such a series of annals there were not some arid tracts. Certainly, there are meagre places, and it makes all the difference whether a writer uses this epithet wisely or as a mere echo. In the following quotation it is justly used :—" For the history of England in the latter half of the tenth century we have, except the very meagre notices of the Anglo-Saxon Chronicles, no contemporary materials, unless we admit the Lives of the Saints of the Benedictine revival."[1] In the latter half of the tenth century the Chronicles really are meagre, and it is a remarkable fact, seeing that the period was one of revived literary activity.

This account of the Chronicles would be incomplete without the mention of a small number of Latin histories which are naturally linked with them. The Latin book of most mark in this connexion is Asser's "Life of Alfred"—a book that has long lain under a cloud of doubt, from which, however, it seems to be gradually emerging. (A foolish interpolation about Oxford which marred the second edition—that by Camden—has left a stigma on the name.) It is not easy to answer all the adverse criticism of Mr. T. Wright; but still I venture to think that the internal evidence corresponds to the author's name, that it was written at the time of, and by such a person as, Alfred's Welsh bishop. The evident acquaintance with people and with localities, the bits of Welsh, the calling of the English uniformly "Saxons," all mark the Welshman who was at home in England. In the course of this biography, which seems to have been left in an unfinished state, there is a considerable extract from the Winchester Chronicles translated into Latin.

But the earliest Latin Chronicle which was founded on the Saxon Chronicles is that of Æthelweard. He is apparently the "ealdorman Æthelwerd," to whom Ælfric addressed certain of his works; and

[1] Professor Stubbs, "Memorials of Saint Dunstan," Rolls Series, p. ix.

he may be the "Æthelwerd Dux" who signs charters, 976–998. His Chronicle closes with the last year of Eadgar's reign. He took much of his material from a Saxon Chronicle, like that of Winchester, but he has also matter peculiar to himself; and this raises a question whether he took such matter from a Saxon Chronicle now lost. He is grandiloquent and turgid to an extent which often obscures his meaning. In him we perceive all the word-eloquence of Saxon poetry, striving to utter itself through the medium of a Latinity at once crude and ambitious.[1]

The Chronicle of Florence of Worcester terminates with 1117; but a continuator carried it on to 1141, making use of the Peterborough Chronicle (E). The work of Florence is often identifiable with the Saxon Chronicles, especially with that of Worcester (D). But he has good original insertions of his own, as in his description of the election and coronation of Harold, on which Mr. Freeman has dwelt, as a record intended to correct Norman misrepresentation.

Simeon of Durham made large use of Florence, and he incorporated the Northumbrian eighth-century Chronicle, of which a specimen has been given above.

Henry of Huntingdon closed his annals at the same date as the latest of the Saxon Chronicles, A.D. 1154. He is a historian of secondary rank, with antiquarian tastes, a fondness for the Saxon Chronicles, and a special fancy for the genealogies and the ballads.

---

[1] Reinhold Pauli, "Life of Alfred," anno 877, note.

To him we owe the earliest known mention of Stonehenge.

All these, except Asser and Æthelweard, are, as regards our Chronicles, subsequent and derivative rather than collateral. They used the chronicles as translators and compilers merely. The first who attempted something more was William of Malmesbury. This remarkable writer (who in 1140 came near to being elected Abbot of Malmesbury) was the first after Beda who left the annal form, and aimed at a more comprehensive treatment of the national history. He recognised the value of traditions from the Saxon times, which in his day were still to be gathered, and it is by the incorporation of such elements that his book has in some respects the character of a supplement to the Saxon Chronicles.

We cannot but be struck with the isolation of the Saxon Chronicles. Great literary products do not grow up alone; but they have, doubtless, a tendency to create a solitude around them. Professor Stubbs apprehends such may have been the case with these Chronicles. He has surmised that probably the Chronicles had the same effect upon the previous schemes of history that Higden's "Polychronicon" had in the fourteenth century, that is to say, it would have prevented the writing of new histories, and caused the neglect or destruction of the old.[1]

[1] Preface to "Chronica Rogeri de Hoveden," Rolls Series, p. xi.

CHAPTER IX.

ALFRED'S TRANSLATIONS.

AROUND the great name of Alfred many attributes have gathered and clustered, some of which are true, some exaggerated, some impossible. It is quite unhistorical that Alfred divided the country into shires and hundreds, or that he instituted trial by jury, or that he founded the University of Oxford. Under the shadow of great names myths are apt to spring, that is to say, unconscious authorless inventions, growing up of themselves round any person or thing which happens to be the subject of much talk and little knowledge. Had the conditions been favourable in England as they were in France, the myths about Alfred might have grouped into an epic cycle, as those about Charlemagne did; and, had the eleventh century produced a great heroic poem analogous to the "Chanson de Roland," it would have formed a graceful and much-needed coping to the now too disjointed pile of Anglo-Saxon literature.

But, when we come to Alfred's literary achievements, we find no tendency to exaggerate or embellish the sober truth. His hand is manifest in the Laws, and strongly surmised in the Chronicles. In both these vernacular products we find a new start, a fresh impulse, under Alfred. But that which stamps a peculiar character on his Translations is that here we discern a new stride in the elevation of the native language to literary rank. Latin was no longer to be the sole medium of learning and education.

The learned language had almost perished out of the island where it had once so eminently flourished. In the north the seats of learning had been demolished; and the monasteries of Wessex, their first use as mission-stations having been discharged, had become secularised in their habits, and had not become seats or seminaries of learning. Alfred found no one in his ancestral kingdom who could aid him in the work of revival. Like Charles the Great, he looked everywhere for scholars, and drew them to his court. In Mercia, the land adjoining scholastic Anglia, he found a few learned men—Werferth, bishop of Worcester; Plegmund, who was elected (A.D. 890) archbishop of Canterbury, and two of obscurer name;[1] he drew Grimbald from Gaul, and John from Old Saxony; Asser, from whose pen we know about these scholars, came to him from South Wales. With the help of such men Alfred gave a new impulse to literature, not as Charles had done, in Latin merely, but as much, or even more, in his own vernacular.

We must not look upon his translations as if they were only makeshifts to convey the matter of famous books to those who could not read the originals. Alfred deplored the low state of Latin,—but then he could substitute his own language for it, and that not merely because he must, but also because the very scarcity of Latin had favoured the culture of English. For

[1] Asser's "Life of Alfred," in "Monumenta Historica Britannica," 487A.

it was in no dull or stagnant time that Wessex had let Latin wane; it was in that vigorous stage of youth and growth when Wessex was fitting herself to take an imperial place at home and raise her head among the nations. In almost all the transactions of life, public and private, where Latin was used in other countries, the West Saxons had for a long time used their own tongue, and hence it came to pass that, when Alfred sought to restore education and literature, he found a language nearer to him than the Latin, and one which was fit, if not to supersede the Latin, yet to be coupled along with it in the work of national instruction.

Of all Alfred's translations, the foremost place is due to that of Gregory's "Pastoral Care."[1] Both internally and externally it is honoured with marks of distinction. The translation is executed with a peculiar care, and a copy was to be sent to every See in the kingdom. The very copy that was destined for Worcester is preserved in the Bodleian; and there it may be seen by any passing visitor, lying open (under glass) at the page with the Worcester address, and the bishop's name (Wærferth) inserted in the salutation. The copy that was addressed to Hehstan, bishop of London, is not extant; but a transcript of it, written (in Wanley's opinion) before the Conquest, is in the Cotton Library, or so much of it as the fire has left. The Public Library at Cambridge has a representative of the copy which was addressed to Wulfsige, bishop of Sherborne. Another Cotton manuscript, which

[1] It was published for the first time in 1871, being edited by Mr. Sweet for the Early English Text Society.

was almost consumed (Tiberius, B. xi.), had happily been described by Wanley before the fire. In this book the place for the bishop's name was blank; and there was this marginal note on the first leaf: ✠ Plegmunde arcebisc'. is agifen his boc. and Swiðulfe bisc'. 7 Werferðe bisc'., *i.e.*, Plegmund, archbishop, has received his book, and Swithulf, bishop, and Werferth, bishop.[1] This book, therefore, of which only fragments now remain, was like the Hatton manuscript in the Bodleian, one of Alfred's originals.

Thus the Bodleian book (Hatton 20, formerly 88), for originality and integrity remains unique; and from it we quote the opening part of Alfred's prefatory epistle:—

Deos boc sceal to Wiogora Ceastre.	This Book is to go to Worcester.
Ælfred kyning hateth gretan Wærferth biscep his wordum luflice and freondlice; and the cythan hate thæt me com swithe oft on gemynd, hwelce wiotan iu wæron gyond Angelcynn, ægther ge godcundra hada ge woruldcundra; and hu gesæliglica tida tha wæron giond Angelcynn; and hu tha kyningas the thone onwald hæfdon thæs folces on tham dagum Gode and his ærendwrecum hersumedon; and hie ægther ge hiora sibbe ge hiora siodo ge hiora onweald innanbordes gehioldon, and eac út hiora	Alfred, king, commandeth to greet Wærferth, bishop, with his words in loving and friendly wise: and I would have you informed that it has often come into my remembrance, what wise men there formerly were among the Angle race, both of the sacred orders and the secular; and how happy times those were throughout the Angle race; and how the kings who had the government of the folk in those days obeyed God and his messengers; and they, on the one hand, maintained their peace, and their customs and their

---

[1] Wanley's "Catalogue," p. 217.

ethel gerymdon; and hu him tha speow ægther ge mid wige ge mid wisdome; and eac tha godcundan hadas hu giorne hie wæron ægther ge ymb lare ge ymb liornunga, ge ymb ealle tha thiowotdomas the hie Gode scoldon; and hu man utanbordes wisdom and lare hieder ón londe sohte, and hu we hie nu sceoldon ute begietan gif we hie habban sceoldon. Swæ clæne hio wæs othfeallenu ón Angelcynne thæt swithe feawa wæron behionan Humbre the hiora theninga cuthen understondan on Englisc, oththe furthum án ærendgewrit of Lædene on Englisc areccean; and ic wene thæt noht monige begiondan Humbre næren. Swæ feawa hiora wæron thæt ic furthum anne ánlepne ne mæg gethencean besuthan Temese tha tha ic to rice feng. Gode ælmihtegum sie thonc thæt we nu ænigne ón stal habbath lareowa.

authority within their borders, while at the same time they spread their territory outwards; and how it then went well with them both in war and in wisdom; and likewise the sacred orders, how earnest they were, as well about teaching as about learning, and about all the services that they owed to God; and how people from abroad came to this land for wisdom and instruction; and how we now should have to get them abroad if we were going to have them. So clean was it fallen away in the Angle race, that there were very few on this side Humber who would know how to render their services in English, or so much as translate an epistle out of Latin into English; and I ween that not many would be on the other side Humber. So few of them were there that I cannot think of so much as a single one south of Thames when I took to the realm. God Almighty be thanked that we have now any teachers in office.

The king goes on to say that he remembered how, before the general devastation, the churches were well stocked with books, and how there were plenty, too, of clergy, but they were not able to make much use of the books, because the culture of learning had been neglected. Their predecessors of a former generation had been learned, but now the clergy had fallen into ignorance. Wherefore, it seemed that there was no remedy but to have the books translated into the language they understood. And this (the king reflected) was according to precedent; for the Old Testament was first written in Hebrew, and then the Greeks in their time translated it into their speech, and subsequently the Romans did the like for themselves. And all other Christian nations had translated some Scriptures into their own language.

Forthy me thincth betre, gif iow swæ thincth, thæt we eac sumæ bec, tha the niedbethearfostæ sien eallum monnum to wiotonne, thæt we tha on thæt gethiode wenden the we ealle gecnawan mægen, and ge don swæ we swithe eathe magon mid Godes fultume, gif we tha stilnesse habbath, thæt eal sio gioguth the nu is on Angelcynne friora monna, thara the tha speda hæbben thæt hie thæm befeolan mægen, sien to liornunga othfæste, tha hwile the hie to nanre otherre note ne mægen, oth thone first the hie wel cunnen Englisc gewrit arædan: lære mon siththan furthur on Læden gethiode tha the mon furthor læran wille and to hieran hade don wille. Tha ic tha gemunde hu sio lar Læden gethiodes ær thissum afeallen wæs giond Angelcynn, and theah monige cuthon Eng-

Therefore to me it seemeth better, if it seemeth so to you, that we also some books, those that most needful are for all men to be acquainted with, that we turn those into the speech which we all can understand, and that ye do as we very easily may with God's help, if we have the requisite peace, that all the youth which now is in England of free men, of those who have the means to be able to go in for it, be set to learning, while they are fit for no other business, until such time as they can thoroughly read English writing: afterwards further instruction may be given in the Latin language to such as are intended for a more advanced education, and to be prepared for higher office. As I then reflected how the teaching of the Latin language had recently decayed through-

lisc gewrit aræden, tha ongan ic on gemang othrum mislicum and manigfealdum bisgum thisses kynerices tha boc wendan on Englisc the is genemned on Læden Pastoralis, and on Englisc Hierde boc, hwilum word be worde, hwilum andgit of andgite, swæ swæ ic hie geliornode æt Plegmunde minum ærcebiscepc and æt Assere minum biscepe and æt Grimbolde minum mæsse prioste and æt Johanne minum mæsse prioste. Siththan ic hie tha gelornod hæfde swæ swæ ic hie forstod, and swæ ic hic andgitfullicost areccean meahte, ic hie on Englisc awende; and to ælcum biscepstole on minum rice wille ane onsendan ; and on ælcre bith an æstel, se bith on fiftegum mancessa. Ond ic bebiode on Godes naman thæt nan mon thone æstel from thære bec ne do, ne tha boc from thæm mynstre. Uncuth hu longe thær swæ gelærede biscepas sien, swæ swæ nu Gode thonc wel hwær siendon ; forthy ic wolde thæt hie ealneg æt thære stowe wæren, buton se biscep hie mid him habban wille oththe hio hwær to læne sie, oththe hwa othre biwrite.

out this people of the Angles, and yet many could read English writing, then began I among other various and manifold businesses of this kingdom to turn into English the book that is called "Pastoralis" in Latin, and "Shepherding Book" in English, sometimes word for word, sometimes sense for sense, just as I learned it of Plegmund, my archbishop, and of Asser, my bishop, and of Grimbald, my priest, and of John, my priest. After that I had learned it, so as I understood it, and as I it with fullest meaning could render, I translated it into English; and to each see in my kingdom I will send one ; and in each there is an "æstel," which is of the value of 50 mancusses. And I command in the name of God that no man remove the "æstel" from the book, nor the book from the minster. No one knows how long such learned bishops may be there, as now, thank God ! there are in several places ; and therefore I would that they (the books) should always be at the place; unless the bishop should wish to have it with him, or it should be anywhere on loan, or any one should be writing another copy.

Here we have a direct statement that the "Pastoral" was translated by King Alfred himself, after a course of study in which he had been assisted by Plegmund, Asser, Grimbald, and John. His interest in this book seems to show that his estimate of it was something like that of Ozanam, who said that Gregory's "Pastoral Care" determined the character of the Christian hierarchy, and formed the bishops who formed the nations.

Gregory's "Dialogues," on the contrary, were translated, not by the king, but by Werferth, bishop of Worcester, as we are informed by Asser.[1] This translation is extant in manuscripts, but it has not yet been edited. It is, perhaps, the most considerable piece of Anglo-Saxon literature that yet remains to be made public. And it is striking, though not unaccountable, that a book which was one of the most popular ever written,[2] which retained its popularity for centuries, and which has left behind it in literature and in popular Christian ethics bold traces of its influence, should, in the modern revival of Anglo-Saxon, have been so long neglected. As this book is practically inaccessible, and as it was moreover a book peculiarly germane and congenial to the average intelligence of these times, it seems to claim a somewhat fuller notice.

Here, as in other translations, the king wrote a few words of preface.

[1] "Monumenta Historica Britannica," 486 E.
[2] "The 'Dialogues' were printed as early as the year 1458."—T. D. Hardy in Willelmi Malm. "Gesta Regum," i., 189.

Ic Ælfred gyfendum Criste mid cynehades mærnesse geweorthad hæbbe cuthlice ongiten, and thurh haligra boca rædunge oft gehyred . thæt us tham God swa micele healicnysse woruld gethingtha forgifen hæfth . is seo mæste thearf thæt we hwilon ure mod gelithian and gebigian to tham godcundum and gastlicum rihte . betweoh thas eorthlican carfulnysse . and ic fortham sohte and wilnode to minum getrywum freondum thæt hy me of Godes bocum be haligra manna theawum and wundrum awriton thas æfterfyligendan lare . thæt ic thurh tha mynegunge and lufe getrymmed on minum mode hwilum gehicge tha heofenlican thing betweoh thas eorthlican gedrefednyssa . Cuthlice we magan nu æt ærestan gehyran hu se eadiga and se apostolica wer Scs Gregorius spræc to his diacone tham wæs nama Petrus . be haligra manna thæawum and life, to lare and to bysne eallum tham the Godes willan wyrceath . and he be him silfum thisum wordum and thus cwæth :—

I, Alfred, by the grace of Christ, dignified with the honour of royalty, have distinctly understood, and through the reading of holy books have often heard, that of us to whom God hath given so much eminence of worldly distinction, it is specially required that we from time to time should subdue and bend our minds to the divine and spiritual law, in the midst of this earthly anxiety ; and I accordingly sought and requested of my trusty friends that they for me out of pious books about the conversation and miracles of holy men would transcribe the instruction that hereinafter followeth ; that I, through the admonition and love being strengthened in my mind, may now and then contemplate the heavenly things in the midst of these earthly troubles. Plainly we can now at first hear how the blessed and apostolic man St. Gregory spake to his deacon whose name was Peter, about the manners and life of holy men for instruction and for example to all those who are working the will of God ; and he spake about himself with these words and in this manner :—

ALFRED'S TRANSLATIONS.

Sumon[1] dæge hit gelamp thæt ic wæs swythe geswenced mid tham geruxlum and uneathnessum sumra woruldlicra ymbhegena. for tham underfenge thyses bisceoplican folgothes. On tham woruld scirum we beoth full oft geneadode thæt we doth tha thing the us is genoh cuth thæt we na ne sceoldon. Tha gelyste me thære diglan stowe the ic ær on wæs on mynstre. seo is thære gnornunge freond. fortham man simle mæg his sares and his unrihtes mæst gethencean gif he ana bith on digolnysse. Thær me openlice æt ywde hit sylf eall swa hwæt swa me mislicode be minre agenre wisan. and thær beforan minre

On a certain day it happened that I was very much harassed with the contentions and worries of certain secular cares, in the discharge of this episcopal function. In secular offices we are very often compelled to do the things that we well enough know we ought not to do. Then my desire turned towards that retired place where I formerly was in the monastery. That is the friend of sorrow, because a man can always best think over his grief and his wrong, if he is alone in retirement. There everything plainly showed itself to me, whatever disquieted me about my own occupation; and there, before the eyes of my heart distinctly

---

[1] Here Gregory begins. The translation sometimes deviates from the text:—"Quadam die nimis quorundam sæcularium tumultibus depressus, quibus in suis negotiis plerumque cogimur solvere etiam quod nos certum est non debere, secretum locum petii amicum mæroris, ubi omne quod de mea mihi occupatione displicebat, se patenter ostenderet, et cuncta quæ infligere dolorem consueverant, congesta ante oculos licenter venirent. Ibi itaque cum afflictus valde et diu tacitus sederem, dilectissimus filius meus Petrus diaconus adfuit, mihi a primævo juventutis flore amicitiis familiariter obstrictus, atque ad sacri verbi indagationem socius. Qui gravi excoqui cordis languore me intuens, ait: Num quidnam tibi aliquid accidit, quod plus te solito mæror tenet? Cui inquam: Mæror, Petre, quem quotidie patior, et semper mihi per usum vetus est, et semper per augmentum novus."

heortan eagan swutollice comon ealle tha gedonan unriht the gewunedon thæt hi me sar and sorge ongebrohton. Witodlice tha tha ic thær sæt swithe geswenced and lange sorgende. tha com me to min se leofesta sunu Petrus diacon se fram frymthe his iugothhades mid freondlicre lufe wæs hiwcuthlice to me getheoded and getogen. and he simle wæs min gefera to smeaunge haligre lare. and he tha lociende on me geseah thæt ic wæs geswenced mid hefigum sare minre heortan. and he thus cwæth to me, "La leof gelamp the ænig thing niwes. for hwan hafast thu maran gnornunge thonne hit ær gewunelic wære?" Tha cwæth ic to him, " Eala Petrus seo gnornung the ic dæghwamlice tholie symle heo is me eald for gewunan. and simle heo is me niwe thurh eacan.

came all the practical wrongs which were wont to bring upon me grief and sorrow. Accordingly, while I was there sitting in great oppression and long silence, there came to me my beloved son Peter the deacon, who, from his early youth, with friendly love was intimately attached and bound to me; and he was ever my companion in the study of sacred lore. And he then looking on me saw that I was oppressed with the heavy grief of my heart, and he thus said to me, "Ah, sire, hath anything new happened to thee, by reason of which thou hast more grief than was formerly thy wont?" Then said I to him, "Alas, Peter, the grief which I daily endure it is to me always old for use and wont; and it is to me always new through the increase of it."

The edifying stories are sometimes as grotesque as the strangest carvings about a mediæval edifice:—

A nun,[1] walking in the convent garden, took a fancy to eat a leaf of lettuce, and she ate, without first making the sign of the cross over it. Presently she was found to be possessed. At the approach of the abbot, the fiend protested it was not his fault;

---

[1] An nunne. This word is of two syllables; there is no silent e final in Anglo-Saxon.

that he had been innocently sitting on a lettuce, and she ate him.[1]

In the Dialogues we recognise that peculiar ideal of sanctity which we identify not so much with Christianity as with mediæval Christianity. The bright samples of Christian virtues are too like those types which have afforded material to caricature. For example, Æquitius, the good abbot, whose virtues adorn a series of narratives, practises in the following manner the virtue of humility:—

Sothlice he wæs swithe waclic on his gewædum and swa forsewenlic thæt, theah hwilc man him ongean come the hine ne cuthon, and he thone mid wordum gegrette, he wæs forsewen thæt he næs ongean gegreted; and swa oft swa he to othrum stowum faran wolde, thonne wæs his theaw thæt he wolde sittan on tham horse the he on tham mynstre forcuthost findan mihte, on tham eac he breac hælftre for bridele, and wethera fella for sadele.	Moreover, he was very mean in his clothing, and so abject, that though any one met him (of those who knew him not), and he greeted him with words, he was so despised that he was not greeted in return; and as often as he would travel to other places, then was it his custom to sit on the horse that he could find the most despicable in the abbey, on which, moreover, he used a halter for a bridle, and sheepskins for saddle.

Constantius was the name of a sacristan who completely despised all worldly goods, and his fame was spread abroad. On one occasion, when there was no oil for the lamps, he filled them with water, and they gave light just as if it had been oil. Visitors were attracted by the report of his sanctity. Once a countryman came from a distance (com feorran sum

[1] Ic sæt me on anum leahtrice, tha com heo and bát me!

ceorl) to see a man of whom so much was said. When he came into the church, Constantius was on a ladder trimming the lamps. He was an undergrown, slight-built, shabby figure. The countryman inquired which was Constantius; and, being told, was so shocked and disappointed, that he spoke sneeringly, " I expected to see a fine man, and this is not a man at all ! "

Mid tham the se Godes wer Constantius tha this gehyrde, he sona swithe blithe forlet tha leoht fatu the he behwearf, and hrædlice nyther astah and thone ceorl beclypte and mid swithlicre lufe ongann mid his earmum hinc clyppan and cyssan and him swithe thancian, thæt he swa be him gedemde, and thus cwæth : "Thu ana hæfdest ontynde eagan on me and me mid rihte oncneowe."

When Constantius the man of God heard this, he forthwith in great joy left the lamps he was attending to, and nimbly descended and embraced the countryman, and with exceeding love began to hold him in his arms, and kiss him, and heartily thank him, that he had so judged of him ; and thus he quoth :—"Thou alone hadst opened eyes upon me, and thou didst rightly know me."

Our next and last example is a story of a well-known type, and perhaps the oldest extant instance of it :—

Eac on othrum timan hit gelamp thæt him to becom for geneosunge thingon swa swa his theaw wæs Servandus se diacon and abbod thæs mynstres the Liberius se ealdorman iu getimbrode on suth Langbeardena landes dælum. Witodlice he geneosode Benedictes mynster gelomlice . to tham thæt hi him betwynon

Also at another time it happened that there came to him for a visit, as his custom was, Servandus, the deacon and abbot of the monastery that Liberius the patrician had formerly built in South Lombardy (*in Campaniæ partibus*). In fact, he used to visit Benedict's monastery frequently, to the end that in each other's com-

ALFRED'S TRANSLATIONS. 199

gemænelice him on aguton tha swetan lifes word . and thone wynsuman mete thæs heofonlican etheles . thone hi tha gyta fullfremedlice geblissiende thicgean ne mihton . huru thinga hi hine geomriende onbyrigdon . for tham the se ylca wer Servandus eac fleow on lare heofonlicre gife. Sothlice tha tha eallunga becom se tima hyra reste and stillnysse . tha gelogode se arwurtha Benedictus hine sylfne on sumes stypeles upflora . and Servandus se diacon gereste hine on thære nyther flore thæs ylcan stypeles . and wæs on thære ylcan stowe trumstæger mid gewissum stapum fram thære nyther flora to thære up flora. Wæs eac æt foran tham ylcan stypele sum rum hus . on tham hyra begra gingran hi gereston . Tha tha se drihtnes wer Benedictus behogode thone timan his nihtlican gebedes tham brothrum restendum . tha gestod he thurhwacol æt anum eahthyrle biddende thone ælmihtigan drihten . and tha færinga on tham timan thære nihte stillnysse him ut lociendum geseah he ufan onsended leoht afligean ealle tha nihtlican thystru . and mid swa micelre beorhtnesse scinan thæt thæt leoht the thær lymde betweoh tham thys-pany they might be mutually refreshed with the sweet words of life, and the delectable food of the heavenly country, which they could not, as yet, with perfect bliss enjoy, but at least they did in aspiration taste it, inasmuch as the said Servandus was likewise abounding in the lore of heavenly grace. When, however, at length the time was come for their rest and repose, the venerable Benedict was lodged in the upper floor of a tower, and Servandus the deacon rested in the nether floor of the same tower; and there was in the same place a solid staircase with plain steps, from the nether floor to the upper floor. There was, moreover, in front of the same tower a spacious house, in which slept the disciples of them both. When, now, Benedict, the man of God, was keeping the time of his nightly prayer during the brethren's rest, then stood he all vigilant at a window praying to the Almighty Lord; and then suddenly, in that time of the nocturnal stillness, as he looked out, he saw a light sent from on high disperse all the darkness of the night, and shine with a brightness so great that the light which then gleamed in

trum wæs beorhtre thonne dæges leoht. Hwæt tha on thysre sceawunge swythe wundorlic thing æfter fyligde . swa swa he sylf syththan rehte . thæt eac eall middaneard swylce under anum sunnan leoman gelogod . wære be foran his eagan gelæded . Tha tha se arwurtha fæder his eagena atihtan scearpnysse gefæstnode on thære beorhtnesse thæs scinendan leohtes . tha geseah he englas ferian on fyrenum cliwene in to heofenum Gérmanes sawle . se wæs bisceop Capuane thære ceastre . He wolde tha gelangian him sylfum sumne gewitan swa miceles wundres . and Servandum thone diacon clypode tuwa and thriwa . and ofthrædlice his naman nemde mid hreames micelnysse. Servandus tha wearth gedrefed for tham ungewunelican hreame swa mæres weres . and he up astah and thider locode . and geseah eallunga lytelne dæl thæs leohtes. Tham diacone tha wafiendum for thus mycelum wundre . se Godes wer be endebyrdnysse gerehte tha thing the thær gewordene wæron . and on Casino tham stoc wic tham eawfæstan were Theoprobo thær rihte bebead . thæt he on thære ylcan nihte asende sumne mann to Capuanan

the midst of the darkness was brighter than the light of day. Lo then, in this sight a very wonderful thing followed next, as he himself afterwards related ; that even all the world, as if placed under one ray of the sun, was displayed before his eyes. When, now, the venerable father had fastened the intent observation of his eyes on the brightness of that shining light, then saw he angels conveying in a fiery group into heaven the soul of Germanus, who was bishop of the city Capua. He desired then to secure to himself a witness of so great a wonder, and he called Servandus the deacon twice and thrice; and repeatedly he named his name with a loud exclamation. Servandus then was disturbed at the unusual outcry of the honoured man, and he mounted the stairs and looked as directed, and he saw verily a small portion of that light. And, as the deacon was then amazed for so great a wonder, the man of God related to him in order the things that had there happened ; and forthwith he sent orders to the faithful man Theoprobus in Casinum the chief house, that he in the self-same night should send a man to the city of Capua,

þære byri. and gewiste and him eft gecythde hwæt wære geworden be Germane tham bisceope. Tha wæs geworden þæt se the thyder asended wæs gemette eallunga forthferedne thone arwurthan wer Germanum bisceop. and he tha smeathancollice axiende on cneow þæt his forsith wæs on tham ylcan tyman the se drihtnes wer oncneow his upstige to heofenum.

Petrus cwæth: "This is swithe wundorlic thing and thearle to wafienne." Book ii., c. 35.

and should ascertain and report to him what had happened about Germanus the bishop. Then it came to pass that he who was thither sent found that the venerable man, Germanus the bishop had indeed died; and he then cautiously enquiring, discovered that his departure was at that very time that the man of God had witnessed his ascent to heaven.

Peter said: "This is a very wonderful thing, and greatly to be marvelled at."

In the translation of the "Comfort of Philosophy," the translator makes his greatest effort and exerts the utmost capabilities of his language. He is not bound by any verbal fidelity to his author; he rather adapts the book to his own use and mental exercitation. In the original the author is visited in affliction by Philosophy, and with this heavenly visitant a dialogue ensues, interspersed with choral odes. Alfred sinks the First Person of the author, and makes the dialogue run between Heavenly Wisdom and the Mind (thæt Môd).

The choral odes (generally called the Metres of Boethius) must have been very hard for Alfred to translate, and they are done somewhat vaguely. We have them in two translations, one in prose and the other in verse. There is no doubt that the poetical version was made from the prose version, without any fresh reference to the Latin. The two are often verbally identical, with a little change in the order of words, and some necessary additions to satisfy the alliteration, or fill out the poetic rhythm. It was long ago observed by Hickes that the style of these poems differed little from prose; but it was Mr. Thomas Wright who first noticed that they were, in fact, merely a versified arrangement of the prose translation.

The same critic gave reasons for thinking that the versified metres were by some later hand, and not by King Alfred. This has been recently the subject of a very interesting discussion in the German periodical "Anglia," it being maintained by Dr. M. Hartmann that they are by Alfred, and the opposite view (that of Mr. T. Wright) being advocated by Dr. A. Leicht.

When the Boethian metres make their appearance in Anglo-Saxon poetic dress, they are considerably expanded. The original prose translation is itself expansive, because the poetry of Boethius is exceedingly terse, and cannot be rendered into readable prose without enlargement. The work of the Saxon versifier is attended with further expansion, because of the mechanical exigencies of the poetic form.

The twentieth metre (iii. 9) offers an extreme case of this kind. Here the original consists of twenty-six hexameters, and the Anglo-Saxon poem has 281 long lines. In this case, however, the poetic expansion is not wholly mechanical; the poet has made some real additions to the thought. The chief of these is a new simile, in which the poising of the Earth in space is illustrated by the yolk of an egg. The prose translation runs thus :—

Thu gestatholadest eorthan swithe wundorlice and fæstlice thæt he ne helt on nane healfe . ne on nanum eorthlic thinge ne stent ne nanwuht eorthlices hi ne healt . thæt hio ne sige . and nis hire thonne ethre to feallanne of dune thonne up.	Thou hast established the earth very wondrously and firmly that it does not heel[1] over on any side : and yet it stands not on any earthly thing, nor does anything earthly hold it up that it sink not; and yet it is no easier for it to fall down than up.

The poetic version enlarges as follows :—

Thu gestatholadest
     thurh tha strongan meaht
 weroda wuldor cyning
     wunderlice
 eorthan swa fæste
     thæt hio on ænige
 healfe ne heldeth
     ne mæg hio hider ne thider
 sigan the swithor
     the hio symle dyde.
 Hwæt hi theah eorthlices
     auht ne haldéth
 is theah efn ethe
     up and of dune
 to feallanne
     foldan thisse :
 thæm anlicost
     the on æge bith
 geoleca on middan
     glideth hwæthre
 æg ymbutan .
     Swa stent eall weoruld
	Thou didst establish
	     through strong might
	 glorious king of hosts
	     wonderfully
	 the earth so fast
	     that she on any
	 side heeleth not
	     nor can hither or thither
	 any more decline
	     than she ever did.
	 Lo nothing earthly though
	     at all sustains her,
	 it is equally easy
	     upwards and downwards
	 that there should be a fall
	     of this earth :
	 likest to that
	     which we see in an egg;
	 the yolk in the midst
	     and yet gliding free
	 the egg round about.
	     So standeth the world

---

[1] See Skeat, " Etym. Dict.," *v*. "heel" (2).

still on tille	still in its place,
streamas ymbutan	while streaming around,
lagufloda gelac	water-floods play,
lyfte and tungla	welkin and stars,
and sio scire scell	and the shining shell
scritheth ymbutan	circleth about
dogora gehwilce .	day by day now
dyde lange swa .	as it did long ago.

The translation of Orosius embodies a considerable piece of original matter. Orosius had given, in the opening of his work, a geographical sketch of Europe and Asia. In the translation a large addition is made to the geography of Europe, and it was an addition not merely to this book, but (so far as appears) to the stock of existing geographical knowledge. This insertion consists of three parts. 1. A map-like description of Central Europe ; 2. Narrative of Ohthere, who had voyaged round the North Cape ; 3. Voyage of Wulfstan from Denmark along the southern and eastern coasts of the Baltic. Ohthere's Narrative is connected with King Alfred by name :—"Ohthere sæde his hlaforde Ælfrede kynincge thæt he ealra Northmanna northmest bude," *i.e.*, Ohthere said to his lord, King Alfred, that he of all Northmen had the most northerly home.

The translation of Beda skips lightly over much of the twenty-two preliminary chapters, giving good measure, however, to the description of Britain and to the martyrdom of St. Alban. All about Gregory and Augustine is full. So also about Eadwine, Oswald, Aidan, Oswy, and St. Chad. (But all that famous section (iii. 25, 26) which describes the crisis between the churches, the synod of Whitby, and the

Scotian departure, is omitted altogether). Full measure is given to Theodore, the synod of Hertford, Wilfrid, Queen Ætheldrith, Hilda, and Cædmon. So also Cuthbert and John of Hexham. Fully rendered are the failure of the Irish and the success of the Anglian missions to Germany; also the visions which we may call Dantesque. (The whole section about Adamnan's influence and writings (v. 15, 16, 17) is omitted.) But about Aldhelm and his writings; also Daniel, bishop of Winchester; the end of Wilfrid; and about Albinus, the successor of Adrian, is fully rendered.

The Anglo-Saxon Gospels must be mentioned here. This is a book about which we have no external information, and the manuscripts are comparatively late. But the diction leads us to place it in or about the times of Alfred.

It is probable that the "Beowulf" is the product of the same reign; while the volume of sacred poetry that is designated by the name of "Cædmon" appears (at least the first part of it) to be either of this time or possibly older.

If with the above we embrace in our view the Laws of this reign and the evidence of contemporary work in the Chronicles, we must be struck with the extent of this great muster of native literature. But we shall hardly do it justice unless we remember that this is the first national display of the kind in the progress of modern Europe. Native poetry had been cultivated in the Anglian period, and there had been a vernacular apparatus to assist the study of Latin, but of a varied and comprehensive literature in English or any other European vernacular, we find no trace until now. We must not look upon Alfred's translations as mere helps to the Latin. What with the freedom and independence of treatment, and what with the original additions, they have a large claim to the character of domestic products. The very scheme itself, that of using translation as a medium of culture, which is now so familiar to us, was then quite a novel idea. In his preface to the "Pastoral," the king casts about for precedents, and he finds none but the translations of Scripture into Greek and into Latin, and these do not, in fact, make a true parallel. But he could hardly have used this argument without a conscious pride that he had in his mother tongue an instrument not unpractised, and not altogether unworthy to be the first of barbarian languages to tread in the footsteps of the Greek and Latin.

This, then (I comprise the matter of three previous chapters and of three that are to follow) is the "Anglo-Saxon"[1] literature, properly so called; for that expression, if used with technical exactness, affords a term of distinction for the later literature of the south as against the earlier literature of the north, which has been called the Anglian period.

[1] This term appears in charters of the tenth century; also Asser styles the king "Ælfred Angulsaxonum rex," "Mon. Hist. Brit.," 483 C. See Freeman, "Norman Conquest," vol. i., Appendix A.

CHAPTER X.

ÆLFRIC.

ALFRED died in 901. From this to the Norman Conquest there are 165 years, and the middle of this period is characterised by the works of the greatest of Anglo-Saxon prose-writers. The productions of Alfred and the scholars that surrounded him, are to be understood as extraordinary efforts, and as beacons to raise men's minds rather than as specimens of the state of learning in the country, or even as monuments of attainments that were likely soon to become general. Although the literary movement under Alfred was so far sustained that it did not subsequently die out, yet it would perhaps be too much to say that he achieved a complete revival of learning. In the inert state of the religious houses, the soil was unprepared. Still, a taste was kindled which continued to propagate itself until the time when the religious houses became active seats of education. This did not happen until the second half of the tenth century, when the reform of the monasteries by Æthelwold and Dunstan produced that great educational and literary movement of which the representative name is Ælfric.

The impetus which Alfred had imparted did not cease with his life. If we look into the Chronicles, we see that the Alfredian style of work is continued down to the death of his son Edward, in 924, and that from that point the stream of history dwindles and becomes meagre. This may be typical of what happened over a wider surface. The impulse given to translation may be supposed to have continued, and we may specify two translations likely to have been made at this time. These are the Four Gospels[1] and the poetical Psalter.[2]

A feature of the Gospels is that the name of Jesus is regarded as a descriptive title, and subjected to translations. It never appears in its original form, but always as " Se Hælend "—that is, The Healer, The Saviour.

To this period, the first half of the tenth century, must be assigned some translations of another sort. There are some considerable remains of a translating period that gave to the English reader a mass of apocryphal, romantic, fantastic, and even heretical reading ; and that period can hardly be any other than this. I imagine that now as a consequence of

[1] The Anglo-Saxon Version of the Holy Gospels, ed. Thorpe, 1842.

[2] Edited by Thorpe from the eleventh-century manuscript at Paris ; Oxford, 1835. This contains Psalms li.-cl. in poetry ; the first fifty are in prose. Dietrich (in Haupt's "Zeitschrift") pointed out that the prose was eleventh-century work, but the poetical version was much older. He surmised that the prose translation had been made for the purpose of giving completeness to a mutilated book, and that the whole Psalter had once existed in Anglo-Saxon verse. Since then some fragments of the missing psalms have been found. See Grein, " Bibliothek der Angelsächs. Poesie," vol. ii., p. 412.

the new literary interest awakened by King Alfred, many old book-chests were explored, and things came to light which had been stored in the monasteries of Wessex ever since the seventh and eighth centuries. These writings claim a manifest affinity with the early products of the Gaulish monasteries, and from these they would naturally have been diffused in southern Britain. But, since the religious life of Gaul had been touched and quickened with the reform of the second Benedict in the ninth century, some old things would have been condemned and rejected there, which might still enjoy credit with the old-fashioned clergy of Wessex.

Of apocryphal materials in Anglo-Saxon literature there are several varieties. First, there is the so-called Gospel of Nicodemus. This is from a Latin version of the Greek "Acts of Pilate," and it is our earliest extant source for that prolific subject, the Harrowing of Hell. The Greek text laid claim to a Hebrew original :—

| ——her onginnath tha gedonan thing the be urum Hælende gedone wæron . eall swa Theodosius se mæra casere hyt funde on Hierusalem on thæs Pontiscan Pilates domerne . eall swa hyt Nychodemus awrat . eall mid Ebreiscum stafum on manegum bocum thus awriten : | ——here begin the actual things that were done in connexion with our Saviour, just as Theodosius the illustrious emperor found it in Jerusalem in Pontius Pilate's court-house ; according as Nicodemus wrote it down all with Hebrew writing on many leaves as follows. |

The "Dialogues of Solomon and Saturn" belong to a legendary stock that has sent its branches into all the early vernacular literatures of Europe. The

P

germ is found in the Bible and in Josephus. In 1 Kings x. 1, we read that, when the Queen of Sheba heard of the fame of Solomon, she came to prove him with hard questions. Josephus, in the "Jewish Antiquities," vii. 5, tells a curious story about hard questions passing between Solomon and Hiram, king of Tyre. From such a root appear to have grown the multiform legends in various languages which passed under such names as the "Controversy of Solomon," the "Dialogues of Solomon and Saturn," or of "Solomon and Marculfus." This became at length a mocking form of literature; often a burlesque and parody of religion. Mr. Kemble traces these legends to Jewish tradition; but of all the examples preserved he says "the Anglo-Saxon are undoubtedly the oldest. . . . . With the sole exception of one French version, they are the only forms of the story remaining in which the subject is seriously and earnestly treated; and, monstrous as the absurdities found in them are, we may be well assured that the authors were quite unconscious of their existence."[1] There are, however, some places in which one is moved to doubt whether the extravagance is the product of pure simplicity, and without the least tinge of drollery.

But the reader may judge for himself. The fragments preserved are partly poetical and partly in prose: the poetry is rather insipid; our quotation shall be from the prose. The subject is the praise

[1] "The Dialogue of Solomon and Saturnus, with an Historical Introduction." By John M. Kemble, M.A. Ælfric Society, 1848, p. 2. See Dean Stanley, "Jewish Church," ii. 170.

and eulogy of the Lord's Prayer, which is personified and anatomised. Saturnus asks, "What manner of head hath the Pater Noster?" And, again, "What manner of heart hath the Pater Noster?" We quote from the answer to the latter question:—

Salomon cwæth. His heorte is xii thusendum sitha beohtre thonne ealle thas seofon heofenas the us sindon ofergesette, theah the hi syn ealle mid thy domiscan fyre onæled, and theah the eal theos eorthe him neothan togegnes birne, and heo hæbbe fyrene tungan, and gyldenne hracan, and leohtne muth inneweardne. . . . . he is rethra and scearpra thonne eal middangeard, theah he sy binnan his feower hwommum fulgedrifen wildeora, and anra gehwylc deor hæbbe synderlice xii hornas irene, and anra gehwylc horn hæbbe xii tindas irene, and anra gehwylc tind hæbbe synderlice xii ordas, and anra gehwylc ord sy xii thusendum sitha scearpra thonne seo an flan the sy fram hundtwelftigum hyrdenna geondhyrded . And theah the seofon middangeardas syn ealle on efn abrædde on thisses anes onlicnesse, and thær sy eal gesomnod thætte heofon oththe hel oththe eorthe æfre acende, ne magon hy tha lifes linan on middan ymb	Solomon said: His heart is 12,000 times brighter than all the seven heavens that over us are set, though they should be all aflame with the doomsday fire, and though all this earth should blaze up towards them from beneath, and it should have a fiery tongue, and golden throat, and mouth lighted up within. . . . . he is fiercer and sharper than all the world, though within its four corners it should be driven full of wild deer, and each particular deer have severally twelve horns of iron, and each particular horn have twelve tines of iron, and each particular tine have severally twelve points, and each particular point be 12,000 times sharper than the arrow which had been hardened by 120 hardeners. And though the seven worlds should be all fairly spread out after the fashion of this one, and everything should be there assembled that heaven or hell or earth ever engendered, they may not encircle the girth of his body at the middle. And

fæthmian. And se Pater Noster he mæg ana ealla gesceafta on his thære swithran hand on anes wæxæpples onlicnesse gethŷn and gewringan. And his gethoht he is springdra and swiftra thonne xii thusendu haligra gasta, theah the anra gehwylc gast hæbbe synderlice xii fetherhoman, and anra gehwylc fetherhoma hæbbe xii windas, and anra gehwylc wind twelf sigefæstnissa synderlice. —Kemble, pp. 148—152.

the Pater Noster, he can by himself in his right hand grasp and squeeze all creation like a wax-apple. And his thought it is more alert and swifter than 12,000 angelic spirits, though each particular spirit have severally twelve suits of feathers, and each particular feather-suit have twelve winds, and each particular wind twelve victoriousnesses all to itself.

I do not undertake to assert that this piece is as old as the first half of the tenth century; it is placed here only because this seems to be the most natural place for the group of literature to which it belongs. As I said, the reader must judge for himself whether this is perfectly serious. I believe that these "Dialogues" are the only part of Anglo-Saxon literature that can be suspected of mockery. The earliest laughter of English literature is ridicule; and if this ridicule seems to touch things sacred, it will, on the whole, I think, be found that not the sacred things themselves, but some unreal or spurious use of them, is really attacked. So here, if there is any appearance of a sly derision, the thing derided is not the Pater Noster, but the vain and magical uses which were too often ascribed to the repetition of it.

Here we must find a place for the translation of "Apollonius of Tyre." This has all the features of a Greek romance, but it is only known to exist in a Latin text, so that it has been questioned whether

this Latin romance is a translation from a Greek
original, or a story originally Latin in imitation of the
Greek romancists. With those who have investigated
the subject, the hypothesis of translation is most in
favour, and for the following reason. The story presents an appearance of double stratification, such as
might naturally result if a heathen Greek romance
had been translated into Latin by a Christian. Although the phenomenon could be equally explained
by supposing a Latin heathen original which had been
re-written by a Christian editor, yet the former is the
more natural and the more probable hypothesis.[1]

We now come to the Blickling Homilies, a
recently-published book of great importance. It is
not a homogeneous work, but a motley collection of
sermons of various age and quality. Some of the
later sermons are not so very different from those of
Ælfric; but these are not the ones that give the book
its character. The older sort have very distinct
characteristics of their own, and they furnish a deep
background to the Homilies of Ælfric. They are
plainly of the age before the great Church reform of
the tenth century, when the line was very dimly drawn
between canonical and uncanonical, and when quotations, legends, and arguments were admissible which
now surprise us in a sermon. Indeed, one can hardly
escape the surmise that the elder discourses may come
down from some time, and perhaps rather an early
time, in the ninth century. One of the sermons bears
the date of 971 imbedded in its context; and this,

---

[1] Rohde, "Der Griechische Roman," p. 408.

which is probably the lowest date of the book, is twenty years before the Homilies of Ælfric appeared. Speaking of that frequent topic of the time, the end of the world, which is to take place in the Sixth Age, the preacher says :—

——and thisse is thonne se mæsta dæl agangen, efne nigon hund wintra and lxxi. on thys geare.—P. 119.

—and of this is verily the most part already gone, even nine hundred years and seventy-one, in this year.

Perhaps there is no book which has been published in the present generation that has done so much for the historical knowledge of Anglo-Saxon literature. Speaking generally, we may say that it represents the preaching of the times before Ælfric; that it contains the sort of preaching that Ælfric sat under in his youth (when not at Abingdon or Winchester); the sort of preaching, too, that Ælfric set himself to correct and to supersede. It is a book whose value turns not so much upon its own direct communications, as on the light it throws all around it, showing up the popular standards of the time, and enabling us to recognise the true setting of many a waif and stray of the old literature. But it is upon the work of Ælfric that it sheds the most valuable light. There is in Ælfric's Homilies a certain corrective aim, which was but faintly seen before, and when seen could not be distinctly explained; but now we have both the aim and the occasion of it rendered comparatively clear.

These Homilies supply to those of Ælfric their true historical introduction. They support the reasons which Ælfric assigns for producing homilies. In his preface he speaks of certain English books to which he designs his sermons as an antidote. He had translated his discourses (he says) out of the Latin, not for pride of learning, "but because I had seen much heresy (*gedwild*) in many English books, which unlearned men in their simplicity thought mighty wise." Not only do the Blickling Homilies contain enough of unscriptural and apocryphal material to justify the charge of "*gedwild*" in its vaguer sense of error, but we have also documentary grounds for believing that a careful theologian of that time, such as Ælfric undoubtedly was, would have brought them under the indictment of heresy.

It used to be thought that the oldest extant list of condemned books proceeded from Pope Gelasius, and was of about A.D. 494; but now that list is assigned to the eighth or even ninth century. In this Index we find sources for much of the literature which we have been considering in this chapter; we find the "Acts of Pilate," "Journeys of the Apostles," "Acts of Peter," "Acts of Andrew the Apostle," "The Contradiction of Solomon," "The Book Physiologus."[1] The material which gives the Blickling collection its peculiar character is largely apocryphal, and, in the light of the above list, heretical.

A new vitality is imparted to Ælfric's sermons by their contrast with these older ones. It is plain that there is a common source behind both sets of sermons; the well-established series of topics for each occasion seems clearly to point to some standard col-

[1] The list may be seen in the "Dictionary of Christian Antiquities" *v*. Prohibited Books.

lection of Latin homilies now lost.[1] The evident identity of the lines on which the discourses run makes comparison the easier and the more satisfactory. In the sermon for Ascension Day, Ælfric's treatment is in pointed contrast with the older book. The Blickling is full of the signs and wonders; some, indeed, Scriptural, but far more apocryphal; and it is effusive over these. Whereas Ælfric teaches that the visible miracles belonged to the infancy of the Church, and were as artificial watering to a newly-planted tree; but, when the heathen believed, then those miracles ceased. Now (he says) we must look rather for spiritual miracles. The Homily on St. John Baptist is a good example. According to the old book, John is called "angelus," because he lived on earth the angelic life, but Ælfric takes it as messenger, and this may hint the difference of treatment. In the same discourse there is a contrast which touches the chronology. The old Homily says that there are only two Nativities kept sacred by the Church—that of the Lord and that of His forerunner. Ælfric takes up this topic with a difference. He says that there are three Nativities, which are celebrated annually, adding that of the Blessed Virgin to the previous two. Now, it was precisely in the tenth century that this third began to be observed in the churches of the West;[2] and the change took place in the interval that separates these two sets of homilies.

On the Assumptio St. Mariæ, the elder homily is

[1] The series that goes by the name of Eusebius of Emesa has much general similarity to the required collection.
[2] "Dictionary of Christian Antiquities," vol. ii., p. 1143.

a jumble of apocryphal legend. Here Ælfric presents a contrast, and manifestly an intentional one. In the preamble he recalls certain teaching of Jerome, "through which he quashed the misguided narrative which half-taught men had told about her departure." Then, after an exposition of the Gospel for the day, he returns to the Assumption in a passage which, when read in the light of the elder Homily, is very pointed:—"What shall we say to you more particularly about this festival, except that Mary was on this day taken up to heaven from this weary world, to dwell with Him, where she rejoices in eternal life for evermore? If we should say more to you about this day's festival than we read in those holy books which were given by God's inspiration, we should be like those mountebanks who, from their own imaginations or from dreams, have written many false stories; but the faithful teachers, Augustine, Jerome, Gregory, and other such, have in their wisdom rejected them. But still these absurd books exist, both in Latin and in English, and misguided men read them. It is enough for believers to read and to relate that which is true; and there are very few men who can completely study all the holy books that were indited by God's Holy Spirit. Let alone those absurd fictions, which lead the unwary to perdition, and read or listen to Holy Scripture, which directs us to heaven."

The Homilies of Ælfric are in two series, of which the first was published in 990, and addressed to Sigeric, Archbishop of Canterbury; the second in 991, after that Danish invasion in which Byrhtnoth fell. These were long ago published by the Ælfric

Society. But there is another set, appropriated to the commemoration of saints, after the manner of the Benedictine hagiographies.[1] These have a Latin preface, pointedly agreeing with the prefaces to the previous series. If their miraculous narratives sometimes contain what we should not have expected from Ælfric, and if this leads us to doubt the authorship, we may reflect that the contrast is not so great as that between the "Cura Pastoralis" and the "Dialogues" of Gregory.

As a slight specimen of the character of these latter discourses, I will give a few lines from that on St. Swithun:—

Eadgar cyning tha æfter thysum tacnum . wolde thæt se halga wer wurde up gedon . and spræc hit to Athelwolde tham arwurthan bisceope . thæt he hine upp adyde mid arwurthnysse . Tha se bisceop Athelwold mid abbodum and munecum dyde up thone sanct mid sange wurthlice . and bæron into cyrcan sce Petres huse . thær he stent mid wurthmynte . and wundra gefremath.	King Eadgar then, after these tokens, willed that the holy man should be translated, and spake it to Athelwold, the venerable bishop, that he should translate him with honourable solemnity. Then the bishop Athelwold, with abbots and monks, raised the saint with song solemnly. And they bare him into the church St. Peter's house, where he stands in honoured memory, and worketh wonders.
* * *	* * * *
Seo ealde cyrce wæs eall be hangen mid criccum . and mid créopera sceamelum fram énde	The old church was all hung round with crutches and with stools from one end to the other,

---

[1] This third set of Homilies is now for the first time in course of publication by the Early English Text Society, under the editorship of Professor Skeat.

oth otherne . on ægtherum wáge . the thær wurdon ge hælede . and man ne mihte swa theah macian hi healfe up.	on either wall, of cripples who there had been healed : and yet they had not been able to put half of them up.

Ælfric's place in literature consists in this :—That he is the voice of that great Church reform which is the most signal fact in the history of the latter half of the tenth century. Of this reform, the first step was the restoration of the rule of Benedict in the religious houses. The great movement had begun in Gaul early in the ninth century, and its extension to our island could hardly be delayed when peaceful times left room for attention to learning and religion. Both in Frankland and in England the religious revival followed the literary one; only there it followed quickly, and here after a long interval.[1]

The chief author of this revival was Odo (died 961), and the chief conductors of it were Æthelwold, Dunstan, Oswald. The leaders of this movement were much in communication with the Frankish monasteries, especially with the famous house at Fleury on the Loire. Various kinds of literature were cherished, but that which is most peculiar to this time is the biographies of Saints. Lanferth, a disciple of Æthelwold, wrote Latin hagiographies, and from his Latin was derived the extant homily of the miracles of St. Swithun. Wulstan, a monk of Winchester and a disciple of Æthelwold, was a Latin poet, and wrote hagiography in verse; among the rest, he versified the work of Lanferth on St. Swithun.

---

[1] In like manner the literary revival of the fifteenth century was followed by the religious revival of the sixteenth.

Ælfric was an alumnus of Æthelwold at Winchester, and perhaps at Abingdon earlier; from Winchester he was sent to Cernel (Cerne Abbas in Dorsetshire), to be the pastor of Æthelweard's house and people, and there he wrought at his homilies. The highest title that we find associated with his name is that of abbot; and this probably is in relation to Egonesham (Ensham, Oxon), where Æthelweard founded a religious house, and Ælfric superintended it. In Æthelweard the ealdorman we have our first example of a great lay patron of literature: much of Ælfric's work was undertaken at the instance of Æthelweard.

It was at his request that he engaged in the translation of the Old Testament, and when he had done the Pentateuch (with frequent omissions), and some parts of Joshua and Judges,[1] he ceased, and declared he would translate no more, having a misgiving lest the narration of many things unlike Christian morality might confuse the judgment of the simple. This is the earliest recorded instance of a devout Christian withholding Scripture from the people for their good. And, when we take it in conjunction with the authorised diffusion of the Benedictine hagiographies of the time, we see what was approved placed by the side of that which was mistrusted.

The so-called "Canons of Ælfric" are a mixed composition, in which some matters of historical and doctrinal instruction are united with directions and regulations and exhortations for correcting the practices of the ignorant priests. They were compiled

[1] "Heptateuchus," ed. Thwaites, 1698 : reprinted by Grein.

by Ælfric, at the request of Wulfsige, Bishop of Sherborne (A.D. 992-1001), for the benefit of his clergy. The reformation of the monasteries had already made considerable progress, and this seems like an extension of the same movement to embrace the secular clergy. Among the divers matters touched in the Articles are these :—The relative authority of the councils; the first four are to be had in reverence like the four gospels (Tha feower sinothas sind to healdenne swa swa tha feower Cristes bec)—the vestments, the books, and the garb of the priest; the seven orders of the Christian ministry; some points of priestly duty as regards marriages and funerals; of Baptism and the Eucharist, with rebuke of superstitious practices; the priest to speak the sense of the Gospel to the people in English on Sundays and high days, as also of the Lord's Prayer and the Creed; but, withal, the immediate practical aim of the whole seems, above all things, to be the celibacy of the clergy.[1]

Ælfric was the author of the most important educational books of this time that have come down to us—namely, his "Latin Grammar," in English, formed after Donatus and Priscian; his "Glossary of Latin

[1] "A Collection of all the Ecclesiastical Laws, Canons, &c., &c., of the Church of England, from its First Foundation to the Conquest, that have hitherto been published in the Latin and Saxonic Tongues. And of all the Canons and Constitutions Ecclesiastical, made Since the Conquest and Before the Reformation . . . . now first translated into English . . . . by John Johnson, M.A., London, 1720." A New Edition, by John Baron, of Queen's College (now Dr. Baron, Rector of Upton Scudamore), Oxford, John Henry Parker, 1850. In two volumes, 8vo. Vol. i., p. 388.

Words"; and his "Colloquium," or conversation in Latin, with interlinear Saxon.[1]

But for us, as for the men of the sixteenth century, the most important of Ælfric's works are his Homilies. The English of these Homilies is splendid; indeed, we may confidently say that here English appears fully qualified to be the medium of the highest learning. And their interest has been greatly enhanced of late years by two important additions to our printed Anglo-Saxon library. The first of these was the "Blickling Homilies," edited by Dr. Morris, which threw a new light upon Ælfric, and added greatly to the significance of his Homilies.

The circuit of Anglo-Saxon homiletic literature has again been greatly enlarged by a more recent publication, namely, that of the "Homilies of Wulfstan."[2] These homilies are quite distinct in character from all the preceding. There is nothing of controversy, and little in the shape of argument: simply the assertion of Christian dogma and the enforcement of Christian duty. The one topic that lies beyond these was more practical, in the view of that day, than it is in our view—I mean the repeated introduction of Antichrist and the near approach of the end of the world. In the quotation the þ and ð (for th) are kept, as in Mr. Napier's text.

---

[1] See above, p. 40. The "Colloquium" is printed in Thorpe's "Analecta."

[2] Wulfstan, "Sammlung der ihm zugeschriebenen Homilien nebst Untersuchungen über ihre Echtheit: Herausgegeben von Arthur Napier. Erste Abtheilung: Text und Varianten. Berlin 1883."

Uton beon â urum hlaforde holde and getreowe and æfre eallum mihtum his wurðscipe ræran and his willan wyrcan, forðam eall, þet we æfre for rihthlafordhelde doð, eal we hit doð us sylfum to mycelre þearfe, forðam ðam bið witodlice God hold, þe bið his hlaforde rihtlice hold; and eac ah hlaforda gehwylc þæs for micle þearfe, þæt he his men rihtlice healde. And we biddað and beodað, þæt Godes þeowas, þe for urne cynehlaford and for eal cristen folc þingian scylan and be godra manna ælmessan libbað, þæt hy þæs georne earnian, libban heora lif swa swa bec him wisian, and swa swa heora ealdras hym tæcan, and began heora þeowdom georne, þonne mægon hy ægþer ge hym sylfum wel fremian ge eallum cristenum folce. and we biddað and beodað, þæt ælc cild sy binnan þrittigum nihtum gefullad; gif hit þonne dead weorðe butan fulluhte, and hit on preoste gelang sy, þonne ðolige he his hâdes and dædbete georne; gif hit þonne þurh mæga gemeleaste gewyrðe, þonne þolige se, ðe hit on gelang sy, ælcere eardwununge and wræcnige of earde oððon on earde swiðe deope gebete, swa biscop him tæce. eac we læirað, þæt man ænig ne læte unbiscpod to

Let us be always loyal and true to our Lord, and ever by all means maintain his worship and work his will, because all that ever we do out of sincere loyalty, we do it all for our own great advantage, inasmuch as God will assuredly be gracious to the man who is perfectly loyal to his lord; and likewise it is the bounden duty of every lord, that he his men honourably sustain. And we entreat and command, that God's ministers, who most intercede for our royal lord, and for all Christian folk, and who live by good men's alms, that they accordingly give diligent attention to live their life as the bookes guide them, and so as their superiors direct them, and to discharge their service heartily; then may they do much good both to themselves and to all Christian people. And we entreat and command that every child be baptised within thirty days; if, however, it should die without baptism and it be along of the priest, then let him suffer the loss of his order and do careful penance; if, however, it happen through the relatives' neglect, then let him who was in fault suffer the loss of every habitation, and be ejected from his dwelling, or else in his dwelling undergo

lange, and witan þa, ðe cildes onfôn, þæt heo hit on rihtan geleafan gebringan and on gôdan þeawan and on þearflican dædan and â forð on hit wisian to ðam þe Gode licige and his sylfes ðearf sy; þonne beoð heo rihtlice ealswa hy genamode beoð, godfæderas, gif hy heora godbearn Gode gestrynað.
Homily xxiv.

very severe penance, as the bishop may direct him. Also we instruct you, that none be left unbishopped too long; and they who are sponsors for a child are to see that they bring it up in right belief, and in good manners and in dutiful conduct, and always continually guide it to that which may be pleasing to God and for his own good; then will they verily be as they are called, "godfathers," if they train their god-children for God.

Hitherto Wulfstan has been represented in print by one sermon only, the most remarkable, indeed, of all his discourses—being an address to the English when the Danish ravages were at their worst, A.D. 1012, the year in which Ælfheah, Archbishop of Canterbury, was martyred. In this discourse the miseries of the time are ascribed to the vengeance of God for national sins; and the coming of Antichrist is said to be near. Wulfstan was Archbishop of York from 1003 to 1023. Beautiful and valuable as his sermons are in themselves, their value is greatly increased by their connexion with the preceding series, and by the continuity they give to this branch of our old literature. With the "Blickling Homilies," in all their variety, and those of Ælfric, and those of Wulfstan, in our possession, it is hardly too much to say that we have a vernacular series of sermons that fairly represents the Anglo-Saxon preaching for a period of one hundred and fifty years.

CHAPTER XI.

THE SECONDARY POETRY.

How still the legendary lay
O'er poet's bosom holds its sway.
MARMION.

BETWEEN the Primary and the Secondary Poetry we must acknowledge a wide borderland of transition. Some poetical works lying in this interval we have already found occasion to notice, and have given them such space as we could afford. We have spoken of the Cædmon, and of the poetical Psalter; and with these I must group the "Judith," a noble fragment, which is found in the Cotton Library in the same manuscript volume with the Beowulf. This fragment preserves 350 long lines at the close of a poem which appears—by the numbering of the Cantos—to have been of about four times that length. This remnant contains what would naturally have been the most vigorous and stirring parts of the poem: the riotous drinking of Holofernes, the trenchant act of Judith, her return with her maid to Bethulia, their enthusiastic reception, the muster for battle, the anticipation of carnage by the birds and beasts of prey, the destruction of the invading host.

The poetry which is distinctly Secondary is contained—the best specimens of it—in two famous books, that of Exeter, and that of Vercelli; and in both of these books it is largely connected with the name of a single poet, Cynewulf. Here is at once an indication of the secondary poetry; not merely that we have a poet's name, for we also entitle poems by Cædmon's name; but that the poet himself supplies us with his name, and has left it—vailed and enigmatic—for posterity to decipher.

Curiously and fancifully did Cynewulf interweave into the lines of his verse the Runes which spelt his name; and it needed the skill of Kemble to explain it to us. There are three of the extant poems in which he has thus left his mark, namely two in the Exeter book and one in the Vercelli book. In two cases out of the three this ingenious contrivance is at the close of the poem. In the Vercelli book it occurs in the Elene, the last of the poems in the manuscript, and Mr. Kemble remarked that it was "apparently intended as a tail-piece to the whole book."[1] This naturally suggests the inference, which indeed is generally accepted, that all the poems in the Vercelli book are by Cynewulf.

But when a like inference is drawn for the Exeter

[1] In Wright's "Biographia Literaria," Anglo-Saxon Period, p. 502, *seq.*, these three Runic passages are collected and translated. In Bosworth's "Anglo-Saxon Dictionary," ed. Toller, v. Cynewulf; the Runic passage is quoted from the Elene, and translated. This poet's Runic device affects us somewhat as when, at the end of a volume of Coleridge's poems, we come upon his epitaph, written by himself:—

"Stop, Christian passer-by!—Stop, child of God!
And read with gentle breast. Beneath this sod
A poet lies, or that which once seem'd he—
Oh, lift one thought in prayer for S. T. C.!"

book, inasmuch as the same Runic device is there found in two pieces, that therefore the book is simply a volume of Cynewulf's poems, there seems less reason to acquiesce. That a large part of the book is Cynewulf's poetry will be generally thought probable. The first thirty-two leaves of the manuscript, which correspond to the first 103 pages in Thorpe's edition, contain a series of pieces which are really parts of one whole, as was shown by Professor Dietrich, of Marburg[1]; and, as one of these connected pieces has Cynewulf's Runic mark, it seems to follow that the whole "Christian Epic" is by him. Again in the middle of the volume from the 65th to the 75th leaf there is the poem of St. Juliana with the Runes of Cynewulf's name at its close, and this is therefore undoubtedly his. This brings us to Mr. Thorpe's 286th page. The four pieces which lie between the above, more especially two of them, St. Guthlac and the Phœnix, may well be his. But from the close of St. Juliana (Thorpe, p. 286) the pieces become shorter and more miscellaneous, exhibiting greater diversity both of subject and of quality, being altogether such as to suggest that they have been collected from various sources and are of different ages. So that on this view the volume might be interpreted as containing (1) Poems by Cynewulf; and (2) a miscellaneous collection. Thus Cynewulf's part would close with "St. Juliana," which ends with the Runic device, like the Elene closing his poems in the Vercelli book.[2] About the person of this poet

[1] In Haupt's "Zeitschrift," ix.
[2] We have already seen in the chapter on the West Saxon

nothing is known, beyond what the poems themselves may seem to convey. His date has been variously estimated from the 8th to the 11th century. The latter is the more probable. If we look at his matter, we observe its great affinity with the hagiology of the tenth century, the high pitch at which the poetry of the Holy Rood has arrived, and the expansion given to the subject of the Day of Judgment. If we consider his language and manner, we remark the facility and copious flow of his poetic diction, but with a something that suggests the retentive mind of the student; his cumulation of old heroic phraseology not unlike the romantic poetry of Scott, joined occasionally with a departure from old poetic usage which seems like a slip on the part of an accomplished imitator.[1] Occasionally he has a Latin word of novel introduction.

All these signs forbid an early date, but they agree well with Kemble's view of the time and person of Cynewulf. He proposed to identify our poet with that Kenulphus who in 982 became abbot of Peterborough, and in 1006 became (after Ælfheah) bishop

laws, that a bookmaker of the Saxon period appended the laws of Ine to the laws of Alfred, as if he found it natural to treat the old material as an appendix to the new.—But there is also something on the other side. In the after part of the Exeter book there are three batches of riddles, and the first riddle of the first series (Thorpe, p. 380), is a charade upon the name of Cynewulf, as was shown by Heinrich Leo. This has naturally led to the surmise that Cynewulf has had more to do with the riddles than simply to preface them in his own honour.

[1] Thus:—" ofer ealne yrmenne grund." Juliana *init ;* and in the same poem we find " bealdor " used of a woman!

of Winchester. To this prelate Ælfric dedicated his Life of St. Æthelwold, and he is praised by Hugo Candidus as a great emender of books, a famous teacher, to whom (as to another Solomon) men of all ranks and orders flocked for instruction, and whom the abbey regretted to lose when after fourteen years of his presidency he was carried off to the see of Winchester by violence rather than by election.[1]

The Canto in the "Christian Epic" in which the Cynewulf-Runes appear, is on the near approach of Domesday. This piece closes with a prolonged and detailed Simile, such as occurs only in the later poetry. Life is a perilous voyage, but there is a heavenly port and a heavenly pilot :—

Nu is thon gelicost swa we on laguflode ofor cald wæter ceolum lithan geond sidne sæ sund hengestum flod wudu fergen.	Now it is likest to that as if on liquid flood over cold water in keels we navigated through the vast sea with ocean-horses ferried the floating wood.
Is thæt frecne stream ytha ofermæta the we her onlacath	A frightful surge it is of waves immense that here we toss upon.

---

[1] All this is marred by William of Malmesbury, who represents him as having trafficked for this promotion, and as having been cut off before he had long enjoyed it. And yet the two pictures are not incompatible. The poetry sets before us a poet of the most splendid gifts, but I know nothing that indicates a superiority of character. Indeed, the comparison with Solomon suggests a moral type to which the known and supposed writings of Cynewulf aptly correspond.

geond thas wacan woruld
   windge holmas
ofer deop gelad.
	through this uncertain world—
	   windy quarters
	over a deep passage.

Wæs se drohtath strong
ær thon we to londe
   geliden hæfdon
ofer hreone hrycg—
   tha us help bicwom
thæt us to hælo
   hythe gelædde
Godes gæst sunu :
	It was discipline strong
	ere we to the land
	   had sailed (if at all)
	o'er the rough swell—
	   when help to us came,
	so that us into safety
	   portwards did guide
	God's heavenly Son :

And us giefe sealde
thæt we oncnawan magun
   ofer ceoles bord
hwær we sælan sceolon
   sund hengestas
ealde yth mearas
   ancrum fæste.
	And he gave us the gift
	that we may espy
	   from aboard o' the ship,
	place where we shall bind
	   the steeds of the sea,
	old amblers of water,
	   with anchors fast.

Utan us to thære hythe
   hyht stathelian
tha us gerymde
   rodera waldend
halge on heahthum
   the he heofnum astag.
	Let us in that port
	   our confidence plant,
	which for us laid open
	   the Lord of the skies,
	(holy port in the heights)
	   when he went up to heaven.

The grandest of the allegorical pieces is that on the Phœnix. Of the pedigree of the fable we have already spoken; as also of the Latin poem which the Anglo-Saxon poet followed. It is rather an adaptation than a translation, and it has a second part in which the allegory is explained. At the close there is a playful alternation of Latin and Saxon half-lines, which does not at all lessen the probability that the poet may have been the ingenious Cynewulf.

THE SECONDARY POETRY. 231

Hafað us alysed	Us hath a-loosed
lucis auctor,	the author of light,
þæt we motun her	that we may here
merueri,	worthily merit,
god dædum begietan	with good deeds obtain
gaudia in celo,	delights in the sky,
þær we motun	where we may be able
maxima regna	magnificent realms
secan, and gesittan	to seek, and to sit
sedibus altis,	in heavenly seats,
lifgan in lisse	live in fruition
lucis et pacis,	of light and of peace,
agan eardinga	have habitations
alma letitiæ,	happy and glad,
brucan blæd daga ;—	brook genial days :—
blandem et mitem	gentle and kind
geseon sigora frean	see Victory's Prince
sine fine,	for ever and ever,
and him lof singan	and praise to him sing,
laude perenne,	perennial praise,
eadge mid englum	happy angels among
alleluia.	Alleluia !

Of the other allegorical pieces the Whale was derived from the book Physiologus, and probably the Panther also. The whale is used as a similitude of delusive security. The story reappears in the Arabian Nights, where it is the chief incident in the first voyage of Sindbad. The monster lies on the sea like an island, and deludes the unsuspecting mariner.

Is þæs hiw gelic	In look it is like
hreofum stane,	to a stony land,
swylce worie	with the eddying whirl
bi wædes ofre	of the waves on the bank,
sond beorgum ymbseald	with sandheaps surrounded

sæ ryrica mæst,[1]	a mighty sea-reef ;
swa þæt wenaþ	so they wearily ween
wæg liþende,	who ride on the wave,
þæt hy on ealond sum	that some island it is
eagum wliten ;	they see with their eyes ;
and þonne gehydaþ	and so they do fasten
heah stefn scipu	the high figure-heads
to þam únlonde	to a land that no land is
oncyr rapum ;	with anchor belayed ;
setlað sæ mearas	sea-horses they settle
sundes æt ende.[2]	no farther to sail.

When they have lighted their fires, and are getting comfortable, then all goes down. This is an apologue of misplaced confidence in things earthly.

But the great and absorbing subject of poetry in this age is Hagiography. We still see the old discredited apocryphal literature in occasional use, but it retires before the more approved medium of popular edification, the Lives and Miracles of the Saints. These offer material very apt for poetical treatment. Even the Homilies, when on the lives of Saints, are often clothed in the poetic garb.

In the Exeter book there are two of this class of poems ; St. Guthlac and St. Juliana. In St. Juliana, a characteristic passage is that in which the tempter visits her in the guise of an angel of light, advising her to yield and to sacrifice to the gods. At her

---

[1] "Dorsum immane mari summo." Æneid i.

[2] Milton has set this to his own deep music :—

"Him haply slumb'ring on the Norway foam,
  The pilot of some small night-founder'd skiff,
  Deeming some island, oft, as seamen tell,
  With fixed anchor. . . ."

prayer, the fiend is reduced to his own shape, reminding us of a famous passage in Milton. St. Guthlac is distressed by fiends, and among the trials to which he is exposed, one is this, that he sees in vision the evil life of a disorderly monastery. When he has endured his trials, and he returns to his chosen retreat, the welcome of the birds is very charming.

But the greatest pieces of this sort are the two in the Vercelli book; the Andreas and the Elene.

In the Andreas we have an ancient legend which is now known only in Greek, but which no doubt lay before the Anglo-Saxon poet in a Latin version. In this story Matthew is imprisoned in Mirmedonia, and he is encouraged by the hope that Andrew shall come to his aid. Andrew is wonderfully conveyed to Mirmedonia, where he arrives at a time of famine, and he finds the people casting lots who shall be slain for the others' food. On the intervention of Andrew the devil comes on the scene and suggests that he is the cause of their troubles. Then follows a long series of tortures to which the saint is subjected. When his endurance has been put to extreme proof, the word of deliverance comes to him and he puts forth miraculous power. He calls for a flood, and it comes and sweeps the cruel persecutors away. But the whole ends in a general conversion, and the drowned are restored to life. He is escorted to his ship and has a happy voyage back to Achaia like the return of any hero crowned with success. Here we are reminded of the return of Beowulf; and widely different as the two poems are, they have not only points of similarity but also a certain likeness of type. There is, however, this great dissimilarity, that in the Andreas the poet stops to speak of himself and of his inadequate performance, but still he will give us a little more. The most novel and extraordinary part is the voyage of Andrew to Mirmedonia. The ship-master is a Divine person, and the instructive conversation which the saint addresses to him, is exceedingly well managed, for while it verges on the humorous, it is perfectly reverent; a strong contrast with the free use of such situations in the later mediæval drama. Another feature which calls for notice is the sarcasm with which the drowning people are told there is plenty of drink for them now.

The " Elene " opens with the outbreak of barbarian war, and Constantine in camp on the Danube, frightened at the multitude of the Huns. In a dream of the night he sees an angel who shows him the Cross, and tells him that with this " beacon " he shall overcome the foe. II. Comforted by his dream, he had a cross made like that of the vision, and under this ensign he was victorious. Then he assembles his wise men to inquire of them who the god was that this sign belonged to? No one knew, until some christened folk, who (according to this poet) were then very few, gave the required information. Constantine is baptised by Silvester. III. Zealous to recover the true Cross, he sends his mother, Elene, with a great equipment to Judea. IV. She proclaims an assembly, and 3,000 come together, and she requires of them to choose those who can answer whatever questions she may ask. V. They select 500 for that purpose. When they are come to the queen, she addresses a chiding speech to them about their blindness in rejecting Him who came according to prophecy; but she does not reveal her aim. Afterwards, the Jews in consternation discuss among themselves what the imperial lady can mean. At length one Judas divines that she wants the Cross which is hidden, and which it is of the greatest consequence to keep from discovery; for his grandfather Zacheus, when a-dying, told his son, the speaker's father, that whenever that Cross was found the power of the Jews would end. VI. The speaker further said that his father told him the history of the Saviour's life, and how his son Stephen had believed in him and had been stoned. The speaker was a boy when his father told him this, and seems to have thus learnt about his brother Stephen for the first time.[1] VII. When they are summoned into the imperial presence they all profess to know nothing about the subject of her inquiry, they had never heard of such a thing before! She threatens. Then they select Judas as a wise man who knows more than the rest, and they leave him as a hostage. VIII. The queen will know where the Rood is. Judas pleads that it all happened so long ago that he knows nothing about it. She says it was not so long ago as the Trojan war, and yet people know about that. When he persists, she orders him to be imprisoned and kept without food. He endures

---

[1] The reader will not stumble at a few historical inaccuracies in a narrative where a speaker in Helena's time is a brother of the protomartyr.

for six days, but on the seventh he yields. IX. Released from prison he leads the way to Calvary. He utters a fervent supplication in Hebrew, in which he pleads that He who in the famous times of old revealed to Moses the bones of Joseph would make known by a sign the place of the Rood, vowing to believe in Christ if his prayer is granted. X. A steam rises from the ground. There they dig, and at a depth of twenty feet three crosses are found. Which is the holy Rood? A dead man is carried by; Judas brings the corpse in contact with the crosses one after another, and the touch of the third restores life. XI. Satan laments that he has suffered a new defeat, which is all the harder as the agent is "Judas," a name so friendly to him before! He threatens a persecuting king who shall make the newly-converted man renounce his faith. Judas returns a spirited answer, and Helena rejoices to hear the new convert rise superior to the Wicked one. XII. The report spreads, to the joy of Christians and the confusion of the Jews. The queen sends an embassy to the emperor at Rome with the happy tidings. The greatest curiosity was displayed in the cities on their road. Constantine, in his exaltation, sent them quickly back to Helena with instructions to build a church in their united names on the sacred spot of the discovery. The queen gathered from every side the most highly-skilled builders for the church; and she caused the holy Rood to be studded with gold and jewels, and then firmly secured in a chest of silver :—

| Tha seo cwen bebeád | Then the queen bade |
| cræftum getŷde | of craftsmen deft |

sundor âsecean
 tha selestan
  tha the wrætlicost
   wyrcan cuthon
stân-gefôgum
 on tham stede-wange
  girwan Godes tempel
   swa hire gasta weard
reórd of roderum .
 Heo tha rôde heht
  golde beweorcean
   and gimcynnum
mid tham æthelestum
 eorcnanstânum
  besettan searocræftum ;
   and tha in seolfren fæt
locum belûcan .
 Thær thæt lifes treó
  sêlest sigebeáma
   siththan wunode
æthelu anbroce .

at large to seek
 the skilfullest,
  the most curious
   and cunning to work
structures of stone ;—
 upon that chosen site
  God's temple to grace
   as the Guarder of souls
gave her rede from on high.
 She the Rood hight
  with gold to inlay
   and the glory of gems,
with the most prized
 of precious stones
  to set with high art ;—
   and in a silver chest
secure enlock :—
 so there the Tree of life
  dearest of trophies
   thenceforward dwelt ;
fabric of honour.

XIII. Helena sends for Eusebius, "bishop of Rome," and he, at her bidding, makes Judas bishop in Jerusalem, and changes his name to Cyriacus. Then she inquires after the nails of the crucifixion, and, at the prayer of Cyriacus, their hiding-place is revealed. When the nails were brought to the queen she wept aloud, and the fountain of her tears flowed over her cheeks and down upon the jewels of her apparel. XIV. She seeks guidance by oracle as to the disposal of the nails. She is directed to make of them rings for the bridle of the chief of earthly kings. He who rides to war with such a bridle should be invincible; and a prophecy to that effect is quoted! Helena obeys, and sends the bridle over sea to Constantine,—

"no contemptible gift!" Helena assembles the chief men of the Jews, bids them submit to Cyriacus, and keep up the anniversary of the Finding of the Cross. Finally, for those who keep the day is proclaimed a benediction so unmeasured and profuse as to leave behind it an air in which the solemn evaporates in the histrionic.

Here more than in any other piece of Anglo-Saxon poetry we feel near the mediæval drama. Almost every canto is like a scene; and little adaptation would be required to put it upon the stage. The narrative at the beginning is like a prologue, and then after the close of the piece we have an epilogue, in which the author speaks about himself, and weaves his name with Runes into the verses in the manner already described.

The briefest fragment in the Vercelli book is about False Friendship; and it contains a long-drawn simile in which the bee is rather hardly treated.

Anlice beoð	Likened they are
swa þa beon berað	to the bees who bear
buton ætsomne;	both at one time,
arlicne anleofan	food for a king's table,
and ætterne tægel	and venomous tail
habbað on hindan;	have in reserve;
hunig on muðe	honey in mouth,
wynsume wist:	delectable food:
hwilum wundiað	in due time they wound
sare mid swice	sorely and slyly
þonne se sæl cymeð.	when the season is come.
Swa beoð gelice	Such are they like,
þa leasan men,	the leasing men,
þa þe mid tungan	those who with tongue
treowa gehatað	give assurance of troth

THE SECONDARY POETRY. 239

fægerum wordum,
    facenlice þencað;
þonne hie æt nehstan
    nearwe beswicað:
habbað on gehatum
    hunig smæccas,
smeðne sib cwidê;
    and in siofan innan
þurh deofles cræft
    dyrne wunde.

with fair-spoken words,
    false in their thought;
then do they at length
    shrewdly betray:
in profession they have
    the perfume of honey,
smooth gossip so sweet;
    and in their souls purpose,
with devilish craft,
    a stab in the dark.

The "Runic Poem"[1] is a string of epigrams on the characters of the Runic alphabet, beginning with F, U, Þ, O, R, C, according to that primitive order, whence that alphabet was called the " Futhorc." Each of these characters has a name with a meaning, mostly of some well-known familiar thing, apt subject for epigram.

When learned men began to look at the Runes with an eye of erudite curiosity, they often ranged them in the A, B, C order of the Roman alphabet; hence it gives the Rune poem some air of antiquity that it runs in the old Futhorc order. And, indeed, some of the versicles may perhaps be ancient; that is, they may possibly date from a time when Runes were still in practical use. But certainly much of this chaplet of versicles must be regarded as late and dilettante work. The Rune names are not all clearly authentic; for example, "Eoh" is rather dubious; but the poet treats the name as meaning Yew, and gives us an interesting little epigram on the Yew-tree:—

[1] Kemble, "Runes of the Anglo-Saxons," pp. 13-19. Grein, vol. ii., p. 351; and literary notice at p. 413.

EOH bith utan	YEW is outwardly
unsmethe treow	unpolished tree;
heard hrusan fæst	hard and ground-fast,
hyrde fyres	guardian of fire;
wyrtrumum underwrethed	with roots underwattled
wynan on æthle.	the home of the Want.[1]

The Riddles are mostly after Simphosius and Aldhelm;[2] but some are aboriginal. The form is mostly that of the epigram, only instead of having the name of the subject at the head of the piece as with epigrams, these little poems end with a question what the subject is. These Riddles are found in the Exeter book in three batches; Grein has drawn them all together, and made eighty-nine of them. That on the Book-Moth, of which the Latin has been given above, p. 88, is unriddled by the translator:—

Moððe word fræt;	Moth words devoured;
me þæt þuhte	to me it seemed
wrætlicu wyrd	a weird event
þa ic þæt wundor gefrægn;	when I the wonder learnt;
þæt se wyrm forswealg	that the worm swallowed
wera gied sumes	sentence of man
þeof in þystro	(thief in the dark)
þrymfæstne cwide	document sure,
and þæs strangan staðol.	binding and all.
Stælgiest ne wæs	The burglar was never
wihte þy gleawra	a whit the more wise
þe he þam wordum swealg.	for the words he had gulped.

[1] It may not be known to all readers, that this is an English word; and historically, perhaps, the best English name, for the mole (talpa). Along the Elbe it appears in a form nearer to that of the text: "Win worp oder Wind-worp, *der Maulwurf*." Bremisch-Niedersächsisches Wörterbuch.

[2] See Prof. Dietrich in Haupt's "Zeitschrift," xi.

Toward the end of the period, the poetic form becomes much diluted. The poetic diction wanes, so does the figured style and the parallel structure; and what remains is an alliterative rhythmical prose, which, from the nature of the subjects treated, appears to have been very taking for the ear of the people. Of this sort is the Lay of King Abgar, which Professor Stephens assigns to the reign of Cnut. The Abgar legend is in Eusebius (died 340) "History," i. 13. Abgar, king of Edessa, being sick, wrote a letter to the Saviour (it being the time of His earthly ministry) praying him to come and heal him, and adding, that if, as he hears, the Jews seek to persecute Him, his city of Edessa, though a little one, is stately, and sufficient for both.

. . . and ic wolde the biddan thæt thu gemedemige the sylfne thæt thu siðige to me and mine untrumnysse gehæle for than the ic eom yfele gehæfd. Me is eac gesæd thæt tha Judeiscan syrwiath and runiath him betwynan hu hi the berædan magon, and ic hæbbe ane burh, the unc bam genihtsumath.	. . . and I would thee pray, that thou condescend to come unto me, and my infirmity cure, for I am in evil case. To me is eke said that the Jews are plotting and rowning together how they may destroy thee; and I have a burgh large enough for us both.[1]

The impression which this secondary poetry leaves is, that the old ancestral form could no longer furnish an adequate poetry for the growing mind of the nation. In contrast with the expanding prose, it

[1] Prof. Stephens, "Tvende Old-Engelske Digte," Kiöbenhavn, 1853.

seems to shrink and fade before our eyes. Its only means of enlargement seems to be in forgetting its own traditions and assimilating itself to the prose. Moreover, we have traces of various tentative sallies; one poet trying rhymes,[1] another trying hexameters,[2] which reminds us of the efforts and essays of the unsatisfied poetic genius in the middle of the sixteenth century. The Benedictine revival had drawn off the interest from the old native themes of song to subjects less fitted for poetry, or with which the poetry of the time was not yet skilled to deal. The old poetry fitted the old heroic themes with which it had grown up; and now it throve better on apocryphal and legendary fables than on the verities of the faith which were rather beyond its strength. In the new zeal the old vein of poetry was lost or neglected, and its place was not yet appropriately filled.

For this want a provision was already making in the south. A fresh spirit of poetry had risen in the region where Roman and Arabic fancy met, and, after kindling France, was coming to England on the wings of the French language. With the new romances came new models of poetic form. A long struggle ensued between the native garb of English poetry and that of the French. Both lived together until the fourteenth century, when the victory of the French form was finally determined in Chaucer; and France set the fashion in poetry to England, as it did generally to modern Europe.

[1] "The Riming Poem," Cod. Exon. ed. Thorpe, p. 352.
[2] Stubbs, "St. Dunstan," Preface.

CHAPTER XII.

THE NORMAN CONQUEST AND AFTER THAT.

THE first of these chapters took a brief survey of the literature that preceded and elevated the Anglo-Saxon literature: this concluding chapter must be still briefer in sketching the manner of its decline. It would be true to say that the Norman Conquest dealt a fatal blow to Anglo-Saxon literature; but it would also be true to say that the cultivation of Anglo-Saxon literature never came to an end at all. I will presently endeavour to reconcile this seeming contradiction; but first I have some little remainder to tell of the main narrative.

There are two small sets of writings which have not yet been described. These are the liturgical and scientific remains. Of liturgical, we have the "Benedictionale of Æðelwold,"[1] and we have the so-called "Ritual of Durham," with its interlinear Northumbrian gloss. But the most famous book of this kind is that which is called "The Leofric Missal," because

---

[1] Written and illustrated with miniatures by order of Æðelwold, Bishop of Winchester, A.D. 963-984. Hexameter verses in a superior style of penmanship, namely, the old Latin rustic, record the history of the book, and give the scribe's name as Godeman, perhaps the Abbot of Thorney, who began A.D. 970. The illuminations are engraved in "Archæologia," xxiv.

Leofric, the first Bishop of Exeter (of Crediton, 1046–1050; of Exeter, 1050–1072) gave it to his cathedral. It is now in the Bodleian Library. "It is one of the only three surviving Missals known to have been used in the English Church during the Anglo-Saxon period," the other two being the Missal of Robert of Jumièges, Archbishop of Canterbury, now in Rouen Library, and the "Rede Boke of Darbye," in the Parker Library at Cambridge.[1]

It may seem almost idle to talk of the "scientific" remains of Anglo-Saxon times. For Science, in its grandest sense,—the recognition of constant order in nature and the reign of law,—had not yet dawned upon the world. Science, in this sense, dates only from the seventeenth century, and its patriarchal names are Copernicus, Galileo, and Kepler. But, nevertheless, the earlier and feebler efforts at the explanation of phenomena have a real and a lasting value for human history, and what they lack in scientific quality has somehow the effect of throwing them all the more into the arms of the literary historian.

There is, however, one small Anglo-Saxon writing which needs not this apology, and which may be considered as a real contribution even to science. I mean the Geography which King Alfred inserted into his translation of Orosius. All our other scientific relics are but compilation and translation in the primitive paths of Medicine, and Botany, and Astronomy.

[1] The "Leofric Missal," edited by F. E. Warren, B.D., Clarendon Press, 1883.

We have some considerable lists of Anglo-Saxon Botany. The vernacular names of plants, many of them, seem to indicate a Latin tradition dating from Roman times.[1] In the medical treatises we see the practice of medicine greatly mingled with superstition. Witchcraft is reckoned among the causes of disease, and formulæ are provided for breaking the spell. The "Leech Book" contains a series of prescriptions for divers ailments, with directions for preparation and medical treatment. One batch of these prescriptions is said to have been sent to King Alfred by Elias, Patriarch of Jerusalem. A very popular book was the Herbarium of Apuleius. It was translated into Anglo-Saxon, and four manuscripts of this translation are still extant.[2]

On astronomical and cosmical matters there exists a well-written little treatise of unknown authorship. It has been attributed to Ælfric, and it is most likely a work of his time. It seems to have been very popular.[3] It is, as it professes to be in the prologue, a popular abridgment of Beda, "De Natura Rerum." It begins with a succinct

[1] Particulars may be found in my "English Plant Names from the Tenth to the Fifteenth Century," Oxford, Clarendon Press, 1880.
[2] The medical treatises have been collected in three volumes (Rolls Series) by Mr. Cockayne, under the title of "Saxon Leechdoms."
[3] There are four copies of it in the Cotton Library, and one in Cambridge University library; some also in other collections. It has been printed from a Cotton manuscript written, the editor says, about A.D. 990. "Popular Treatises on Science," edited by T. Wright, 1841.

abstract of the creation, the sixth day being thus rendered :—

On ðam syxtan dæge he gescop eall deor cynn, ꞇ ealle nytena þe on feower fotum gað, ꞇ þa twegen menn Adam ꞇ Efan.

On the sixth day he created all animal-kind, and all the beasts that go on four feet, and the two men Adam and Eve.

The eclipse of the moon is well explained. After saying that Night is the shade of the earth when the sun goes down under it, before it comes up the other side,—

Woruldlice uðwitan sædon, þ seo sceadu astihð up oð ðæt heo becymð to þære lyfte ufeweardan, and þonne be yrnð se mona hwiltidum þonne he full byð on ðære sceade ufeweardre, and faggeteð oððe mid ealle asweartað, for þam þe he næfð þære sunnan leoht þa hwile þe he þære sceade ord ofer yrnð oð ðæt þære sunnan leoman hine eft onlihton.

Worldly philosophers said, that the shadow mounts up until it arrives at the top of the atmosphere, and then sometimes the moon when he is full runs into the upper part of the shadow, and is darkened or utterly blackened, forasmuch as he hath not the sun's light so long as he traverses the shadow's point until that the sun's rays again enlighten him.

The Norman Conquest gave the death-blow to our old native literature, in the sense that the use of the literary Anglo-Saxon in its first integrity, as at once a learned language and a spoken language, did not extend beyond the generation that witnessed that great dynastic change. In this strict sense we might point to the close of the Worcester Chronicle in 1079 as the termination of Anglo-Saxon literature. There is, indeed, a Saxon Chronicle that was even begun after that date, one which comprises the whole Saxon period, and was continued by original writers down to 1154, but it is not written in normal Anglo-Saxon. It represents the flectional decay which the living and popular English was undergoing.

It exhibits, also, something of that new growth which was to compensate for the loss of flection. And it already bears marks of that French influence which was so largely to affect the whole complexion of the language. I quote from the last Annal in the Saxon Chronicle of Peterborough:—

1154. On þis gær wærd þe King Stephan ded and bebyried þer his wif and his sune wæron bebyried æt Faures feld, þet minstre hi makeden. Þa þe King was ded. þa was þe eorl beionde sæ. and ne durste nan man don oþer bute god for þe micel eie of him. Þa he to Engle land com. þa was he under fangen mid micel wurtscipe. and to king bletcæd in Lundene on þe Sunnen dæi be foren midwinter dæi. and held þær micel curt.

In this year was King Stephen dead and buried where his wife and his son were buried at Feversham, the minster he made. When the King was dead, then was the earl beyond sea, and no man durst do other than good for the great awe of him. When he came to England, then was he received with great worship, and consecrated king in London on the Sunday before Christmas Day; and he held there a great court.

Here, then, at the very latest, we must close the canon of Anglo-Saxon literature. And here our subject branches in two; we have to follow with a brief glance what happened in two divergent lines of succession. As when, in the early mountainous course of some growing river, a broken hill has fallen across its bed, the old water-way is choked, and the descending waters make new channels to the right and to the left; so it was with the fortunes of our native language and literature after the Norman Conquest. The stream of largest volume was the spontaneous and popular utterance which amused in hall and taught in church; the lesser stream was the artificial maintenance of Anglo-Saxon literature which went on in the old seats of religion and learning.

The Norman Conquest brought in a vast body of romantic literature. Heroic or entertaining tales in a ballad form were at that time highly popular; and a peculiar talent for this sort of narrative was developed in France and among the Normans. The oldest French romances were those of which the central figure was Charles the Great. It was one of these, the "Song of Roland," that animated the conquering Normans at Senlac. According to high authorities, it was in the next generation after the Conquest that the "Chanson de Roland" took that final epic form which now it bears, and probably the poet's home was in England.[1] For a long time the speech of the upper society was wholly French. The two languages quickly met one another in the market, and in all the necessary business of life; but in respect of literature they long stood apart. Such was the state of things in this island during the time in which the Carling cycle prevailed. With that cycle the English language never came into contact at all in its palmy days; and the few Carling poems that exist in English are of later date, and are of a mixed nature. When at length, towards the close of the twelfth century, a literary

---

[1] "La Chanson de Roland," par Léon Gautier, ed. 7 (1880), Introduction.

intercourse had sprung up between the two languages, the hero of popular song was no longer Charles, but Arthur. In the English poetry of Layamon (1205), founded upon the French of Robert Wace, we see the story of Arthur in that early stage where it still purports to be history rather than romance. Layamon represents the first great step from the old literature to the new; and he is the first to give an English home to that ideal king who was to be the chosen theme of Spenser and of Tennyson. We will quote the death of Arthur and his funeral cortège :—

THE PASSING OF ARTHUR.
Line 28,582.

Tha nas ther na mare,	Then was there no more
i than fehte to laue,	in that fight left alive,
of twa hundred thusend monnen,	out of 200,000 men,
tha ther leien to-hawen ;	that there lay cut to pieces ;
buten Arthur the king one,	but Arthur the King only
and of his cnihtes tweien.	and two of his knights.
Arthur wes forwunded wunderliche swithe.	Arthur was wounded dangerously much.
Ther to him com a cnaue,	There to him came a youth
the wes of his cunne ;	who was of his kin ;
he wes Cadores sune,	he was son of Cador,
the eorles of Cornwaile.	the earl of Cornwall.
Constantin hehte the cnaue ;	Constantine hight the youth ;
he wes than kinge deore.	to the king he was dear.
Arthur him lokede on,	Arthur looked upon him,
ther he lai on folden,	where he lay on the ground,
and thas word seide,	and these words said,
mid sorhfulle heorte.	with sorrowful heart.
Constantin thu art wilcume,	Constantine thou art welcome,
thu weore Cadores sune :	thou wert Cador's son :

ich the bitache here,
mine kineriche :
and wite mine Bruttes,
a to thines lifes :
and hald heom alle tha laȝen,
tha habbeoth istonden a mine
daȝen :
and alle tha laȝen gode,
tha bi Vtheres daȝen stode.
And ich wulle uaren to Aualun,
to uairest alre maidene ;
to Argante there quene,
aluen swithe sceone :
and heo scal mine wunden,
makien all isunde,
al hal me makien,
mid haleweiȝe drenchen.
And seothe ich cumen wulle
to mine kineriche :
and wunien mid Brutten,
mid muchelere wunne.
Æfne than worden,
ther com of se wenden,
that wes an sceort bat lithen,
sceouen mid vthen :
and twa wimmen therinne,
wunderliche idihte :
and heo nomen Arthur anan,
and aneouste hine uereden,
and softe hine adun leiden,
and forth gunnen hine lithen.

Tha wes hit iwurthen,
that Merlin seide whilen ;
that weore unimete care,

of Arthures forth-fare.

I here commit to thee,
my kingdom ;
and guide thou my Britons
aye to thy life's cost ;
and assure them all the laws,
that have stood in my days :

and all the laws so good,
that by Uther's days stood.
And I will fare to Avalon,
to the fairest of all maidens ;
to Argante the queen,
elf exceeding sheen :
and she shall my wounds,
make all sound ;
all whole me make,
with healing drinks.
And sith return I will,
to my kingdom :
and dwell with Britons,
with mickle joy.
Even with these words,
lo came from sea wending,
that was a short boat moving,
driving with the waves :
and two women therein,
of marvellous aspect :
and they took Arthur anon,
and straight him bore away
and softly down him laid,
and forth with him to sea they
gan to move away.
Then was it come to pass
what Merlin said whilome ;
that there should be much
curious care,
when Arthur out of life should
fare.

Bruttes ileueth ȝete,	Britons believe yet,
that he beo on liue,	that he be alive,
and wunnie in Aualun	and dwelling in Avalon,
mid fairest alre aluen :	with the fairest of all elves :
and lokieth euere Bruttes ȝete,	still look the Britons for the day
whan Arthur cume lithen.	of Arthur's coming o'er the sea.

In this poetry there is a new vein of popularity. Since we left the primary poetry we have been on the track of a literature whose spring was in book-learning. A foreign erudition had thrown the lore of the native minstrel into the shade. But some relics of domestic material reappear with the new gush of popular song in the 13th century. Among the mass of stories which fill that time, we find here and there an old English tale, and sometimes it is a translation back from the French. The romance of King Horn is one of these. The names of the personages, and the general course of the plot —the Saracens notwithstanding—are essentially Saxon. There are lines which are almost pure Saxon poetry, and there are incidents that recall the Beowulf.

The story is as follows :—Horn was the son of the King of Suddene; he was of matchless beauty, and he had twelve companions, among whom two were specially dear to him; they were Athulf and Fikenild, the best and the worst. The land was conquered by Saracens, who slew the king, but sent off Horn and his twelve in a ship to perish at sea. They came to a land where the king was Aylmar, who thus addressed them :—

Whannes beo ȝe, faire gumes,
That her to londe beoth icume,
Alle throttene
Of bodie swithe kene.

"Whence be ye, fair gentlemen, that here to land are come? All thirteen of body very keen. By him that made me, so fair a band saw I at no time; say what ye seek?" Horn tells his story, and Aylmar likes him, and bids Athelbrus, his steward, teach him woodcraft, and the harp and song, and also to carve and be cupbearer :—

> Bifore me to kerve
> And of the cupe serve.

The Princess Rymenhild falls in love with Horn, and this is an occasion to prove the loyalty of Athulf. She orders Athelbrus to send Horn to her; but he, fearing the consequences, and being specially responsible for Horn, sends Athulf instead. Athulf finds that the princess has been deceived, and declares at once that he is not Horn. When at length Horn does meet Rymenhild, he points out to her the inequality of his rank. She gets her father to knight him. She also gives him a ring, in which the stones are of such virtue that if he looks on them and thinks of her he need fear no wounds :—

> The stones beoth of suche grace
> That thu ne schalt in none place
> Of none duntes beon of drad.

He rides forth in search of adventures to prove his knighthood. He falls in with a crew of Saracens, slays 100 of them, and brings the head of the master Saracen on the point of his sword to the king, where he sits in hall among his knights, and presents it in acknowledgment of his dubbing (compare p. 130 above). Fikenild tells Aylmar of Horn's love for his daughter, and Aylmar banishes Horn. Departing, he promises Rymenhild to return in seven years or she shall be free to marry another. He leaves the faithful Athulf behind to look after Rymenhild. He arrives at the court of King Thurston, and there he calls himself Cutberd. The land is infested by pagan invaders. Cutberd slays a giant and many of the Saracens who were with him. Thurston offers him his daughter and the kingdom with her. Cutberd tells the king that it must not be so, but that he will claim his reward when he has relieved the king of all his troubles, which will be at seven years' end (compare p. 131 above).

Meanwhile, Rymenhild is sought in marriage by King Modi, and the day is fixed. In her distress she sends in all directions to seek Horn; her messenger finds Horn and delivers his message, but he never returns to the princess, because he is drowned. Now Horn tells King Thurston his story, and entreats his help. He adds that he will provide a worthy husband for his daughter, namely, Athulf, one of the best and truest of knights. Thurston assembles his men and they go with Horn. Horn leaves them under the wood while he goes towards the palace. He meets a palmer and changes clothes with him. In the palace he takes his place with the beggars, and when Rymenhild rises to offer wine to the guests he gets speech of her and lets her see the ring she had given him. This leads to a full recognition and the betrothal of Horn with Rymenhild. Such is the tale of King Horn.

But, of all the old native stories that crop up in

this later time, the most remarkable is the "Lay of Havelok the Dane," a large subject which we can only just indicate here.[1]

Of the learned branches a good deal continued unbroken by the Conquest. Such was mostly the case with Homilies and Lives of saints, and Poetry of the allegorical and instructive kind.

In the Exeter Song-book we saw pieces that had been taken from the old book "Physiologus." This allegorical poetry retained its place through all the changes.[2]

---

[1] This poem, of which there are many external traces, had long been given up as lost, was deplored by Tyrwhitt and by Ritson, and was accidentally discovered in a Bodleian manuscript, latent amidst legends of saints. From this unique MS. it was edited by Sir F. Madden; and again (1868) by the Rev. W. W. Skeat, who says in his preface :—"There can be little doubt that the tradition must have existed from Anglo-Saxon times, but the earliest mention of it is presented to us in the French version of the Romance. . . . . The story is in no way connected with France ; . . . . From every point of view, ... the story is wholly English," p. iv.

[2] An old English Miscellany, containing a "Bestiary," &c., ed. R. Morris (E. E. T. S.), 1872, p. 17. The "Phisiologus" is quoted in Chaucer, apparently from this very "Bestiary"; and Dr. Morris says that scraps of it are found even in Elizabethan writers. I add a translation of the piece quoted :—
"Whilst that weather is so bad, the ships that are driven about on the sea (death is unwelcome, men love to live) look about them and see this fish; they ween it is an island. They are very glad of it, and with all their might they draw towards it, make the ships fast, and all go ashore. With stone and steel and tinder they make a good fire on this monster, and warm themselves well, and eat and drink; the whale feels the fire and makes them sink, for he quickly dives to the bottom, he kills them all without wound."

THE NORMAN CONQUEST AND AFTER THAT. 255

Here is a passage from the "Whale," in the language of the thirteenth century :—

> Wiles that weder is so ille,
> the sipes that arn on se fordriven
> (loth hem is deth, and lef to liven)
> biloken hem and sen this fis;
> an eilond he wenen it is.
> Thereof he aren swithe fagen,
> and mid here migt tharto he dragen,
> sipes onfesten,
> and alle up gangen.
> Of ston mid stel in the tunder
> wel to brennen one this wunder,
> warmen hem wel and heten and drinken;
> the fir he feleth and doth hem sinken,
> for sone he diveth dun to grunde,
> he drepeth hem alle withuten wunde.

These examples may suffice to represent that new literature which began to rise after the violent removal of the old. They do not belong to the history of Anglo-Saxon literature except indirectly as a foil and a contrast. They show how ready were new forms to take the place of the old. But while the English language was thus following the natural and spontaneous course of its development, there still survived a powerful interest in the old classical Englisc. The seat of this literature was in the old monasteries, which became strongholds of ancient culture and tradition. The old books were perused and re-copied, and a scholarly knowledge of the old language was made an object of study. This was sustained not only by sentiment, and curiosity, and literary taste, but also by a sense of corporate interest. The titles of the old monasteries to their lands were wholly or very largely contained in Saxon writings, and these grew in importance with the growing habits of documentary legality under Norman rule. A language which was at once native and recondite, far more recondite than the Latin of the ordinary scholar, could not but be impressive as a documentary medium. The number of extant Saxon books and deeds which were either originally composed after the Conquest, or at least re-copied and re-edited, is quite enough to prepare us to receive what Matthew Parker said in the Latin preface to his edition (1574) of " Asser " :—

"Furthermore; inasmuch as the medium of many legal documents and venerable memorials and royal charters preserved in archives, dating, some before, some after, the coming of the Normans into England, is Saxon both in language and in writing, I will advise all who study the institutions of this realm, to undergo the slight and insignificant labour which is necessary to make themselves masters of this language. If they will but do this, they will doubtless make discoveries daily, and will bring to light things which now lie hidden and remote; yea, they will without effort clear up the intricacies and perplexities of a great number of things. And in ages past there were societies of religious persons who were ordered by our forefathers for this work, that some among them might be trained in the knowledge of this tongue, and might transmit the same in succession to those who came after. To wit, in Tavistock Abbey, in the county of Devon, and in many other fraternities (within my memory) this was an established thing; to the end, as I suppose, that acquaintance with a literature whose language is antiquated might not perish for lack of use."

Thus we see that in the centuries between the Conquest and the Reformation the old ENGLISC was a recognised subject of study; and that it enjoyed, as the Latin did, the honours of an ancient language which was too much esteemed to be allowed to perish. And, therefore, it was said above that the Anglo-Saxon language and literature never died out; for the knowledge of it was kept up till the time when, through the general Revival of learning, new motives were supplied for its diligent study, and the very man in whom the new movement is impersonated is he who testifies that the study had lasted down to a time within his own memory.

INDEX.

ABGAR, Lay of, 241
Abingdon Chronicle, 32, 173
Ælfric, Abbot, 23, 40, 67, 207, 213, 221, 245
—— Bata, 40
Ælfheah, Archbishop, 224
Æthelberht, 81
Æthelred's Laws, 164
Æthelweard, 183, 220
Æthelwold, Bishop, 25, 51, 181, 207, 219, 243
Aidan, Bishop, 99
Alcuin, 23, 99, 117
Aldhelm, 21, 53, 86
Alfred, 15, 24, 186 ff., 207, 244
Alfred Jewel, 49
Alfred's Laws, 154 ff.
Andreas, the, 90, 233 f.
"Anglo-Saxon," 206
Apollonius of Tyre, 18, 212
Apuleius, 245
Architecture, 52
Arnold, Thomas, 121, 136
Arthur, 59, 249
Arundel Marbles, 48
Ashburnham House, 32
Ashmolean Museum, 49
Asser, 43, 183, 187, 256
Athelstan's Laws, 159
Augustine, Archbishop, 52
Avitus, Bishop, 14

BALLADS, the, 145 ff.
Baron, Dr., 221

Beda, 21, 64, 81, 102 ff., 204, 245
Benedict of Nursia, 15
—— of Aniane, 209
Beowulf, the, 32, 45, 58, 68, 71, 120 ff., 225
Biscop, Benedict, 86, 99
Blickling Homilies, 47, 139. 213 ff.
Blume, Dr., 46
Bodleian Library, 34
Boëthian Metres, 71, 202 ff.
Boëthius, 14, 201 ff.
Boniface (Winfrid), 21
Bosworth, Dr., 44, 226
Bradford-on-Avon, 53
Buckley, Professor, 40
Burials, Saxon, 55
Byrhtnoth, 217

CÆDMON, 14, 22, 39, 68, 99, 111
Cæsar, 62
Camden, William, 43, 183
Canons of Ælfric, 67, 220
Canterbury, 20, 79, 98
Carling Romances, 248
Cenwalh, 180
Ceolfrid, Abbot, 102
Charles the Great, 187, 248
Chaucer, 27, 242, 254
Chronicles, the, 20, 22, 61, 169 ff.
Cockayne, Oswald, 245
Colman, Bishop, 99

260   ANGLO-SAXON LITERATURE.

Conybeare, 45
Cotton Library, 32, 245
Cotton, Sir Robert, 31, 35
Coxe, Henry Octavius, 39, 40
Cuthbert, St., 99, 104
Cynewulf, 226 ff.

DANIHEL, Bishop, 21
Dasent, Sir George, 68
Day, John, 35, 42
Days of the Week, 73
Dialogues, Gregory's, 16, 36, 193 ff.
—— of Solomon, &c., 210 ff.
Dietrich, Professor, 208, 227, 240
Documents, Legal, 167
Dunstan, Archbishop, 25, 43, 207, 219
Durham Ritual, 111, 243

EADMER, 52
Ebert, Adolf, 103, 118
Edda, the, 65, 72
Eddi, 21, 99
Edwin, King, 98
Egbert, Archbishop, 21, 99
Elene, the, 90, 234 ff.
Epinal Gloss, 91, 97
Ettmüller, Ludwig, 121, 134
Eusebius of Cæsarea, 241
—— of Emesa, 216
Evesham, 69
Exeter Book, 29, 88, 225 ff., 254
Eynsham, 220

FELIX, Bishop, 80
Florence, 184
Floriacum, 25
Frankish Art, 51
—— Graves, 56
Freeman, E. A., 54, 141, 184, 206
Futhorc, the, 239

GIBSON, Edmund, 45
Gildas, 60
Glossaries, 90
Godeman, 243
Gospels in A.-S., 73, 205, 208
Gough, Richard, 39
Gregory the Great, 15, 20, 85
—— of Tours, 18, 19, 85
Grein, Dr., 121, 135, 208, 220, 239
Grettir, Saga of, 137
Grimbald, 187
Grimm, Jacob, 46, 73, 153
Grundtvig, Dr., 121
Guthlac, St., 227, 232
Guthrum, 156, 159

HADRIAN, Abbot, 21, 85
Harley, Robert, 34
Hatton, Lord, 36
Havelok the Dane, 254
Heliand, the, 22, 23, 68, 116
Henry of Huntingdon, 184
Heyne, Moritz, 121
Hickes, George, 44
Hickey, E. H., 144
Higden, 185
Hild, Abbess, 100
Homilies of Ælfric, 74, 102, 214 ff.
—— of Wulfstan, 222 ff.
—— see Blickling.
Horn, Romance of, 251 ff.
Hugo Candidus, 229

ILLUMINATED Books, 51
Ine's Laws, 151
Inscriptions, 47
Irish Teachers, 86
Isidore of Seville, 85

JARROW, 102
Jerome, 217
Jewellery, 49
John of Saxony, 187
Joscelin, 43

INDEX.

Judith, the, 225
Juliana, St., 227, 232
Junius, Franciscus, 37, 44, 112

KEMBLE, J. M., 90, 121, 154, 210, 226, 228, 239
Kentish Dialect, 84, 90, 97
—— Laws, 80

LAMBARDE, William, 150
Lanferth, 219
Lappenberg, J. M., 46, 169
Laud, Archbishop, 34
Laws, the, 66, 150 ff.
Layamon, 27, 249
Leofric, Bishop, 28, 244
—— Missal, 29, 243
Lumby, Professor, 103
Lindisfarne, 117
—— Gospels, 33, 51, 111

MACRAY, W. D., 34
Madden, Sir F., 254
Maidulf, 86
Maine, Sir H., 154, 163
Marshall, Dr., 44
Matthew Parker, 29, 42, 256
Mayor, Professor, 103
Metcalfe, F., 44
Milton, John, 14, 112, 115, 232
More, Bishop, 41, 101
Morfil, W. R., 148
Morley, Henry, 134
Morris, Dr. R., 222, 254
Müllenhof, Dr. Karl, 134

NAPIER, Arthur, 222
Nicodemus, Gospel of, 209
Northumbria, 21
Northumbrian Dialect, 111
Notker, 15

ODIN, 75
Odo, Archbishop, 25, 219
Orm, 27
Orosius, 13, 204

Oswald, Bishop, 219

PALGRAVE, Sir Francis, 152, 164
Panther, the, 231
Parker, Archbishop, 29, 42, 256
Parker, J. H., 54
Parker Library, 44, 244
Pastoral Care, the, 16, 36, 188 ff.
Paulinus, Bishop, 98
Pauli, Reinhold, 169
Paulus Diaconus, 23
Pericles (Shakespeare), 18
Peterborough Chronicle, 26, 36, 178, 181, 184
Phœnix, the, 9, 227, 230
Physiologus, the, 215, 231, 254
Pilate, Acts of, 209
Plegmund, Archbishop, 187
Psalter (Kentish), 94
—— (Poetical), 90, 208

RAWLINSON, Richard, 38, 45
Riddles, 87, 240
Robert of Jumièges, 244
Rochester Book, 26
Ruined City, the, 140
Rule of St. Benedict, 40
Runes, 78, 111, 226, 238
Runic Poem, 239
Rushworth, John, 38
Ruthwell Cross, 111

SANDERS, W. Basevi, 41
Schaldemose, 121
Schmid, Reinhold, 150
Scott, Sir Walter, 150, 228
Sculpture, 55
Sievers, Edouard, 116
Sigeric, Archbishop, 217
Simeon of Durham, 177, 184
Simposius, 10, 240
Skeat, Professor, 44, 111, 218, 254
Smaragdus, 23
Solomon and Saturn, 209 ff.
Somner, William, 44

Spell, 75
Spelman, Sir Henry, 43, 44
—— Sir John, 44
Spenser, Edmund, 136, 249
St. Augustine's, Canterbury, 20, 35
Stallybrass, J. S., 70
Stephens, Professor George, 47, 111, 117, 241
Stubbs, Professor, 162, 183, 185
Sweet, Mr., 33
Swithun, St., 69, 218, 219

TACITUS, 62
Tavistock, 256
Tennyson, Alfred, 136, 147, 249
Theodore, Archbishop, 21, 85, 100
Thorkelin, G. J., 45, 121
Thorney, 243
Thorpe, Benjamin, 46, 121, 150, 208, 222
Thwaites, Edward, 220
Trial by Jury, 163 ff.

VERCELLI Book, 46, 90, 225, 233 ff.
Vigfusson, Dr. Gudbrand, 138

WACE, Robert, 27, 249
Walahfrid Strabo, 23
Waldhere (Fragment), 47

Wanley, Humphrey, 45
Warren, F. E., 244
Watson, R. Spence, 113
Wearmouth, 102
Weland, 58, 70
Werfrith, Bishop, 36, 187, 189, 193
Westwood, Professor, 30, 39, 51
Whale, the, 231, 255
Wheloc, Abraham, 43, 150
Whitby, 99
Widsith, the, 148
Wilfrid, 99, 100
Wilkins, Bishop, 150
Willebrord, 99
William of Malmesbury, 185
Winchester Chronicle, 171, 178,
Winfrid (Boniface), 21, 99
Winton Book, 26
Woden, 66
Worcester Chartulary, 26
—— Chronicle, 32, 173
Wordsworth, Canon, 48
Wright, Thomas, 183, 226, 245
Wülcker, Professor, 112, 140
Wulfstan, Archbishop, 224
Wulstan, Latin poet, 219

YORK, 21, 98, 177

ZEUNER, Rudolf, 33
Zupitza, Julius, 41

THE END.

CORRIGENDA.

Page 103, Heading, *for* "Anglican" *read* "Anglian."
,, 115, line 22, *for* "vora" *read* "wora."
,, 150, ,, 23, *for* "Lombarde" *read* "Lambarde."
,, 154, ,, 16, *for* "History" *read* "history."
,, 208, ,, 12, *for* "translations" *read* "translation."